MARTIN LUTHER KING, JR. AND THE CIVIL RIGHTS MOVEMENT

Edited by David J. Garrow

A CARLSON PUBLISHING SERIES

The Student Nonviolent Coordinating Committee

THE GROWTH OF RADICALISM IN A CIVIL RIGHTS ORGANIZATION

Emily Stoper

PREFACE BY DAVID J. GARROW

CARLSON
Publishing Inc

BROOKLYN, NEW YORK, 1989

Library of Congress Cataloging-in Publication Data
Stoper, Emily
    The Student Nonviolent Coordinating Committee.

    (Martin Luther King, Jr., and the Civil Rights
Movement ; 17)
    Includes bibliographical references.
    1. Student Nonviolent Coordinating Committee.
2. Civil rights movements—United States—History—20th
century. 3. Afro-Americans—Civil rights—History—20th
century. 4. United States—Race relations. 5. Civil
rights workers—United States—Interviews. 6. Radicalism
—United States—History—20th century. I. Title.
II. Series.
E185.61.S876   1989   323.3'08'8375   89-22265
ISBN 0-926019-11-2

This book was written as a doctoral dissertation at Harvard University in 1968. It has been edited, proofread, typeset and indexed for publication here. The interviews were not included in the dissertation.

Typographic design: Julian Waters

Typeface: Bitstream ITC Galliard

The index to this book was created using NL Cindex, a scholarly indexing program from the Newberry Library.

For a complete listing of the volumes in this series, please see the back of this book.

Printed on acid-free, 250-year-life paper.

Manufactured in the United States of America.

Contents

Series Editor's Preface

The Student Nonviolent Coordinating Committee (SNCC) represented the cutting edge of the southern black freedom struggle from 1960 to 1966. Formed in April of 1960 by southern black college students in the immediate wake of the initial lunch-counter sit-in movement that had begun in Greensboro, North Carolina, on February 1, SNCC's young activists played crucial roles in the 1961 Freedom Ride and then initiated intensive and dangerous local-level grassroots organizing and voter registration projects in a number of rural deep South locales.

The two earliest and most significant SNCC projects were in Mississippi and in southwest Georgia, and aside from Clayborne Carson's valuable *In Struggle* (1981), which functions best as an intellectual history of SNCC's evolution rather than as a comprehensive organizational history, these important early SNCC efforts have not yet received the scholarly attention they deserve. In time John Dittmer's immensely promising work on the black freedom struggle in Mississippi will help to fill at least some of this gap, but at present the overall amount of academic attention being directed toward SNCC is disappointingly small. SNCC's importance and impact as one of the five major organizations involved in national civil rights politics—along with SCLC, CORE, the NAACP, and the National Urban League—has been usefully chronicled in a number of significant works on the movement and its interactions with the federal government, but SNCC's equally if not more important local, grassroots role has not even begun to receive the level of analysis and appreciation that is deserved.

The relative lack of scholarly literature on SNCC is to a considerable extent mitigated by the valuable autobiographical memoirs of James Forman (*The Making of Black Revolutionaries*, 1972) and Cleveland Sellers (*The River of No Return*, 1973), by Howard Zinn's participant-observer *SNCC: The New Abolitionists* (1965), and also by oral history-based academic studies of white movement volunteers that parenthetically offer important perspectives on SNCC: Sara Evans's *Personal Politics* (1979), Mary Aickin Rothschild's *A Case of Black and White* (1982), and Doug McAdam's *Freedom Summer* (1989). Additionally, the extremely rich trove of SNCC papers presently archived at the Martin Luther King, Jr., Center for Nonviolent Social Change in Atlanta offer an especially valuable resource that so far has not been at all adequately mined by scholars or other writers.

Next to Carson's book, however, no other work is more valuable to an academic appreciation of SNCC's development and internal life between 1960 and 1966 than Emily Stoper's important but until now little-utilized 1968 Harvard dissertation. Based upon fifty-one lengthy and substantive interviews conducted in 1966-1967, Stoper's work is a very early and extremely important history that traces the internal development of SNCC, its growing disillusionment with the federal government, and its often troubled relations with other civil rights organizations such as the NAACP and SCLC. Particularly in her sections on the interrelationships between different civil rights groups, and in Chapter Three's pioneering discussion of SNCC's attitudes towards leadership and structure, Stoper's analyses give prescient articulations of themes and interpretations that in subsequent years would figure heavily both in activists's memoirs and historian's overviews. Additionally, Stoper's organizational analysis of SNCC as a "moralist" or "redemptive" group—see her notable 1977 *Journal of Black Studies* essay which is reprinted in this series's *We Shall Overcome*, Volume Three, pp. 1041-1062—is likewise an insightful contribution to our understanding of SNCC.

I am very pleased both that Carlson Publishing's series of volumes on *Martin Luther King, Jr., and the Civil Rights Movement* is able to include Emily Stoper's significant work and also that this book is able to provide as an appendix extensive transcriptions and selections from Stoper's extremely valuable and almost uniquely early oral history interviews with important activists such as Jane Stembridge, Charles Jones, and John Lewis. This volume should be a notable contribution to future scholarly appreciation of SNCC's history and importance.

David J. Garrow

Preface 1989

Re-reading my twenty-year-old dissertation on SNCC sent me on a journey back into the familiar/strange world of that peculiar epoch of American political history known as the '60s. I quickly became absorbed in both the pleasures of contemplating an antique for its own sake and in musings on its meaning from the perspective of today.

When I originally wrote about SNCC I saw it as a particular kind of political organization, a "moralist" (later renamed "redemptive") organization. As I re-read the work, several alternative interpretations came to mind. For example, it seems odd to me that I did not also see SNCC in terms of the rise and fall of the New Left. Probably I was too absorbed in the New Left myself at the time to be able to stand back and look at it as a historical phenomenon. But today it is apparent to me that SNCC's emphasis on community organizing, its attempt to build parallel institutions, its moralism, its belief in the need for and the possibility of redeeming America, its increasing sense of frustration and disillusionment, its interest in the idea of violence in its later years—all seem fairly typical of SDS and other New Left groups. SNCC's eventual demise can be seen as having been caused in large part by the same causes as the demise of the New Left in general—the sense by its own participants that their original idealistic aims had ended in bitter and futile conflicts and the fact that these conflicts in turn antagonized much of the American public. Even more deeply, the New Leftists as a group came to feel that the original reforms they had sought—integration, an end to the Vietnam War, more rights for certain disenfranchised groups—could be granted without really satisfying them, because they were looking for something else, though what it was they were not entirely sure. The Freedom High in SNCC seemed to foreshadow an important development of the '70s, a turning inward by a great many individuals to examine their own deeper values and motivations, in many cases through the personal growth movement.

As I read the dissertation again, I also saw in retrospect the foreshadowing of another phenomenon of the '70s, namely, the women's movement. During the time I was completing this work in 1968, I was quite blind to the beginnings of a movement that was to profoundly alter my world view just a year or two later. When Charlie Jones, one of the many perceptive black men I interviewed, predicted that the next big movement would be of women, I just gave him a superior smile, as if to say, "How could *I* be an oppressed person?" My dissertation is full of sexist language, such as the generic use of "man" and "he." This future staunch feminist even referred to males in SNCC as "men" and females as "girls." Probably even worse, I failed to notice the prominence of women among the local leaders organized by SNCC (my thanks to Dave Garrow for pointing this out recently). Nor did I see fit to remark on the fact that all three Mississippi blacks who were the FDP's candidates for Congress in the 1965 Congressional Challenge were women.

In many mays, SNCC reminds me even more of radical feminism than of the New Left—in the rejection of the idea of leadership, in the emphasis on somehow transforming the society by organizing alternative institutions, in the glorification of the qualities of the oppressed group, in the view of sexism (a concept modelled on racism) as the essence of the problem with the larger society. Radical feminists, though, never rested their hopes on political change; perhaps they knew better, since many of them were veterans of the New Left and even of SNCC itself.

I have spoken of SNCC as foreshadowing the personal growth movement and radical feminism. But SNCC's history is most obviously an episode in the evolution of American race relations. The period spanned by SNCC's rise and fall (1960-68) is a watershed for black people in this country. It marks the end of certain easy and arrogant assumptions on the part of white Northerners: that racism was merely a regional phenomenon, a nasty Southern habit; that integration could be achieved by simply getting people to choose right over wrong—after which there would be no more race problem; that black people would and should blend into the melting pot of American society, given the opportunity and enough time. I think that most white Americans in 1960 had no idea how angry many blacks were; by 1968, black anger could not have escaped anyone's notice. SNCC's rising anger, its growing disillusionment with non-Southern whites and with integration, and its increasingly strong insistence on black people's right to define themselves, speak for themselves and take power for themselves—all paralleled similar developments among many black people outside SNCC. SNCC helped to articulate this trend but it surely did not create it. Someone with roots in the black community might have seen this, rather than the organizational ethos, as the most plausible explanation for SNCC's development.

One final alternative perspective on SNCC's history comes to mind—as an exploration of the limits of democracy. The story told here really asks the question: can democracy be practiced in any meaningful sense by the poorest and least educated members of a society? What is the appropriate relationship to them for organizers from outside? Even those whose own parents or grandparents were members of this group will have personal goals and values that do not coincide with those of the people they are organizing. Are the poorest people always too easily either terrorized or bought off? Can they ever hope to make significant changes by operating in the same polity as the elites who may benefit from their poverty and powerlessness and who certainly do not share their priorities?

These questions have relevance today for the black underclass in the cities, to whom Jesse Jackson has tried to make a political appeal, and also for the roughly one-fifth of humanity that lives in chronic absolute poverty in the Third World. It is fashionable to call for a development strategy that involves mobilizing the political and economic energies of the very poorest people, many of whom live in countries that are far less democratic or open even than Mississippi in the 1960s. SNCC's experiences may offer some caveats for those who attempt such organizing work.

This document offers an opportunity to look back at the way we were during the 1960s, a practice that seems to have come into fashion now. That period—and the story of SNCC in particular—offers us a rich lode of political experience that we have only just begun to mine. Readers of this work are invited to relate SNCC's story to their own political experiences and concerns but also to cherish SNCC itself for its sustained courage and vision in pushing the limits of the American political process.

Emily Stoper
December, 1988
Oakland, California

Acknowledgments

The author gratefully acknowledges the encouragement and excellent advice she received from Professor James Q. Wilson of Harvard University at every stage of the work. Thanks are also due to Professor Howard Zinn of Boston University, who read and criticized this manuscript.

This work would not have been possible without the assistance of the large number of members of the Student Nonviolent Coordinating Committee who have spent hours of their time in describing and interpreting their organization. The author would like to thank them for their very generous aid and advice. Miss Miriam Cohen, in particular, was a valued source of inspiration and advice in the planning of the work. A great many people offered hospitality and assistance of various kinds in the course of the interview project; to all of them, the author expresses her gratitude.

The author also wishes to thank the Southern Regional Council and the Freedom Information Service for giving her access to their files.

Finally, she expresses deep appreciation to her husband, Arnold Stoper, for his aid in preparing this manuscript and for his constant patience and understanding.

This work was researched and written during the tenure of two New York State Regents College Teaching Fellowships. The Frank G. Thomson Fund at Harvard University paid most of the author's travel expenses.

The Student Nonviolent Coordinating Committee

Introduction

In July 1966, there was a small riot in Atlanta, Georgia. Stokely Carmichael, the chairman of the Student Nonviolent Coordinating Committee (SNCC), was photographed by the national news media angrily exhorting a crowd of black people to seize their rights from the oppressive white man. He was later accused of inciting the riot. Only two months before, Carmichael had been elected chairman of SNCC, replacing John Lewis, a man with a deep commitment to nonviolence. A little over six years before that, SNCC had been founded, for the purpose of coordinating the lunch-counter sit-ins which were then sweeping the South. The leaders of the sit-ins were SNCC's first members. These were quiet, respectable black college students, devoted to the religious principle of nonviolence, who seemingly asked only the right to be served a cup of coffee at a dime-store lunch counter.

What had happened? In the months following the Atlanta riot, the American public acquired a new interest in SNCC, an interest which was fed by a spate of newspaper and magazine articles. It looked to some journalists as if Carmichael's succeeding Lewis was the result of a victory of a small group of violent, bitter young men from the North, who had seized control of the organization from the rather conventional, religious Southern students who had run it earlier.[1] In seeking explanations for this change of leadership, many liberals recalled that SNCC had experienced continual frustrations and violent persecutions in the South. Other liberals and some conservatives, like Ralph McGill, stated or hinted that SNCC had been infiltrated by Communists.[2]

Neither of these explanations is particularly satisfying. The Southern-persecution hypothesis leaves unanswered the question why the thrust of Carmichael's anger seemed to be not against Southern sheriffs but against Northern white liberals. The Communist-takeover theory, even if true, explains nothing about the nature of the organization which had supposedly made possible such an outcome.

How and why did SNCC change in so few years from a religiously oriented group with moderate, integrationist goals to a cadre of political organizers dedicated to Black Power? When had the seeds of Black Power been planted in SNCC, and under what circumstances had they begun to sprout? In seeking the answer to this question, I soon learned that most SNCC members believed that all white Americans had a distorted view of their organization's development. This discovery led me to questions about the character of SNCC's relationship with established organizations and institutions. In order to answer these questions, I had to delve into the nature of SNCC as an organization. What held it together? Why was it no larger in 1967 than in 1961? Was it true that it had been taken over by Communists—or, for that matter, by any other group? Does SNCC resemble other black-advancement organizations or other American radical groups? Or is it perhaps a new phenomenon, unlike either?

When I began my study in 1966, I was faced with an almost total lack of published material on SNCC that might help me answer these questions. There was at that time only one book about SNCC, Howard Zinn's *SNCC: The New Abolitionists*,[3] which gives a very good account of external events up to 1964 but does not deal with the internal workings of the organization. This emphasis on events was also true of almost all the periodical articles about SNCC. I was therefore forced to rely for information about SNCC's internal dynamics on my own interviews.

I did fifty-one interviews, almost all of them with present or former SNCC members, eighteen of them with whites. Since I myself am white and have never belonged to SNCC, I received some refusals (perhaps half a dozen), but fewer than expected. I chose my sample by the following method. First, I interviewed perhaps a dozen SNCC members at random, asking each one who were the leaders or others I should try to interview. I then tried to interview all those who had been mentioned more than twice. For this purpose, I visited Boston, New York, New Haven, Newark, Chicago, Washington, D.C., Atlanta and Albany, Georgia, and several towns in Mississippi. I failed to obtain interviews with three important leaders, Stokely Carmichael, Bob Moses and James Forman; however, at least some of the opinions of all three of them are available in published forms. I did interview almost all others whom I was able to identify as leaders between 1960 and 1966, as well as a number of ordinary members.

The interviews were long, loosely structured and deep. I asked broad questions concerning the "important areas" and only when I felt the direction of the interview had been determined did I make specific inquiries. Such inquiries varied from one person to another, depending on the capacity of the person to answer them (i.e., where and when he had worked). This method allowed the "shape" of the study (the subjects and lengths of the chapters) to be determined by SNCC members themselves. I feel that such an approach was particularly appropriate to an initial study of an organization. A questionnaire would have provided more accuracy in detail but possibly not in broad direction.

The number and depth of my interviews provide assurance that my conclusions about SNCC's character and development are correct. The interviews rarely contradicted each other, and where they did I have presented all opinions. I was troubled somewhat by the problem of memory distortion. To what extent has SNCC's early history been mythologized? Is it possible that statements about the early years which were repeated in 1966 and 1967 even by a great many early members reflected only the kind of group-wide distortion which may occur so easily in a small, close organization? I have some evidence that this kind of distortion did occur. For example, many early members seem to have forgotten the extent to which SNCC continued to sponsor direct-action demonstrations between 1961 and 1964, probably because this type of activity become rare later on. There are a large number of press releases and clippings which prove the prevalence of these demonstrations. However, the interviews do reflect the more significant fact that these demonstrations were not considered important. SNCC apparently did not emphasize in its communications to the outside world the same things which were seen as important within the organization. Another example of this gap between news stories and interviews is in the area of nonviolence. This ideal appears to have declined in SNCC long before its statements to the press—or the press's treatment of those statements—began to reflect that decline.

Only a series of depth interviews done in 1962 and 1963 similar to the ones I did in 1966 and 1967 could fully insure against memory distortion. In the absence of such interviews, I stressed to my informants the importance of remembering how they felt then, in many cases by asking them to recall in detail specific events—and then I measured these responses against the documents and news stories available to me. Broadly speaking, the documents and news stories told me what events had occurred; the interviews gave me the reactions of SNCC members to those events. Since most of my interviews were with people who no longer work for SNCC, I did not simply receive the Black Power interpretation of SNCC's history. The fact that I interviewed people who had been in SNCC at different periods helped me to distinguish broadly held views from the distortions characteristic of a particular period. This mitigated the problem of memory distortion. Although my method does not guarantee the accuracy of every statement, it should insure that my broad conclusions are correct.

In an effort to gain a participant-observer perspective without bringing my objectivity into question, I worked in Mississippi for about two weeks for the Poor People's Corporation (PPC), a SNCC spin-off group. I did not have access to SNCC's files, but I did see a number of documents in the archives of the Southern Regional Council in Atlanta and the Freedom Information Service in Jackson, Mississippi, as well as in the private collections of some SNCC members. My experience with the PPC and my perusal of documents further confirmed the conclusions I had drawn from the interviews.

Many SNCC people questioned whether a white person should be doing a study of SNCC; they felt that black people should write their own history. I agree that they should do so, and I welcome studies on SNCC by black people which concentrate on its place in the history of race relations. My own study is focused on organizational behavior and deals with race relations only secondarily. It discusses only the period before the summer of 1966; I have not even attempted to deal with the Black Power period. In any case, I cannot accept the view that white people should cease completely to write about black people or about race relations.

The question of the scholar's perspective is certainly a valid one, though, especially since the subject is so current and so emotionally charged. I did not, of course, approach SNCC as a completely neutral observer. At the beginning of my study in August 1966, my bias was broadly sympathetic, although I was puzzled and disturbed by the recent shift away from nonviolence and cooperation with whites. I am now probably even more sympathetic with SNCC's problems, although I disagree with most of its prescriptions for race relations in America. More broadly, I would characterize myself as a liberal with a sympathetic ear to the radical outlook. This thesis would probably be very different if I were a segregationist or a pacifist or a Communist. The very idea of allowing the subjects to help shape the thesis implies a belief in the integrity and importance, if not the validity, of their world-view. I make no claim to ultimate objectivity. What I do claim is that within the context implied by the questions I raised at the start, my findings have both accuracy and significance.

In setting forth these findings, I have found it necessary to offer first a summary of the actual events in SNCC's history, since these events do not seem to be widely known.

ONE

Outline of SNCC's History

Briefly, SNCC's history fell into four phases, as follows:

1. Sit-in Phase, Spring 1960-Summer 1961.
2. Community Organizing Phase I, Summer 1961-Winter 1964.
3. White Politics Phase, Spring 1964-September 1965.
4. Community Organizing Phase II, Spring 1965-present.

Sit-in Phase

SNCC was founded during the weekend of April 15-17, 1960, on the campus of Shaw University in Raleigh, North Carolina. A group of black Southern college students, along with their white Northern supporters, altogether about 300 people, came together for a conference under the sponsorship of the Southern Christian Leadership Conference (SCLC). The Southern students were almost all leaders of the "sit-in" movement which had started on February 1, 1960, when a group of black college students in Greensboro, North Carolina, refused to leave a dime-store lunch counter where they had been denied service. Within days, the sit-in idea had spread to other campuses and by mid-April dozens of Southern college towns and cities were the scenes of sit-ins. Neatly dressed black students, sometimes carrying Bibles or textbooks, sat patiently for hours at lunch counters, waiting to be served, often in the face of abusive language and threats of violence. In Nashville, Tennessee, the students were actually attacked. Meanwhile, Northern students, mostly white, picketed the Northern branches of Woolworth's, one of the stores involved, in order to express their sympathy and to exert financial pressure on the chain.

Ella Baker, a middle-aged black veteran of civil rights activity who was then working for SCLC, conceived the idea of a committee whose purpose would be to coordinate the sit-in activity, keep the leaders in touch with each other, raise funds, increase publicity and perhaps arrange to start sit-ins in places where they had not appeared spontaneously. She called the Raleigh conference for this purpose, and it was there that the Temporary Student Nonviolent Coordinating Committee was founded. The keynote speaker at the conference was James Lawson, a divinity student at the American Baptist Seminary in Nashville, Tennessee. Lawson's speech stressed the power of nonviolent confrontation, as exemplified in the sit-ins, to give courage to the black man and to change the heart of the white. It was this power that Lawson envisaged as the chief weapon of the new organization.

Meanwhile, the sit-ins seemed to be dying down. An agreement was reached in October with several of the nationwide store chains for the integration of all the facilities in their stores. Some sit-in leaders, especially from the very active Nashville Movement, wanted to apply the strategy of nonviolent confrontation to other areas, and movie theatres were proposed as the 1961 target. However, there was little activity in the winter of 1960-61. A brief stir was raised when on the first anniversary of the start of the sit-ins, February 1, 1961, several SNCC leaders, along with members of the Congress of Racial Equality (CORE), went to jail in Rock Hill, South Carolina, after a sit-in. Until that point, the sit-in leaders had generally avoided long jail sentences by being bailed out immediately after their arrests. The Rock Hill sit-in was designed to try out a new tactic: "jail no bail." Since sit-ins were no longer being reported in the Northern papers, it was hoped that the thought of college students on a chain gang would revive Northern interest. However, the interest proved fleeting and the penalty was high: thirty days on the chain gang.

In May 1961, SNCC did finally find a new focus of interest: the integration of interstate buses and bus terminals. On May 1, 1961, an integrated group of CORE leaders and supporters undertook a trip on two buses from Washington, D.C. to New Orleans. The purpose of this "Freedom Ride" was to desegregate the buses and terminal facilities along the way. One of the original riders was John Lewis, a leader of the Nashville movement who was later to become chairman of SNCC. The Ride was fairly uneventful until one of the two buses was burned by white segregationists in Anniston, Alabama. On the same day, the civil rights leaders on the other bus were attacked by a mob in Birmingham. The original riders, many of them seriously injured, here abandoned the trip. The sit-in leaders, especially those from Atlanta and Nashville, sensed an opportunity for a well-publicized and dramatic revival of nonviolent direct action. They decided to continue the Ride on to New Orleans. Martin Luther King, the head of SCLC, in response to a plea for a cooling-off period from Attorney General Robert Kennedy, called for a temporary lull in the Rides. His call was ignored, as students, mobilized by SNCC, poured into Alabama from all over the nation to continue the journey into Mississippi. As the Freedom Riders arrived in Jackson, they were immediately arrested for "not moving on" and similar charges. There in Jackson some of the students chose to serve two-month jail sentences. Among them were Stokely Carmichael and the late Ruby Doris Smith, who in May 1966 were to be elected chairman and executive secretary, respectively, of SNCC.

The Freedom Rides continued all through the summer of 1961, as new reinforcements kept arriving, including many white Northerners. SNCC tried to coordinate these rides but without much success.

Almost all of the early SNCC activists participated in some of the first Freedom Rides and for many of them it was a kind of turning point. The Rides, which had all the features of the sit-ins, at the same time pointed the way to the next phase of SNCC.

SNCC had come into existence because of a new social movement, the sit-ins (actually not completely new; sit-ins had been tried by the National Association for the Advancement of Colored People (NAACP) in border states in the late 1950s). The sit-ins of the 1960s expanded at a great pace for a while, then died down over an extended period and finally underwent a brief but intense revival, the Freedom Rides. After that, the sit-ins no longer really provided a *raison d'etre* for SNCC. Local groups, the NAACP, SCLC, and CORE all seemed well equipped to carry them on. During the Freedom Rides, though, the more moderate groups had shown a reluctance to carry the cause into the heart of the Black Belt after being confronted with the full fury of white violence. SNCC's mustering of college students had enabled the Rides to carry into Mississippi. Some of its members now saw a new goal: to carry the movement into the rural Deep South, hitherto almost completely untouched. In the summer of 1961, SNCC began preparations for doing that. At that point, SNCC was optimistic and reformist in outlook. Most of its members believed that integrating public facilities in the South was a real step toward freedom. Almost all members of SNCC were reformist, but there was a serious quarrel within the organization—over strategies for reform.

One group within SNCC wanted to continue "direct action," meaning the use of the strategy of nonviolent confrontation to integrate all aspects of society. The other group, for a variety of reasons, felt that direct action was of limited value and wanted to try voter registration in the Deep South, with the long-range goal of creating a political base for demands for black equality. At that point, SNCC leaders did not think of "taking over" town or county governments but merely of influencing white politicians to take into account the desires of black people.[1] At a meeting at the Highlander Folk School in Tennessee in August 1961, SNCC almost split into two organizations. But Ella Baker, who had been instrumental in founding SNCC, fought to prevent its dissolution and an agreement was made to divide the organization into two wings. The direct-action wing was to be led by Diane Nash, a member of the Nashville Movement. Charles Jones, another sit-in leader, was appointed head of the voter registration wing.

One reason for the bitterness at the Highlander Folk School meeting was that the direct-action supporters feared that voter registration was a thinly disguised device for depriving the movement of its independence and militancy. They were aware that the effort to register black voters in the Deep South was being supported by the federal government, which promised protection, and by several liberal, white-supported foundations, such as the Taconic, the New World and the Field Foundations. They feared that the movement would lose its uniqueness and moral purity by concentrating on such activity. Voter registration involved politics, both by its nature and by the fact that the federal government was prepared to give concrete support. Politics was believed to be "dirty," in that it necessarily involved the compromise of moral principles. Therefore, voter registration was thought to be a threat to the moral task of SNCC as an organization. By and large, the people who believed this also believed in nonviolence as a matter of principle, rather than in nonviolent direct action as a tactic. Not political deals, they felt, but moral nonviolent confrontation was SNCC's appropriate medium. Thus, it was the nonviolent wing of SNCC which at the start was the most radical in its rejection of standard American politics.

Community Organizing Phase I

In August 1961, Bob Moses, a black man from Harlem, began SNCC's first voter registration in McComb, Mississippi. (He had earlier made an unsuccessful effort to organize Cleveland, Mississippi.) The McComb project soon became involved in direct action as well. Less than a month after SNCC came to McComb, over 100 high school students were mobilized for a demonstration. This use of high school students later became a SNCC hallmark. After numerous arrests, several brutal beatings and a murder (of a black farmer who attempted to register), this project was abandoned after a few months. When the project had started, at least some SNCC staff members thought that, with the expected cooperation of the federal government, it would take only six months to a year to establish the black people's right to vote.[2] The violence and effectiveness of the resistance was something of an eye-opener. McComb was written off as a "pilot project."

For the next few years, SNCC sponsored both voter registration and direct-action projects. The direct-action wing first planned to sponsor a "Move on Mississippi" involving coordinated demonstrations throughout the state, but it soon gave this up for less ambitious projects involving one town at a time. Typically, a direct-action project would be started by one or perhaps two SNCC workers, who usually began their organizing among college students or teenagers. Every few months, there would be a mass march, usually followed by hundreds of arrests. The campaigns involved not only sit-ins and public demonstrations but also economic boycotts. The demands usually were for the integration of public facilities, for the employment of blacks on the basis of merit, and for the establishment of biracial committees. Between 1961 and early 1964, direct-action campaigns sponsored by SNCC took place in Atlanta, Savannah, Americus and Albany, Georgia; in Danville and Farmville, Virginia; in Cambridge, Maryland (where local leadership developed and the project continued for years); on Route 40 in Maryland (in conjunction with CORE); in Clarksdale, Jackson, Greenwood and Greenville, Mississippi; in Pine Bluff and Helena, Arkansas; in Knoxville and Somerville, Tennessee; in Louisville, Kentucky; in Selma, Gadsden and Tuscaloosa, Alabama; and in many other places in the South.

It sometimes took years for a direct-action project to succeed in integrating the public facilities of a town—and then little else would change, and life for the black people would continue as before. Often, the integrated facilities would not be used by black people because they were too expensive.

It is sometimes said by SNCC members that the direct-action wing went to Mississippi and the voter registration wing went to Southwest Georgia, but actually both kinds of activity took place in both states. In fact, in many towns the direct-action project was combined with a voter registration project or was intended as the forerunner to voter registration.[3] Direct action involved the teenagers, who in turn would involve their parents, at least in the raising of bail or bond money. Once the adults were involved, a voter registration project could be started.

In many towns, direct action was considered too dangerous and only voter registration was attempted. But voter registration turned out to be a form of direct action, in that its chief effect was to involve large numbers of people in immediate participation and dramatic confrontation with danger. The standard method of voter registration was to get as many black people in a county as possible to march to the courthouse together to register on a "Freedom Day," which was built up to by weeks of house-to-house organizing and church meetings. On the Freedom Day, there were often hundreds of arrests. Thus, voter registration entailed precisely the same kind of public commitment as direct action. It showed the black people that their worst fears were not justified and it showed both local whites and the courts that black people really did want to vote.

Putting people in a position where they would probably be arrested by the police and then bailed out by SNCC was a way of prying them away from their dependency on the goodwill of white men in power. Getting them arrested *en masse* served chiefly to unify the members of a community against white authority. SNCC sometimes deliberately provoked such mass arrests.[4]

In Selma, Alabama, beginning in 1963, SNCC sponsored a major voter registration project, using not only demonstrations but a serious educational effort to help black people meet the literacy requirement. It still had little success in getting people registered. In voter registration in general, SNCC accomplished as little after years of effort as in direct action. Fewer than six percent of the eligible black voters in Mississippi were registered by the summer of 1963, and the figure was little higher in rural Georgia, Alabama and Arkansas. For many SNCC members, voting and integration, although desirable in themselves, came to be seen primarily as issues around which to organize. The real purpose of SNCC work in the Deep South was thus to awaken the black man's political consciousness and ultimately to make him a political force to be reckoned with.[5] It was mainly for this reason that the distinction between the two wings of SNCC faded in importance after the Highlander Folk School meeting. After only a few months, Charles Jones and Diane Nash got together and agreed there was no further need for separate chairmen.[6] Both direct action and voter registration came to be seen as part of a unified effort to insure for the black man an independent and dignified position in American politics and society.[7]

This awareness of a broader goal kept SNCC workers going in the face of repeated failures to achieve immediate goals. But the people among whom SNCC was working were deeply discouraged by the lack of concrete gains. SNCC was asking Southern blacks, who were in a highly vulnerable position, to take enormous risks in order to register to vote and was offering in exchange only vague ideals like "freedom" or "the exercise of constitutional rights." It was unable even to begin to help with the immediate problems of massive unemployment and underemployment, which were both a cause and an indirect effect of the absence of political rights. Most black people who attempted to register were repeatedly turned away, either by delaying tactics or by the discriminatory use of the literacy test. The small number of black people who did succeed in registering were faced with an almost total absence of meaningful choice of candidates. The Rev. R. L. T. Smith, a black man, had run for the U.S. Senate from Mississippi in 1962, but there were so few registered black voters that he made a very poor showing.

SNCC was finding it increasingly difficult to organize communities around voter registration. Clearly, some new tactics were necessary. The Mississippi Democratic gubernatorial primary in the summer of 1963 offered an opportunity for experimentation. SNCC planned to hold a "vote-in" in which unregistered black people would go to the polls on election day and swear affidavits to the effect that they had been illegally prevented from registering. Under a Reconstruction statute designed to protect whites, they could then be permitted to vote. Threats by election officials of fines or imprisonment for unlawfully attempting to procure registration caused this effort to fizzle. SNCC collected a number of affidavits anyway and presented them to the federal government as proof that black people in Mississippi really did want to vote.

Then it decided to dramatize the exclusion of black people from the franchise by setting up polling places on primary day in black churches and homes where unregistered people could vote for one of the two regular candidates for the gubernatorial nomination, Paul Johnson and J. P.

Coleman. This "Freedom Vote" aroused such interest and activity that SNCC decided to repeat it in the November election. This time, the Freedom Ballot contained the names of the Democratic and Republican candidates for governor and also that of a "Freedom" candidate, Aaron Henry, a black druggist who was state chairman of the NAACP. The name of a sympathetic white man, the Rev. R. Edwin King, candidate for lieutenant governor, appeared on the Freedom Ballot as well. Henry and King received 70,000 to 80,000 votes, in spite of a press blackout and continual harassment of the campaign workers.

White Politics Phase

The Freedom Ballot won considerable publicity in the North, mainly because about seventy white students from Yale and Stanford Universities participated in the campaign. Their activities and their jailings and beatings were reported in their hometown and college papers. The result was a flood of donations to SNCC. Two months after the election, SNCC[8] decided to expand enormously the successful elements of the Freedom Ballot by holding a "Freedom Summer" in Mississippi. The summer was to involve not seventy but about a thousand white student volunteers. Like the Freedom Vote, it was to be centered around a dramatization of the exclusion of black people from the political process, this time in the case of the selection of delegates to the Democratic National Convention. SNCC was going to challenge the right of the regular Democratic Party of Mississippi to send delegates to the convention in Atlantic City. It formed the Mississippi Freedom Democratic Party (FDP), which chose its delegates in a manner exactly parallel to the regular Democratic Party, except that no one was excluded. (Of course, virtually no whites took advantage of the opportunity to participate in the Freedom Democratic Party's deliberations.)

About 700 Northern students descended on Mississippi in the summer of 1964. One of them, Andrew Goodman, was murdered during his first week there, along with James Chaney and Michael Schwerner. The others spent the summer working on voter registration, setting up and running community centers and "freedom schools," and preparing for the "challenge" to the white Democrats in Atlantic City in August. At the convention, the credentials committee offered the Freedom Democrats seats for two delegates-at-large, while seating the regulars as the delegation from

13

Mississippi. The FDP rejected this compromise and the credentials committee did not file a minority report, so the issue of who was to be seated was never brought to the convention floor.

Mississippi was not the only place where SNCC encouraged black political candidates. In Albany, Georgia, Thomas Chatmon and Slater King, both black men active in the Albany Movement, ran for city commissioner and mayor, respectively, in 1963. Slater King's brother, C. B. King, ran for Congress in 1964. There were also SNCC-backed candidates for Congress in 1964 in Selma, Alabama, Danville, Virginia, and Enfield, North Carolina. All lost.

After the summer of 1964, SNCC found itself exhausted and uncertain where to turn next. Partly for lack of a more promising type of activity, four FDP candidates for the U.S. Congress, who had just won a "Freedom Election," challenged the regular Mississippi delegation in January 1965. The regulars were temporarily seated, but a final decision about the seats was postponed until the following September. That spring and summer, many SNCC people worked on this second FDP challenge. Several hundred white students were brought to Washington in week-long shifts to lobby for the challenge during the summer. But most SNCC members had little hope for the success of the challenge and were tired of devoting their efforts to projects that were certain of failure.

The Arkansas project was still engaging in a great deal of voter registration and direct-action activity in 1965. Since it had been only indirectly affected by the events of the summer of 1964, it actually flourished in 1965. In the summer of 1965, it ran a summer project with about fifty student volunteers, half of them black. The Arkansas project did not go into decline until after the enunciation of the slogan "black power" and the consequent resignation of the state project director, the Rev. Ben Grinage. But by early 1965, SNCC in Mississippi was floundering.

A large number of whites had been added to the staff after the Mississippi summer project in 1964 and they presented acute problems. During the fall of 1964 and the winter of 1965, SNCC went through a period of great internal upheaval. As a result, its organizational structure was changed and the whites began to drift out of the organization. SNCC was at loose ends; it did not know what to undertake next. The failure of the convention challenge had convinced it that it could not make significant headway through the regular political process because its most important ally, the national Democratic Party, had only a very limited commitment to its cause.

14

The FDP was working on the congressional challenge, but most SNCC members were very pessimistic about it.

Community Organizing Phase II

In March 1965, SNCC members participated in the Selma-to-Montgomery March led by the Rev. Martin Luther King. While marching through Lowndes County, Alabama, the population of which is eighty percent black, several SNCC members decided that this might be a good place to start a new project. It was in Lowndes County that Mrs. Viola Liuzzo was killed during the March, and no other national group seemed to want to undertake its political organization. Stokely Carmichael, who had been working for SNCC in the Deep South for about a year and in Lowndes County for a few months, and one or two others began organizing the county in earnest. In November 1965, they formed the Lowndes County Freedom Organization (LCFO), whose symbol was the Black Panther. It became famous as the Black Panther Party. With the help of the 1965 Voting Rights Act, hundreds of black people were registered. No appeals to conscience were made in Lowndes; the explicit goal was power right from the start. In November 1966, the LCFO ran its own candidates for the offices of sheriff, coroner, tax assessor, tax collector and member of the Board of Education (all county offices). In all these cases, there was a real hope that the black candidates would win. All lost, however, partly because of election irregularities and partly because many black people voted for white candidates.

Meanwhile, in the spring of 1965, SNCC helped found the Mississippi Freedom Labor Union (MFLU), which organized cotton pickers and choppers to resist a cut in wages from $3.00 a day to $1.75. When many of the strikers were evicted from their homes, the MFLU set up a tent city for them near Greenville, Mississippi. The tent city still exists, but the MFLU disappeared when its strike was broken. At the height of the 1965 cotton-chopping season, there had been 2,000 strikers. But the introduction of mechanization made it possible for the plantation owners to do without their unskilled workers completely. SNCC then founded the Poor People's Corporation of Mississippi (PPC) which runs a series of craft-producing cooperatives employing mostly people who have been thrown off the land.

15

The PPC still exists but it is a marginal operation and has little connection with SNCC.

Meanwhile, in early 1965, SNCC began trying to re-establish its original campus base by founding a "campus travelers' group" of seven members. Then, in the summer of 1965, a group of SNCC members were active in operating the Child Development Group of Mississippi (CDGM), a part of the Office of Economic Opportunity's Head Start program. The following winter there was increasing pressure in Washington to take CDGM out of SNCC's hands or else destroy it. After being discontinued twice and partially replaced by a rival agency, CDGM's existence was finally assured—but not without a long fight on its behalf by the United Automobile Workers (UAW), the National Council of Churches and other national liberal organizations. SNCC was particularly bitter when its old ally from the NAACP, Aaron Henry, cooperated with the moderate whites in the battle over CDGM.

SNCC found itself once again floundering. Its old ideas and strategies—community organizing, nonviolence, the use of white organizers, a certain amount of reliance on the federal government—seemed to have led it to a dead end. No SNCC-initiated project, using these strategies, had ever achieved a clear success. Some of the short-range goals SNCC had set for itself had been accomplished by other means (for example, the registration of large numbers of black voters in Mississippi with the help of federal registrars). Thus, SNCC had been deprived of both techniques and issues for political organizing.

This frustration had led one group of members, who were working in Atlanta's ghettoes, to become particularly bitter and anti-white. In early 1964, there had been a very active nonviolent direct-action project in Atlanta centered around the integration of Toddle House restaurants. By mid-1965, the people in the Atlanta project were doing little organizing and a great deal of talking about black consciousness, the coming race war, etc.[9]

SNCC workers left Lowndes County after the election and began to try to develop "freedom organizations" in other places, including Northern ghettoes. A freedom organization was conceived as a multi-purpose community group. It might register people to vote, run its own political candidates where they had a chance of winning, conduct economic boycotts on behalf of black employment, encourage draft resistance, etc. All of the above would be viewed as techniques; its central purpose would actually be to arouse "black consciousness." SNCC's greatest success had been in awakening among black people awareness and anger rather than in achieving concrete gains. A freedom organization would be a sort of miniature SNCC, only much more openly aimed at black minds rather than at substantial reform. It would also differ from the old SNCC in not attempting to penetrate the Democratic Party and in not relying in any way on the goodwill of whites. It would instead develop "pockets of power," the idea of which had been discussed in SNCC for years.[10] Thus, a freedom organization was an acceptable vehicle for the growing anti-white group in SNCC. It seemed that SNCC's old concern about integration had all but disappeared.

Finally, in May 1966, there was a formal transfer of leadership. John Lewis, the early sit-in leader who had been chairman for almost three years, was voted out of office and replaced by Stokely Carmichael, the pioneer of the freedom organization, whose work in Lowndes County had given him a great reputation for militancy. The executive secretary, James Forman, resigned and was replaced by Ruby Doris Smith, an early leader who was quite anti-white. The following month, during James Meredith's march through Mississippi, Carmichael enunciated the slogan Black Power.

SNCC had come into being as a coordinating committee for the sit-in movement. When that movement died in 1961, SNCC would have died too, but it found a new definition of itself: an organizer of the black people of small rural communities in the Deep South, the places where no other civil rights organization was willing to go. After more than two years of this activity, SNCC found that it had hardly made a dent in the system of political and economic white supremacy there. Its organizing activities were becoming more difficult rather than easier as people saw their danger and unproductiveness. In order to give itself some hope of success, SNCC had to redefine itself in a way that placed much greater reliance on white assistance, both within the organization and in Washington. The enormous conflicts and frustrations brought about by this course almost wrecked the organization. In the spring of 1965, SNCC began to try to pick up the pieces. Its new definition of itself led to an attempt to return to an earlier period, before the adventure in white politics. It was hoped that an extension of the organization outside the South, combined with a new militancy, would create greater success.

All of the above tells what happened to SNCC but not why. What sort of organizational dynamics caused SNCC to react as it did to frustration? Why did it not seek a less hostile environment than the Deep South? Why was it unable to obtain more help from the rest of the country? What kept it going at all after repeated failures?

In discussing these questions, SNCC members generally speak in terms of SNCC's political environment. It seems reasonable that a closer examination of SNCC's experiences with other institutions is necessary to understand what sort of an organization it became and why. This is the subject of the next chapter.

TWO

SNCC's
Political Context

That SNCC's political environment influenced it strongly is beyond question. Every political group is shaped by its environment; different groups react in different ways, but all groups are in some way influenced. Policy to some extent depends on the nature of both enemies and allies.

Most previous writing on SNCC has stressed its environment strongly and in particular one part of that environment: the Deep South, where most of its organizing before 1966 took place. Yet the thrust of SNCC's anger has since 1965 been directed not against white supremacists but against white liberals. It is necessary to examine why this is so, and to do that we will have to look at SNCC's broader environment, the U.S. in the 1960s. We will find that it is not only *white* liberals that incur SNCC's wrath but also more moderate black-advancement organizations, such as the NAACP and SCLC. This chapter then has three parts: the Deep South; Relations with White Allies; and Relations with Black Allies.

A. *The Deep South*

In an open society, liberal reformist political activity seems the most appropriate kind. Exponents of radical change in America generally have difficulty gaining adherents. Even those citizens who see important specific evils are reluctant to sacrifice the advantages of an open and benevolent system, as conspiratorial, radical groups must do. In most parts of America, SNCC would probably have disappeared or become a standard political pressure-group shortly after its appearance on the scene. It was only because it chose to concentrate its activities in the Black Belt, and most especially in Mississippi, that its radical interpretation of American society had plausibility and appeal. There, in the "closed society,"[1] its efforts to obtain what seemed

19

like simple justice were met with violent and unmoving hostility. Did SNCC choose to work in the Deep South because its leaders were already radicals who wished to have their angry views about American society confirmed? It is true that in choosing these areas, the early leaders faced a guarantee of frustration, hardship, isolation, brutality, even deaths, and thus they almost insured that SNCC would maintain a stance outside society. The commonsense approach to Southern injustice would have been to chip away at its edges, in the border states and the big cities, before attacking the hard-core rural Deep South. (This was what other civil-rights organizations were doing.)

Yet the evidence does not support the hypothesis that it was the radical bent of the early leaders that led them to choose the Deep South. Most of the early SNCC members were sit-in leaders. There have been a number of social and psychological studies[2] of sit-in leaders, all of which show that they were overwhelmingly middle-class, religious, patriotic young black people. It is true that the SNCC leaders were the most militant of the sit-in leaders. Yet all of the early SNCC people in my study spoke of a long process of disillusionment with American society which occurred *since* the sit-ins. The few early SNCC leaders who were not sit-in leaders were not radicals either.

SNCC chose the Deep South in part because it was optimistic rather than pessimistic about America, particularly about the support of the federal government. As one early member put it, there was a belief in "a great force that's really fair."[3]

Early SNCC leaders give a variety of other reasons for this decision. The most frequently cited is that Mississippi was a symbol that had to be broken. This is persuasive, especially when one recalls that the move to Mississippi began immediately after the peak of the direct-action movement, with its heavy emphasis on symbolic confrontation. The Freedom Rides ended in Jackson and so Mississippi seemed the logical place to pick up from there. In August 1961, about half a dozen Freedom Riders completed sentences of a few months in jails in Mississippi and decided to stay where they were and attack the system that had jailed them. Bob Moses was beginning work in Mississippi at the same time, and since he was an inspired leader, many people followed him there. Why then did Moses (who had never been a direct-action leader) choose Mississippi?

One of SNCC's original goals had been to try to start sit-in movements in places where they had not begun spontaneously, and it was for this purpose that Moses had originally visited the state in 1960. Mississippi was where people were suffering the worst and where the local college students and the established organizations were doing the least. One early SNCC leader[4] commented that at least there was no problem of organizational rivalry there! In fact, it was an NAACP official, Amzie Moore, who first invited SNCC into Mississippi. He had tried to persuade his own group to work in the rural part of the state, but with no success.

Work in the Deep South was appealing because it was something that SNCC could do and that no other group could or would do. Such work required just the kind of stamina and courage that the young sit-in leaders possessed in a high degree. The Deep South had appeal to the young also because it offered a reassuring moral simplicity: white men seemed really evil; therefore, black men could be really good. Thus, by working there, SNCC leaders could retain both their sense of moral superiority and their feeling of special destiny.

Moreover, Mississippi had an evangelical appeal, which meshed with the religious background of many of SNCC's early members. The conversion of the worst sinner seemed to offer the greatest reward. This belief was expressed in the statement made by many SNCC members that once Mississippi was broken, the rest of the South would follow.

There were other, less frequently mentioned, reasons for choosing the rural South. One is the political potential provided by the heavy concentration of black people combined with the disproportionate weight given to rural areas in Southern apportionment, particularly in the Georgia county-unit system. Still another reason is that many of the sit-in leaders were themselves natives of or only one generation removed from the rural Deep South. This meant that they knew this area and had a strong motivation for wanting to right the wrongs which had been perpetrated on themselves and their ancestors. Perhaps some of those whose parents had been assimilated into the middle class were seeking a sense of identity by returning to their origins. They tended to believe that the culture of poor Deep South black people was the "true" and "pure" black culture, because these black people were the most oppressed and most isolated from the general white culture. Perhaps for this reason, they saw the oppression of these people as symbolic of the plight of all black Americans. In working for the political birth of these people, perhaps they sought a new political birth for all black people, including themselves. The choice of the rural Deep South represented a rejection of the kind of political accommodation chosen by the black middle class, and thus contained the seeds of a rejection of all political accommodation.

Violence

Having determined to tackle the hard-core Deep South, SNCC faced the ever-present shadow of white violence—continual beatings, jailings, even murders. The list of those who were murdered in the cause of civil rights in the South since 1960 is a long one. It includes Herbert Lee, Medgar Evers, Clifton Walker, Michael Schwerner, James Chaney, Andrew Goodman, Lewis Allen, Jimmie Lee Jackson, James Reeb, Viola Gregg Liuzzo, Samuel Younge, Jonathan Daniels, Freddie Lee Thomas and Vernon Dahmer, and probably a number of others whose deaths were not publicized. Most white Americans would recognize only the names of the white people on this list[5] (except for Chaney, who died with two white men, and Evers, who was Mississippi state executive director of the NAACP). No convictions of the murderers have been obtained, except in the spectacular case of Schwerner, Chaney and Goodman, which involved two whites. The conclusion for SNCC was almost unavoidable: the life of the ordinary black man in the Deep South was completely unprotected, either by the press or by the legal system.

Most of the above-mentioned murder victims were not SNCC members, but almost all of them had worked on common projects with SNCC. There had been a great many attempts on the lives of SNCC members. Local white men sprayed bullets into SNCC offices, or burned them down. In February 1963, Bob Moses was shot at as he was riding in a car near Greenwood, Mississippi. His companion, a SNCC worker named Jimmy Travis, was hit by a bullet which almost killed him.[6] A week later, another car containing SNCC members was shot into. All of this happened in Greenwood. Instead of abandoning its project there, SNCC followed a policy of defiance. It had long before resolved never to give in to violence, but rather to "send in ten men if one was shot, to send in 100 if ten were shot." SNCC therefore brought its people from all over Mississippi into Greenwood, and the result was that hundreds of black people marched to the courthouse to register and the town swarmed with Justice Department employees and reporters from all over the nation. At about the same time, ten SNCC and CORE field secretaries, including SNCC executive secretary James Forman, were continuing the march into Mississippi of William Moore, a Baltimore postman who had just been murdered in Alabama. Such bold policies were not without cost, however.[7] Six months later, sixty-two of SNCC's sixty-seven workers (including unpaid volunteers) in Mississippi were in jail. Of the sixty-two, forty-five were doing hard labor on the Leflore County prison farm. (Greenwood is the county seat of Leflore County.) Another sixteen were under maximum security guard in the state penitentiary.[8] The price of concentrating its small forces had been a heavy one for SNCC.

The experience in Greenwood was typical of SNCC experiences all over the Deep South. Virtually every SNCC member before 1964 went to jail at least once, and many went time after time. Three SNCC workers (Don Harris, Ralph Allen and John Perdew) spent sixty-eight days in jail, starting in August 1963, on a charge which carried a possible death penalty. They had been arrested in Americus, Georgia after a meeting in a church. The police beat Harris and other people, several of whom required stitches in the head. The arrested men were indicted for "attempt to incite insurrection" (the capital charge), unlawful assembly, unlawful rioting and the obstruction of a lawful arrest.[9] They were finally released after a federal court ruled unconstitutional the Georgia statute under which they were held.[10] This episode received almost no publicity in the North, even though two of the accused men (Allen and Perdew) were white.

Conditions in prisons in the Deep South were horrible. One SNCC member described an experience in Parcham State Penitentiary in Mississippi:

> We stayed in the hot box two nights. It's a cell about six foot square . . . Long as they don't turn the heat on—with three in there—you can make it. There's no openings for light or air; there was a little crack under the door, but you couldn't see your hand before your face 'less you get down on your knees. When they get ready to feed you they hand the tray through a little door which they close—and then you can't eat unless you get down on your knees by the light comin' in the door—then you can see how to eat. And they had a little round hole in the floor which was a commode . . .[11]

Another SNCC member said he had been put in the "hot box" with twelve other people.

> We were making it okay for about thirty minutes with the fan off, breathing in this oxygen, letting out this carbon dioxide—and the air was evaporating on top of the building, and it got so hot the water was falling off the top of the building, all around the sides like it was raining . . . altogether, I was thirteen days in the hot box . . .[12]

23

Normal cells often contained many more people than bunks. Adding to their misery, SNCC workers before 1964 often went on hunger strikes while in jail.

Almost every male SNCC worker, and a great many of the females, was beaten at least once, either in jail or on the street. Sometimes the police did the beatings, sometimes it was angry white men. On a few occasions, the police introduced white prisoners to their cellmates as integrationists and hinted that the cellmates ought to beat them up; the cellmates did so with alacrity.[13] One SNCC project, in Danville, Virginia, became famous throughout SNCC because of the brutality of the police. During demonstrations there in the summer of 1963, police repeatedly attacked peaceful demonstrators with billy clubs and hoses. The mimeograph machines in the SNCC office ground out hundreds of press releases about the violent persecutions of SNCC workers; few of them were ever printed.

SNCC workers learned to live with the extreme hostility of the white communities of the towns in which they worked. They experienced the fear of being completely at the mercy of someone who hated them and did not care if they died.[14] They came to be continually vigilant, suspicious, cautious while at the same time bold. This psychological tension, even more than the physical hardships of SNCC life, was an important cause of the relatively high rate of turnover among SNCC members. For those who stayed more than a year or two, vigilance and suspicion became a part of their personalities. The more they suffered, too, the more keenly they felt the gap between themselves and the white liberals, who supported them financially but were not prepared to "put their bodies on the line."

The continual fear had an important shaping influence on SNCC. It meant that, as in the sit-ins, the most admired leaders were those who had proved that they were ready to confront the white man and to suffer physically for that confrontation. Further, it meant that the focus of SNCC activity came to be the overcoming of this fear of violence, both in the SNCC people themselves and in those whom they were trying to persuade to register or to demonstrate. A white man who worked in SNCC for several years put it this way:

> Nothing was ever accomplished by anybody, specifically in Albany, Georgia, in 1961-3. On the surface they lost every battle. They never desegregated the buses . . . They never desegregated the schools, they never got the jobs, and so on and so forth . . . (But) the fact of the attack, the willingness of the

people (in Albany) to stand up (and) to suffer in that situation . . . was a signal to other people in . . . many areas of the country . . . Albany gave people courage.[15]

For many SNCC members in the early years this was what SNCC seemed to be about: the overcoming of the paralyzing fear which prevented the black people of the small towns of the Deep South from organizing themselves into politically effective groups. After 1964, as the terror abated somewhat and as other groups began to compete with SNCC in the rural Black Belt, the focus shifted somewhat away from the overcoming of the fear of violence. Significantly, this was the same period when SNCC began to lose its cohesion as an organization. To some extent, the enormous courage that was assumed to go along with membership in SNCC had kept the organization close-knit by insuring the members' respect for each other. Mississippi SNCC had served as a model for the rest of SNCC in part because the state of Mississippi was a symbol of violent resistance to black advancement.

The continual danger affected SNCC's structure, too. Its central office developed along the lines called for by the dangers faced by its members. Besides fund-raising, its main function seemed to be to provide publicity, expedite internal communications and make contacts with the outside world, particularly the Justice Department, all with the purpose of lessening the dangers to field secretaries. It might almost be said that the chief function of SNCC before 1964 was to provide such protections, as well as a sense of solidarity, so that its component projects would not be overwhelmed by their isolation and helplessness in a hostile world.

After the long, slow winter of 1964-5, SNCC experienced a brief revitalization in the spring of 1965, when it entered Lowndes County, within a few weeks after the deaths of Jimmie Lee Jackson, the Rev. James Reeb and Mrs. Viola Liuzzo. It has been declining gradually in membership and in level of activity ever since—possibly in part because the use of public violence has fallen off in the Deep South. SNCC had learned two years before, in Greenwood in 1963, that violence, when inflicted by the whites, could be a great rallying force. It is not inconceivable that it dropped its own strict adherence to nonviolence partly because it sensed that violence could act as such a rallying force when employed by its own members as well as when employed by hostile whites.

The continual physical danger that SNCC members faced was an important factor in keeping alive the sense of moral superiority felt by the early sit-in participants. SNCC members saw themselves as the suffering victims of the local whites, not merely their political rivals. Only a burning belief in the rightness of their cause could have kept them going in the face of the brutality of their opponents—and this brutality itself helped to sustain such a belief. The moral fervor necessary for prolonged membership in SNCC was in turn a cause of SNCC's anger at the federal government, which dealt with the situation as if it were merely a matter of political rivalry. (See Chapter II, section B, on the federal government.) This anger at the federal government and at white Americans in general was one cause of SNCC's dropping the creed of nonviolence.

Violence against SNCC members also played a part in widening the breach between black and white members. It was widely believed in SNCC that whites were far less likely to be beaten than blacks[16] and this form of discrimination was particularly resented by many of the black members. Some of them believed that the contribution of whites could never mean the same as the contribution of black people because whites never had to pay the same penalty for their acts.[17] Even death did not bring equality, because whites who died for civil rights were mourned by the whole nation, whereas blacks who died were quickly forgotten by all except their friends and relatives.

Thus, white violence had a shaping effect on SNCC which it is hard to underestimate. For the first few years of SNCC's existence (before 1964), the overcoming of violence could almost be said to be its paramount goal. After that, the continuing, somewhat abated violence, which was reinforced by the memory of past brutalities, served to accelerate the trends within SNCC away from political accommodation, integration within the organization, and strict nonviolence.

Nonviolence

SNCC's nonviolence was perhaps the most apparent casualty of repeated encounters with white violence. It becomes easy to advocate violence against one's enemies if one believes that they are wicked men while he is a pure and suffering victim. Moreover, if one views nonviolence as merely a tactic of the weak against the violence of the strong, then it is not at all surprising that the continuation of violence by the strong would cause the dropping of the tactic. But for SNCC, at first, nonviolence was more than that. At its birth,

SNCC inherited a doctrine of nonviolence as the center of a way of life from its parent organization, SCLC. SNCC's founding constitution said:

> We affirm the philosophic or religious ideal of nonviolence as the foundation of our purpose, the presupposition of our faith and the manner of our action.
>
> By appealing to conscience and standing on the moral nature of human existence, nonviolence nurtures the atmosphere in which reconciliation and justice become actual possibilities.

This statement, which was written by a man who never worked for SNCC (James Lawson), is much stronger than SNCC's commitment to nonviolence ever was. Nonviolence was strictly adhered to during the sit-in movement because it was an integral part of the direct-action strategy. Direct action depends for its effectiveness on a confrontation with an immediate moral impact on both whites and inactive blacks, and such a confrontation in America cannot be combined with violence. Many of the sit-in leaders saw nonviolence as the foundation of a way of life as well. One of them[18] believed that nonviolence meant not merely "turning the other cheek" but learning to live in a community and to love oneself and thus to love all other human beings. He felt that carrying a gun for self-defense was a hostile act and therefore not nonviolent. In his view, a man should present himself naked and defenseless to those who threaten him with violence and then he can love and live. This very deep adherence to the philosophy of nonviolence was prevalent only in the Nashville Student Movement (SNCC's most important subsidiary during the sit-in phase), which was under the influence of James Lawson. Even in Nashville, there were those who were nonviolent chiefly because it was the popular strategy of the day.[19]This was even more true of the other sit-in centers.

By the summer of 1961, when SNCC began to shift into its first community-organizing phase, the fervor of the nonviolent movement was already waning. For most SNCC workers, a few weeks facing the terrors of organizing work in the Deep South were sufficient to dampen considerably their idealism and their faith in brotherly love. Nonviolence always remained a strict rule during public demonstrations, since SNCC recognized that it was necessary for the effectiveness of the direct-action strategy. However, quite early there were certain exceptions made in other areas. In Mississippi the local black people carried guns for self-defense as a long-established custom; as early as 1962, SNCC began "looking the other way" if those local blacks who worked with SNCC continued to adhere to this custom.[20] In Southwest

Georgia, the SNCC project was directed by the Rev. Charles Sherrod, who led the SNCC members in hymn-singing and in prayers before each meal. This was where those who were committed to nonviolence as a religious principle tended to cluster.[21] Yet Rev. Sherrod himself said in 1967[22] that nonviolence was never promoted as a way of life in the communities where he worked but rather as a technique to achieve certain goals.

SNCC as an organization never attempted to enforce the section on nonviolence in its constitution; the decision was left very much up to the individual project and often to the individual person. The sit-in leaders began to drift out of SNCC, and were replaced by people who had never really experienced the meaning of nonviolence in action. This process apparently took place rather rapidly. One SNCC worker in Southwest Georgia in the early years (Don Harris) estimated that between fifty and seventy percent of the staff in 1961 and in 1962 were opposed to strict adherence to nonviolence. In Southwest Georgia in 1963, there was a story circulating among SNCC workers that SNCC in Albany had once been protected by an armed gang of black teenagers. Whether or not the story was true, it seemed to appeal to SNCC people.[23]

SNCC stopped sponsoring regular workshops on nonviolent philosophy and techniques in 1961,[24] although such workshops were held intermittently until 1964. One SNCC worker suggests that "the press was more fascinated by it than we were."[25] Whatever discussion about nonviolence there was tended to center around marginal issues such as whether a SNCC member who was staying in the home of local black people should use the family's gun to protect them if they came under attack while the men in the family were not at home.

During the period before 1964, the technique of nonviolence even in demonstrations lost some of its usefulness. Bob Moses spoke of nonviolent action as an "annealing process" in which a community is brought to a white heat, then molded while cooling.[26] But this worked only if the nonviolence of the blacks was openly met by white violence. As time passed, the law officers and other white citizens of the Southern states realized this and they stopped cooperating. They learned to beat up civil rights workers only indoors and while no one was looking. This made it much more difficult for SNCC to use persecution as a unifying, community-building force. Even in Mississippi, the police caught on eventually, at least in the bigger towns. For example, in Hattiesburg, in January 1964, COFO sponsored a Freedom Day in which a number of Northern clergymen joined local black people in demonstrating for the right to vote. Their presence attracted Justice Department officials and reporters. The police refused to use terror or mass arrests and instead prevented the black people from registering by delaying tactics and the unfair administration of literacy tests.[27] As the demonstrations stretched on for days, James Forman actually tried to bait the town authorities into ordering the use of billy clubs, in order to break the stalemate, but without success.[28] A few weeks later the same thing happened at Canton, Mississippi. At about the same time in Atlanta, SNCC workers who were demonstrating against segregation fought back against the police. Forman called this a "creative confrontation," but it was not tried again because it was followed by a steep drop in funds from the North.[29]

These incidents make clear that nonviolence, which had at first appeared to be a means for the creative control of discontent, was actually a method of deliberately creating tensions which would rally the black community and force it to confront certain issues. Since after 1961 nonviolence was never a matter of principle for more than a few members of SNCC, it was predictable that SNCC should consider abandoning it once it stopped serving as a useful vehicle for arousing communities. After the first major urban riot (in Harlem in 1964), the usefulness of violence became a subject of open debate among all partisans of black advancement. It was no longer simply assumed that black violence was counter-productive. The riots undoubtedly had an important influence on SNCC's attitude toward nonviolence.

The Mississippi Summer Project of 1964 had given nonviolence a new lease on life. During the preparations for the summer, the question came up at a staff meeting for the first time in a long time when someone asked what the summer volunteers should be told about nonviolence. After some debate, it was decided that a SNCC worker should maintain nonviolence whenever possible.[30] COFO workers were not permitted to carry guns[31] and were trained in nonviolent techniques, but judgment on marginal issues (such as whether to ride in a car with a local black person who was carrying a gun) was left up to individuals.

After the summer, SNCC's militancy increased rapidly. At a closed meeting in May 1965, the executive committee discussed the question whether SNCC workers (not just local people) ought to carry guns. No decision was reached, but it was known that some people on the staff were in fact carrying guns.[32] Nonviolence had gradually become unimportant until finally nobody really cared whether it was being strictly maintained. By the time Stokely Carmichael was elected chairman in May 1966, there were "perhaps three" people in SNCC (including John Lewis) who were philosophically committed to nonviolence.[33] Most of the people in the organization were willing to use nonviolence as a tactic but were not very strongly convinced of its usefulness.[34] This situation with respect to attitudes toward nonviolence had existed for at least two years; there was no sudden change in May 1966. John Lewis lost the chairmanship not because of his views on nonviolence, which had been in conflict with those of the other members of SNCC for several years, but because of his lack of militancy toward the federal government and other organizations.

Violence and militancy were, however, related. Black racial pride was one cause of the dropping of nonviolence. The members of SNCC desired at least equality of standing with the white man. Why, then, should violence be denied to them as a weapon, while the white man used it with impunity? Once SNCC members came to believe that the system offered them no protection against white violence, the demand for equality pointed directly toward black violence.

The gradual abandonment of a firm commitment to nonviolence was not, however, related to a Northern black takeover. It is true that almost all of the original SNCC members who had a deep commitment to nonviolence were Southerners. However, as these original members drifted out of SNCC, they were replaced by both Northerners and Southerners (mostly Southerners) who regarded nonviolence merely as a tactic. Both in the South and in the big cities of the North (the places of origin of these people), violence is very much a part of life for both whites and blacks. One early SNCC member[35] commented that SNCC stopped being "un-American" when it abandoned strict nonviolence. Nonviolence was kept alive to some extent by the rather idealistic and sheltered white Northern college students who joined SNCC in small numbers beginning in early 1963, but mostly it was kept alive by tactical and financial necessity. SNCC was simply not strong enough or rich enough to be able to abandon openly its initial moralistic stance. Nonviolence therefore lingered long after conditions in the Deep South had made it both useless and repugnant to most SNCC members.

Conditions of Southern Black People

Those who possess the least may also have the most to lose. SNCC learned to its sorrow that violence was not the only method by which the black rural Southerner was kept in line, and possibly not even the most important or effective. Many, if not most, of the black people of the rural Deep South are in economic bondage to whites just as medieval serfs were in bondage to their lords. They are tenant farmers or sharecroppers, living on someone else's land and continually in debt, often to their landlords. Even in the early 1960s, there were too many of them for the land to support. Now mechanization has eliminated the need for all but a few of them. By 1966, about ninety-five percent of Mississippi's farm crops were mechanically planted and harvested, a rise from seventy-two percent in 1963.[36] They cannot even strike (as the Mississippi Freedom Labor Union learned) because their labor is not really needed. In 1966, an estimated sixty-four percent of the cotton labor force in Mississippi had no work.[37] Many landlords did not hesitate to put off the land instantly and summarily any black person who attempted to register to vote.[38] These people had been living on a pittance, close to subsistence (three dollars a day was the average wage for cotton pickers and choppers);[39] once thrown off the land they had nothing.

In Leflore County, Mississippi, after SNCC began its project there in 1962, the county government discontinued the Federal Surplus Food Program on the grounds that it could no longer afford to store and distribute the food. All food was cut off from 22,000 people, most of them black.[40] SNCC collected large quantities of supplies in the North; Leflore County was virtually adopted by a group of liberals in Chicago, who became the most active Friends of SNCC chapter in the country.[41] The first truckload of supplies from Chicago was confiscated and the two SNCC drivers were jailed for "possession of narcotics" (aspirin and vitamin pills). SNCC did manage to feed the people of Leflore County, and the Greenwood project finally had to be disposed of by violence and arrests. But it was beyond SNCC's capacity to feed all of the people in all of the areas where it worked, and in many places it made little headway because of the black people's fear of economic reprisals. A man living at subsistence has no leeway in which to take political risks.

In the larger towns of the Black Belt there was a small black middle class. Some segments of it (such as the teachers and officials of the black schools) were just as economically dependent on the whites as were the sharecroppers, and even harder to organize. One SNCC leader, stressing the fact that the Albany Movement included every part of the Albany black community, said, "Why, we even had *teachers* coming to our meetings!"[42] Those who had even a little more than the others were very reluctant to give it up. However, some members of the black middle class were more financially independent of the whites—although even they usually participated in politics only as the white man's voice in the black community.[43] These included ministers and an occasional lawyer, real estate man or other businessman with mainly black customers. SNCC did enlist the cooperation of ministers, especially young ones. However, except in Southwest Georgia, it did not generally make much effort to work with the black middle class. Its purpose was to give political voice to the poorest and most silent of the Deep South's black people, and it saw the existence of a "black bourgeoisie" as an obstacle rather than an aid in accomplishing this purpose. The middle-class blacks, it feared, would give up any chance for real political influence in exchange for a few courtesies and occasional concessions from the "white power structure." Even in the Black Belt, many of these people had already been absorbed by the NAACP, which generally opposed the sort of aggressive political behavior favored by SNCC.

This left students, and SNCC often chose to organize towns where there was a college. High-school students and even elementary-school students in some places also participated. Students could always be counted on to join in demonstrations. However, there were a number of disadvantages to working with them: they had no money; they usually were too young to register to vote; they were often not permanently linked to the town in which they were studying; and they were all too easily subject to expulsion by "Uncle Tom" black school administrations. Still, SNCC did recruit many of its members from among student demonstrators in the years before 1964, and students who lived in town sometimes got their parents involved.

In Southwest Georgia, SNCC generally tried to bring about coalitions among these various groups. In Sumter County, for example, the movement in 1963 consisted of a very old church deacon who lived far out in the country, a family that had been running a funeral home in Americus, the county seat, for fifty years, and a group of students of high-school age and younger. The old deacon had provided a church for SNCC to hold its first meetings; the funeral-home family provided financial backing; and the students were the "troops." When Don Harris, who had been the SNCC organizer in Sumter County, went to jail in August 1963, the movement simply fell apart, because its various components had no organic connection to each other.[44] In general, the only place where SNCC's projects continued to exist after the SNCC organizers left were the towns where one or two strong local leaders emerged—people capable of holding together the various groups necessary for effective political action.

Although SNCC did recruit a number of local young men onto its staff, the emergence of strong local leadership was relatively rare. The chances of strong leaders emerging are rather slender in an environment where, from earliest childhood, initiative, aggressiveness, etc., are punished, while submission, obsequiousness and a capacity for drudgery are rewarded. Those black people who do grow up rebellious and self-confident generally leave the South at an early age. Seventy-nine percent of those black college students in a recent survey who rated the South's race relations as "very poor" planned to live outside the South, as did sixty-four percent of those with a pro-black racial image.[45] Those who stay are usually the ones with the lowest occupations,[46] and economic burdens quickly limit their freedom of action. They early come to believe that only people who are "qualified" can engaged in political activity and hold political office. To be "qualified" means to have a certain number of years of education, a certain amount of wealth and political experience, certain kinds of personal connections—in short, to be "qualified" means to be white. Very few Southern communities have any black office-holders.[47]

SNCC waged a campaign of ridicule against the notion of "qualification" for political leadership. It taught that anyone who had lived among the people and understood their problems was qualified to be their political spokesman and that all of these other skills are irrelevant. In its Freedom Schools, it encouraged people to be proud of their dialect rather than to hasten to learn the white man's way of speaking.[48] According to Stokely Carmichael, "Money, who you know and especially education are what people mean when they use the word *qualified* . . . Alabama Negroes are beginning to believe they don't need to be qualified to get involved in politics. People long accustomed to self-contempt are beginning to believe in their own voice."[49] As long as the notion of "qualified" was accepted by both those in power and the powerless, Carmichael said, politics was just one more of many means of excluding some people from society.

In Lowndes County, Alabama, he was to learn to his sorrow that ignorance and lack of economic independence can indeed be obstacles to free political activity no matter how often people are told they should not be.

When it became apparent in 1966 that a large number of black people were going to be registered under the Voting Rights Act, the plantation owners in Lowndes had their tenants and sharecroppers register and then drove them to the polls by the truckload on Election Day.[50] All the black candidates lost, and the election results showed that many black people must have voted for the white candidates.

The use of trucks by the plantation owners points up a further handicap of SNCC's work among rural black people in the South. Few blacks had telephones and those who did usually shared party lines with whites and therefore did not have assured privacy in their conversations. In many places, mail was not even delivered to black homes but had to be picked up at the post office in town. In any case, mail is not an effective method of initiating a political movement. This meant that it was necessary for the SNCC workers to visit all the local black people at their homes, which were widely scattered. There was always a shortage of SNCC cars, and the few that were available were continually being harassed by the local police. At Mount Beulah, a civil-rights headquarters and training center near Edwards, Mississippi, it was necessary to cross a solid dividing line in order to make a left turn onto or off the road that went past the main entrance. For months, a local police car waited at the entrance and ticketed all cars that did this. Such harassment was not atypical. To SNCC workers in the field, the chief problems of SNCC often seemed to be technical ones: keeping the old cars in operation, finding food and shelter for the field secretaries, keeping open the lines of communication to the outside world. To organize widely scattered, poverty-stricken, powerless people, it was necessary to face all the problems they faced, in addition to those arising from the effort to bring about important changes in a highly conservative environment.

SNCC made a virtue out of this necessity by adopting wholeheartedly the dress, the diet and the lifestyle of the people among whom it worked. The SNCC worker in jeans or overalls was affirming his closeness to the people among whom he worked, for both political and cultural reasons. It was part of SNCC's political purpose to be a clear and unmediated voice of its clientele; it was part of its cultural purpose to provide a link between educated, politically aggressive young black people and their "brothers" who remained in poverty and political thralldom.

Poverty, ignorance, isolation, the habit of submission—SNCC's voter-registration and desegregation campaigns floundered for years on these rocks. Violence could sometimes by overcome by a single bold confrontation or series of confrontations—but the deeper conditions had to be fought continuously. No project could ever be fully insured against economic and psychological erosion. When SNCC first began to do community organizing, its plan was to send a few SNCC organizers to certain towns, to get political movements going there within a matter of months and then to leave the projects in the hands of local leaders, while SNCC organizers went on to other towns. Several early projects collapsed immediately on the departure of the SNCC field secretaries, and SNCC soon realized that it would be necessary for its organizers to settle in communities for years, perhaps indefinitely.[51]

In many places, SNCC work went through cycles of four phases. In the first phase, when SNCC organizers went from house to house, people would not open their doors. In the second phase, they cautiously opened the doors and heard them out. In phase three, they would attend mass meetings—and finally they would actually confront the white community, usually by going to the courthouse *en masse* to register. Then nothing would happen and disillusionment would set in. This mean a return to phase one, at which point SNCC had generally spent many months in the community and did not know what to do next.[52]

A basic problem was that it was very difficult to attack the problem of the sharecropper's lack of political power without simultaneously attacking his lack of economic power. As one leader[53] puts it, "How are you going to get a man to register to vote when his first concern is where his children's next mouthful is coming from?" SNCC did try to deal with the economic problem through such programs as: forming a labor union (the MFLU); giving contraceptive information; distributing food and clothing in some areas; advising on how best to take advantage of available government programs; documenting discrimination in federal programs and in state welfare programs and lobbying with the federal government to end such practices; documenting economic reprisals for civil rights activities; organizing black people to obtain representation on the local committees of the federal Agricultural Stabilization and Conservation Service (which determine acreage allotments), etc.[54] But these efforts did little to change the basic economic fact of white ownership and control of the land and of almost all supplies and services. SNCC simply was not equipped to improve significantly in the short run the immediate circumstances and conditions of its clientele.

This basic frustration was at the root of all of SNCC's later efforts to bring in on its side the rest of white America and the federal government.

35

It was also at the root of SNCC's decision in 1966 to shift the focus of its efforts to the cities, both in the North and the South.

Shift to the Cities

In cities, black people are less likely to be hopelessly submissive than in the rural South, less subject to economic reprisal for political activity (at least on the individual level), more alert and educated, and more easily accessible. Yet all of these factors were present in 1961, when SNCC first began political organizing in the Deep South, and in fact the factors that made the Deep South attractive to SNCC in the beginning were even stronger than in 1961. The North was where its members felt they were mostly likely to be "bought off" through liberal programs and where SNCC would encounter the most competition from other organizations that could be more effective by bargaining for immediate reforms.

Yet, beginning in 1965, SNCC did begin to develop programs in the cities. From the start, groups calling themselves "Friends of SNCC" had existed in Northern cities and on college campuses. However, they had restricted their activities to fund-raising and other forms of support for Southern programs. Then, in 1965, SNCC projects were begun in Montgomery, Birmingham and Atlanta. By the fall of 1965, there were about twenty-five people working full-time for SNCC in Northern offices, ten of them in New York and one or two each in Boston, Detroit, Chicago, Washington, San Francisco, Philadelphia and Los Angeles. These people went to staff meetings and were well enough known to the Southern workers so that they were trusted to begin action programs. One of the first of these programs was the "Free D.C." group founded by SNCC's Washington office. Its first activity was a boycott in January 1966 of the Washington city buses to protest a fare increase. Later it concentrated on pressuring for home rule for the District of Columbia. Other urban SNCC groups ran boycotts, sit-ins, and freedom schools around various issues concerning employment, housing, education, public services and so forth. When Black Power was enunciated, SNCC began to think in terms of expanding these programs still further, to develop a force of militant young blacks in the cities.

When asked about the reasons for the shift to the North, SNCC members stress the lack of a future for black people in the rural Deep South, as mechanization eliminates the need for hand-picking and weeding of the crops. What this means is that the exodus to the cities which began in the 1920s will be speeded up in the next few years and that only those black people who are too old and too set in their life-style to move will be left in the rural Black Belt. These are precisely the people to whom SNCC, manned by adventurous young people, has the greatest difficulty in appealing. SNCC workers in the Deep South urge young people there not to leave, because the areas where they live often have black majorities or near-majorities and therefore would provide a good base for political power—but SNCC knows that this endeavor is in the long run hopeless, since the land cannot provide a living for these people.

A further reason for SNCC's shift to the North is SNCC's new view of the source of the black man's troubles in America. If racism or racist policies derive from the major political and economic institutions, then clearly the place to fight these evils is near the centers of power of these institutions, which in almost all cases are in the North and in cities.

Washington and Newark already have black majorities and other major cities are expected to within the next decade. The North may soon provide the kind of political base that SNCC hoped for in the South. But SNCC is not trying to organize the leading residents of the Northern black sections. Just as it shunned the black middle class in the South for the poor tenant farmers and sharecroppers, it turns in the North to the most outcast members of society—unemployed youth, narcotics addicts, petty criminals, in general, those least likely to be "bought off" by promises of jobs or reforms.[55]

What seems significant is that wherever SNCC worked, whether in the hamlets of the Deep South or on the streets of New York, it did not change its basic conception of itself as a small group of organizers among people who were in some way excluded from American society. Persecution and murder were unable to drive it away from its work among poor black Southerners; agricultural mechanization and then the poverty program, with its irresistible temptation to join the mainstream, did. SNCC then began to follow the migration routes of those who were still excluded. Faced with the challenge of the poverty program, SNCC could not transform itself into a political pressure group working through established channels to obtain more wealth and prestige for its clientele. This would have required tailoring itself to the tastes and demands of white liberals in power—and this SNCC would not do.

B. *Relations with White Friends and Allies*

The frustration SNCC experienced in the Deep South can easily explain its bitterness against Southern racists, but what it cannot explain is the striking fact that the brunt of SNCC's anger is directed less against Southern racists than against the American system as a whole and in particular the federal government and other liberal institutions. In this section, we shall attempt to account for this by discussing SNCC's interactions with the federal government and with white liberals. These relationships were disappointing to all parties concerned.

The Federal Government

SNCC in the early '60s shared with the rest of the nation the view that the South was only an ugly aberration. It assumed that although the conditions of black people in the North were far from ideal, there at least they had the support and cooperation of white people and the federal government in solving their problems.

SNCC first became disillusioned with the federal government because of its role in the Deep South. As far as SNCC was concerned, there were three major aspects of the federal presence in the Deep South: (1) the Justice Department and the federal courts, (2) the Civil Rights laws and Interstate Commerce Commission rulings and (3) the poverty program.

The involvement of SNCC with the Justice Department came early and was very intimate at the start. The Kennedy administration approached SNCC-affiliated sit-in leaders with offers of protection for a voter registration campaign almost immediately on coming to power. Since the general feeling of hope in the country was shared by these leaders, the offer was accepted. One SNCC leader called SNCC in 1961 "an arm of the Justice Department."[56] What he meant was that the impetus to focus on voter registration in the Deep South had come largely from Washington. (The direct-action program was at first geared toward Washington also, in that it focused in the first few years on the testing of Interstate Commerce Commission rulings on segregation in public accommodations.) William Higgs, Timothy Jenkins and some Northerners in SNCC say today that they knew from the start that SNCC and the Justice Department were simply using each other for limited ends—but most others in SNCC had real hope of continuing and substantial support. "Up to and including 1964, the federal government was . . . a person's focus. This is where we go, we go to Washington to protest. We get the government to carry out its responsibilities. (Then) SNCC people began to see that the government wasn't the panacea, wasn't going to be the instrument of curing the ills."[57]

Actually, for most SNCC field secretaries the process of disillusionment began quite early. SNCC's hopes for voter registration in the Black Belt were mainly based on the expectation of federal police protection—an expectation which was soon shattered. A number of field secretaries in the early years underwent the experience of being beaten by the local citizens or even the local police while several FBI agents stood nearby taking notes.[58] The notes were ostensibly to be used in federal courts to obtain injunctions against such anti-SNCC activities or to show illegal interference with the right to vote. The FBI interpreted its mandate as forbidding it to exercise police power by simply stopping the beating. SNCC was unimpressed by this argument; taking notes during beatings was cited again and again by SNCC workers as proof of federal callousness. Further, most SNCC workers were convinced that local FBI agents were not merely indifferent but hostile. They believed that FBI agents generally work in or near the areas from which they are recruited. This means that those from Mississippi are generally Mississippians, with all the racial attitudes one would expect. Moreover, SNCC people knew that the FBI worked closely with the local police in the solution of some crimes and therefore that personal relationships developed. In a number of cases, SNCC suspected the FBI of leaking information to the local police, who were always hostile to SNCC. The FBI advised SNCC to keep it informed at all times of the whereabouts of its field secretaries; after several experiences involving remarkably detailed knowledge by the local police about SNCC doings, most projects stopped following this advice.

For example, SNCC blames the death of Lewis Allen, a Mississippi black man, indirectly on the FBI. Allen had witnessed the fatal shooting of Herbert Lee, a black farmer, by E. H. Hurst, a white state representative, during SNCC's McComb project in 1961. Allen told the FBI that he wished to testify at the grand-jury hearing that the killing was not in self-defense, but that he could only do so if the FBI promised him protection. The FBI said it was unable to provide protection. Allen did not testify and Hurst was exonerated. About six months later, a deputy sheriff broke Allen's jaw with a flashlight, after telling him he knew Allen had told the FBI that Hurst had not shot in self-defense. In January, 1964, Allen was found shot dead in his front yard. The murderer was never caught.[59] (No white man has ever been convicted in the Deep South for killing a lone black civil rights worker. The Schwerner-Chaney-Goodman case involved two whites.)

SNCC's feelings about the Justice Department are summarized in this incident in McComb in 1961 recounted by an early leader.[60]

Well, we got this word that the Klan came down and told some Negroes that they were going to take Bob Moses out of jail. They were taking everybody over to Magnolia, which is the county jail, about eight miles from there. We got the word they were going to take Bob out and kill him. [Herbert] Lee had already been shot by this guy, a state representative [E. H. Hurst], and he was first on the list and Bob moved up to number one on the list of the Klan to be killed. So I called the Justice Department and told them all this and they told me to talk to the local FBI guy and told him where to come to find me and he came up and I told him what the scene was and he said, "oh, I don't think so, I know them people. I've been living with them. I don't think they'd do anything like that." And then I called back [Washington] and I told them to get somebody down here because their guy was from the South and he was saying "oh, I don't think they'd do that." So, John Doar [a Justice Department Civil Rights Division lawyer] . . . I'll never forget this as long as I live. I was sitting back there. People were still in jail and, lord knows, were relying on the Justice Department, to protect people. I called Burke Marshall and told him "get on the FBI, man" and Burke said, "it's a matter of jurisdiction." And I sat right there not knowing when the cops were going to come in. And all of a sudden John Doar walked in and he said, "I'm John Doar." I said, you know, "very good" and I was relaxed and I had all the might of the federal government. I told him the whole scene and he said, "well, I'm sorry but there ain't nothing that I can do."

I don't know why he came but he said, "I'm just as scared of them as you are, man, there's nothing I can do." I looked at him and here was all the force, honor, the military technology, power, of the greatest country, the most powerful country in the history of the world, represented in the form of John Doar, and he says to me, "I'm just scared as you are, man, ain't nothing I can do." And that pretty much completely shook me out of any illusions that I might have had about the federal government.

In the course of the years before 1964, SNCC members actually grew to hate the Justice Department, their ostensible protectors in Washington. They felt that the Justice Department had led them into the perils of voter registration work in the Deep South by offering them protection and had then abandoned them. In fact, the Justice Department in the early '60s had enormously increased the level of its civil rights activities over that of the

Eisenhower administration. For the first time a civil rights division was created. In Mississippi alone, the Justice Department brought nineteen voting suits in the three years of the Kennedy administration. In two broad suits it called for an end to the constitution-interpretation tests for voters (later obtained in the Voting Rights Act of 1965).[61]

SNCC members hardly seem aware of this activity. And in any case they were convinced more or less from the start that lawsuits would not solve the problem. The history of the NAACP, they felt, had demonstrated the limitations of this path. They wanted not lawsuits but justice, immediate and concrete. They understood that it is not positive law but "underlaw" that rules in the Deep South. "Underlaw" is local white custom. Southern state statutes are very similar to those in any state, with a slight tendency toward vagueness in the breach-of-the-peace and vagrancy laws. The local police step into this vague area, providing punishment arbitrarily for activity which might "unreasonably disturb the public." They are backed up by local political officials and by organizations like the White Citizens' Councils. A black man who tried to sue a white man would lose his job; therefore, the existence of higher courts which might rule in his favor is irrelevant.[62] Only the direct intercession of higher authorities can really help.

The fact that the Justice Department was not willing to intercede directly to provide protection seemed to SNCC to be a manifestation of sheer hypocrisy. Its states'-rights-based excuse (that it could not exercise the police power) was not very convincing to SNCC members, especially after the Justice Department actually brought suit, in the middle of the demonstrations in Albany in 1963, against a group of leaders of the SNCC-supported Albany Movement on charges of obstructing justice (because a white juror's store was being picketed on account of the owner's segregationist views) and perjury. In other cases, federal district courts (sometimes presided over by Kennedy-appointed judges) made rulings hostile to civil rights (many of which were, however, overruled by higher courts, sometimes with the help of the Justice Department as *amicus curiae*).

SNCC's skeptical attitude toward the federal courts was matched by its pessimism about civil rights laws. SNCC felt that there were a number of existing laws which provided the basis for federal action and which were not being enforced (see Appendix One). It was therefore dubious about the enforcement of future civil rights legislation. Although it participated in the March on Washington in August 1963, it differed from many other participating groups in not seeing the main purpose of the March as pressure for passage of a civil rights bill.

John Lewis, SNCC's former chairman, puts a great deal of blame on the federal government for the slowing down of the movement's progress; he cites the government's "lack of commitment, lack of caring, and timidity."[63] Others also blame the government for the gradual demise of the movement since 1964, but for different reasons. Julian Bond, SNCC's communications director, says the 1964 and 1965 Civil Rights Acts took the pressure off the country. He feels that people were not as concerned about civil rights after the bills' passage because they felt they had done what they should for black people.

An even more fundamental problem arose from the fact that the Voting Rights Act of 1965 in effect took away SNCC's major immediate goal. For several years, SNCC had geared its whole program around voting in the Deep South—and for almost as long it had been calling for federal marshals to come south and enforce the right to vote. Then, when the marshals finally came, under the terms of the Act, SNCC's program became superfluous. But by that time it had become clear to most SNCC people that voter registration was only a program and not really a goal, that it was a vehicle for the political awakening and radicalization of black Southerners. With the coming of the federal registrars, SNCC lost its vehicle. In Lowndes County, Alabama, between March 1965, when SNCC began in earnest its project there, and August 1965, when the Voting Rights Act was passed, only about fifty or sixty black citizens passed the registration test. After August, when the federal registrars entered the county, the "voting rolls swelled by the hundreds."[64] But many of these hundreds later voted for white candidates and black people were unable to win electoral office in Lowndes County. SNCC's program was thus stolen without its purpose being achieved.

As if "stealing" SNCC's program were not enough, the federal government went on to lure away its personnel by means of the poverty program. When the program first entered Mississippi, SNCC's leading members in the state were approached one by one and offered jobs at such astronomical salaries (for a SNCC man) as $125 a week. Many of them accepted, leaving only the most bitterly anti-government people working for SNCC.

In one interesting case, SNCC actually fought the federal government and Mississippi whites for control of part of the poverty program, the Child Development Group of Mississippi (CDGM). In 1965, the Office of Economic Opportunity (OEO) gave a grant of a million and a half dollars to a civil-rights-affiliated group to run eighty-four pre-school centers and related adult education programs throughout Mississippi during an eight-week summer session. SNCC was the most important of the civil rights groups involved. It felt that the help which would be given to the children was negligible but that CDGM offered an important potential for community action, just as voter registration had. In order to defeat attacks, the OEO also gave grants to some county school boards to set up high-school programs in competition with CDGM. In the white-controlled programs, the emphasis was on discipline and regimentation. In the CDGM programs, the atmosphere was more informal and the emphasis tended to be political. From the start CDGM encountered the same forms of harassment as other SNCC projects, plus pressure by Mississippi's Representative John Bell Williams and Senator John Stennis to take its supervision out of SNCC's hands.[65]

CDGM applied for OEO money to extend its programs after the summer, but Senator Stennis' opposition managed to delay a new grant until the following February. Nevertheless, CDGM managed to continue the program with volunteers drawn entirely from among poor black Mississippians.[66] Yet CDGM was criticized by white Mississippi politicians for being unrepresentative of the community and for using poor administrative and accounting procedures. In October 1966, OEO announced the termination of CDGM. Most of its programs were to be taken over by Mississippi Action for Progress, a board consisting of white moderates like Hodding Carter III and Douglas Wynn and black moderates like Aaron Henry.[67]

SNCC felt that the charges of poor administration were generally unjustified and that the idea of a biracial board representing a "community" in Mississippi was absurd. There are not one but two communities in every town in Mississippi, a white one and a black one, and any biracial board, SNCC believed, was bound to be dominated by the white community. Therefore, the new arrangement in effect gave white Mississippians control over a program in which no white Mississippians participated as students or teachers. Through the CDGM episode, SNCC felt that it had seen once again that the federal government, while appearing to give it aid, would support it only insofar as it could do so without stepping on the toes of white Southerners, which was not very far. SNCC felt that it had done an excellent job in initiating and developing a highly successful program, only to see it taken from its hands by people whose commitment to the beneficiaries of the program was partial at best. SNCC's view that the NAACP was not to be trusted (see below) was further confirmed by the cooperation of Aaron Henry, its state chairman, with the white moderates. It was inconceivable to SNCC that any black group with integrity could cooperate with the new board.

However, this was not the end of the story. A full-scale campaign of pressure on behalf of CDGM was waged by Walter Reuther (president of the United Auto Workers), the National Council of Churches, some individual churches and other liberal groups, and finally, after the President himself intervened through Vice President Humphrey, CDGM was re-funded in January 1967.[68] This demonstration of the efficacy of liberal support does not seem to have affected SNCC's attitude toward liberals, though. Stokely Carmichael believes that the motive of the federal government and the liberals in providing the Voting Rights Act and the poverty program is to control black people. He says the idea is to induce blacks to exchange the possibility of real power for tokenism and patronage by organizing them in the Democratic Party. The new programs give crumbs from the table, in his view, so that they can exercise power through federal control over jobs.[69]

In general, SNCC's experiences with the federal government in the Deep South led it to be highly suspicious of any offer of assistance and aid from Washington. Since the federal government represented white segregationists as well as black people, its loyalties were always divided. The conclusion SNCC drew from this was not that the federal government's aid should be used in limited ways but rather that the federal government was "the enemy" or at best the enemy's ally. During the entire period before May 1966, SNCC continued to seek and receive various forms of federal assistance for itself and for black people in general, but at the same time its members after 1964 always spoke of the government in private with great hostility. In the interviews, those who left SNCC before the summer of 1964 generally seemed to have a more positive orientation toward the federal government than more recent members. Since SNCC's relations with the federal government in the Deep South remained about the same between 1961 and 1966, the ambivalence of this relationship cannot by itself explain this shift in attitude. To explain this change, we must look to events that occurred outside the Deep South.

Even before 1964, SNCC members had developed a profound dislike for Attorney General Robert F. Kennedy, because of their disappointing experiences with the Justice Department. Very little of this animus seems to have been transferred to President John F. Kennedy, though, and at the time of his death in November 1963, SNCC did not yet have a strong generalized antagonism toward the executive branch. John Lewis, who was SNCC's chairman at the time of President Kennedy's assassination, says that Kennedy was an inspiration to many of the students in the sit-ins and Freedom Rides. Lewis was critical of Kennedy for appointing segregationist federal judges, but he still felt that the young president had given the movement hope. "When Kennedy died, something died within a lot of young people."[70]

SNCC shared the early suspicion of President Lyndon Johnson felt by many liberals. When the nation, including the liberals, began to rally around the new president, SNCC began to feel somewhat alienated. Its members have never liked Johnson, and they tend to blame him personally for the non-punishment of murderers of black people and civil-rights workers, for the attack on CDGM, and even in some cases for the assassination of Malcolm X. President Kennedy had raised their hopes, at least briefly; President Johnson dashed them. SNCC members never believed that Johnson had any real commitment to their cause. Nothing in his administration, not even the passage of the civil rights bills, swayed them from this view.

March on Washington

Even before the death of President Kennedy, SNCC had a public disagreement with the liberal "Establishment" which gave a hint of future conflict within the organization between militants and moderates with regard to the "Establishment." In August 1963, SNCC joined hundreds of different groups in a "March on Washington for Jobs and Freedom," one purpose of which was to demonstrate massive public support for a civil rights bill. This was the March at which Martin Luther King gave his famous *I Have a Dream* speech. John Lewis, SNCC's chairman, was also to speak at the March, along with leaders of several other groups. The day before the March, Lewis released his prepared speech to the press. The other March leaders read it and were upset by its tone and by certain statements in it. In particular, Lewis had said that "in good conscience, we cannot support, wholeheartedly, the administration's civil rights bill, for it is too little and too late."[71] He objected to the absence of provisions for protection from police brutality, for the registration of qualified voters who lack a sixth-grade education and for insuring "the equality of a maid who earns $5 a week in the home of a family whose income is $100,000 a year."[72] Some of the other March leaders, including Martin Luther King,[73] objected to SNCC's

45

lack of enthusiasm for the civil rights bill, since support for the bill was one of the important purposes of the March.

Lewis' original speech contained phrases like "the revolution is at hand" and "the black masses are on the march for jobs and freedom."[74] Even though these were juxtaposed with other phrases, such as "we must work for the community of love, peace and true brotherhood," many of the more moderate leaders like Roy Wilkins of the NAACP and Eugene Carson Blake of the National Council of Churches objected to the strong language. Even Bayard Rustin, who defended most the strongly worded speech, objected to Lewis' saying that patience was a nasty word; he feared that the leaders of the Catholic Church might be offended.[75] Still others, including AFL-CIO leaders,[76] objected to a seeming equation of the Democratic and the Republican parties in Lewis' plea, "The party of [John F.] Kennedy is also the party of [Senator James O.] Eastland [of Mississippi]. The party of [Senator Jacob] Javits [of New York] is also the party of [Senator Barry] Goldwater [of Arizona, the Republican nominee in 1964]. Where is *our* party?" And *all* of the March leaders, except Rustin, were offended by the words, "The time will come when we will not confine our marching to Washington. We will march through the South, through the heart of Dixie, the way Sherman did. We shall pursue our own 'scorched earth' policy and burn Jim Crow to the ground—nonviolently."[77] They all felt that the reference to General Sherman would needlessly exacerbate Southern sensibilities, and that others would be put off by the threatening tone, in spite of the amendment "nonviolently."

At the last minute, SNCC leaders were prevailed upon to change radically the wording of the speech. It was too late, though, because the original statement had already been released to the press. The whole nation saw that there was a gap between most of the liberal leaders and SNCC. SNCC members saw it too and they were angry that SNCC had publicly lost the skirmish. Lewis, James Forman and Courtland Cox, who had been responsible for agreeing to the changes, were raked over the coals by many of the other members. They felt that SNCC must always look to poor black people, never to powerful whites, even powerful white allies.

The Freedom Democratic Party and the Challenges

One year later, there was a much more serious dramatic confrontation and break with the national liberal leaders. This occurred at the Democratic National Convention in Atlantic City, New Jersey, in August 1964. At the convention, the Mississippi Freedom Democratic Party (FDP) challenged the seating of the delegates from the regular Mississippi Democratic Party.

The FDP had been founded four months earlier for the purpose of carrying out this challenge. The early leaders of the FDP (Fannie Lou Hamer, Lawrence Guyot, Annie Devine, Victoria Gray, Aaron Henry) came out of COFO, but most of them were, at first, totally committed to SNCC. The idea for the FDP came from Bob Moses and from William Higgs, who had been a SNCC adviser for several years. Since the fall of 1964, it has had only one chairman, Laurence Guyot, who was at first a SNCC member. (The first chairman was Aaron Henry of the NAACP.) The FDP members were all Mississippi black people, although the party did not, of course, exclude whites. SNCC remained very influential in the FDP and long after the convention challenge it contributed ideas, money and people to the FDP's projects. Eventually, however, the two organizations drifted apart. In 1965, all of the people working for SNCC in Mississippi became associated with the FDP—but the FDP failed to take the same direction as the rest of SNCC, and one by one its top leaders dropped their SNCC memberships.

One reason for this gradual break may be the preponderance of older, less educated, more isolated, more religious people in the FDP, people who were not in tune with the mood of urban black youth. Mrs. Hamer, the FDP's most famous member, says, "I think blacks and whites have still got to work together. I'd like to see democracy work—I haven't given up yet. I'm not one of those who go around hating all the time. If I was like that, I'd be a miserable person. I keep remembering that righteousness exalts a nation; hate just makes people miserable."[78] Mrs. Hamer resigned from SNCC in December 1966 after making a plea for keeping whites in the organization at a staff meeting. The religious ring to her words gives some clue as to her reasons for not becoming anti-white, even though she was faced with the same experiences as other SNCC members. She herself attributes the difference in the courses taken by FDP and SNCC to the generation gap created by changing times. She is about fifty years old, and she says she would not have dreamed, as a girl, of defying the white man in ways that her teen-age daughter takes almost for granted. The attitudes acquired in youth do not fade easily.

At the time of the Atlantic City convention there had not yet been any apparent break between SNCC and the FDP. However, FDP people probably had higher hopes for their challenge than SNCC people. Even within SNCC, there were varying expectations. Some people, such as John Lewis and Julian Bond,[79] thought there was actually a possibility of recognition and seating of the FDP. Others felt the purpose of the challenge was to put the Democratic Party on the spot. Still others thought the point was to show the black population the futility of such efforts and also to teach the blacks that they were capable of going through these steps, that they could organize themselves and confront directly something like the Democratic convention.[80] Thus, their rejection of this kind of politics could be based not on a lack of self-confidence but on a knowledge of the corruption of the system. SNCC people were probably somewhat doubtful that the grass-roots FDP people had the same motives that they did; it was probably for this reason that during the crisis over whether to accept a proffered compromise, SNCC did its best to prevent the leaders of the more moderate civil-rights groups from talking to the FDP delegates either collectively or individually.[81]

The legal basis for the challenge was that the Mississippi Democratic Party had systematically excluded black people from its process of delegate selection and moreover had refused to sign the loyalty pledge to the Democratic nominees for president and vice-president in contravention of a convention rule.[82] The FDP on the other hand had excluded no one from its procedures and was willing to sign the loyalty pledge. The FDP counsel was Joseph Rauh, a white man who had been national chairman of the Americans for Democratic Action and who was a convention delegate from the District of Columbia and a member of the convention's Credentials Committee. Rauh, who is a close friend of Hubert Humphrey, is a perfect example of what SNCC members would call an "Establishment liberal." He was chosen as FDP counsel because of his political connections and his inside knowledge of Democratic Party workings.

It was the job of the Credentials Committee to recommend which delegation should be seated. On the opening day of the convention, back-room negotiations were begun for the purpose of working out a compromise. The Administration's spokesmen proposed that all members of both delegations who would sign the loyalty oath be seated, but that the

FDP delegates have no voting rights. This proposal also called for a change to be made in the call of the convention in 1968 to make clear that the Democratic Party in every state must be open to every registered voter without discrimination because of race and that any state party practicing such discrimination would not have its delegation seated. Rauh rejected this in favor of a counter-proposal by Representative Edith Green (D-Ore.) that every member of both delegations who signed the loyalty oath be seated and that Mississippi's vote in the convention be divided proportionately among the delegates seated. This proposal was, however, unacceptable to the Administration because it conceded that the FDP had legal standing, which the Administration denied because the FDP had not held conventions in every county. (Some SNCC members say that the regulars had not actually held all of the county conventions either.)[83]

By the following day (August 25) a new compromise had been worked out whereby all of the regulars who signed the loyalty oath would be seated plus two FDP delegates-at-large, with voting rights but without the right to be seated in the Mississippi seating section. The two delegates, Aaron Henry and Reverend R. Edwin King (a black and a white man respectively), were designated in the compromise. The change in the convention call was also included in the compromise, as was a statement welcoming the other FDP delegates as honored guests of the convention, with similar standing to the delegates from Puerto Rico and the Virgin Islands. This compromise was approved by the convention by voice vote, but rejected immediately by both the Mississippi regulars and the FDP. Almost the entire regular delegation bolted the Party and left the convention. Only three members of it signed the loyalty pledge and took their seats. Even though the FDP had rejected the compromise, Henry and King took their seats, near the seating section for delegates from Alaska. Other FDP delegates sat down in some of the empty seats in the Mississippi section, whereupon the three remaining regulars left. The sergeants-at-arms succeeded in ejecting only one of the FDP delegates. On the following day even more FDP delegates, including King and Henry, took seats in the Mississippi section.

In the meantime, the Credentials Committee was debating whether it should submit a minority report recommending the adoption of Representative Green's compromise. Such a report, requiring the signatures of ten percent of the Credentials Committee members, would have brought the question to the convention floor and required a roll-call vote by states, something which the Administration was eager to avoid. Eleven signatures

49

of Credentials Committee members were necessary and the FDP forces believed at the start of the convention that they had seventeen. The descriptions of the beatings undergone by the black people who had attempted to register to vote, especially that of Mrs. Hamer, had deeply moved the Committee members. However, the Administration was able to find out the names of the seventeen and it exerted enormous pressure on them not to sign a minority report.

When it became clear that Joseph Rauh, the FDP counsel, did not intend to sign the report, the other delegates who had intended to sign decided that it would be futile to do so.[84] Rauh said that the compromise already offered was a significant gain and that it represented more than the FDP had originally hoped to achieve. On the opening day of the Convention, Rauh had said, "We can win on the floor. I think we're going the whole distance."[85] Some SNCC members were outraged at this example of what they considered to be liberal perfidy, although others said they had never expected Rauh to stand by the FDP beyond a certain point. It was generally believed in SNCC that Rauh had deserted the FDP because of his friendship with Vice President Humphrey. It was also assumed by virtually all SNCC people that Humphrey had been ordered by President Johnson to work out a compromise short of full FDP recognition, under threat of being deprived of the vice-presidential nomination. Humphrey did in fact take the lead in the negotiations for the compromise, which were held in his hotel suite, and it is also true that the President refrained until the last day of the convention from announcing the identity of his running mate.

Throughout the entire dispute about the seating of delegates, there was a general state of non-comprehension and suspicion of the motives of other parties. When asked about the President's reasons for opposing Representative Green's compromise, SNCC members generally reply that he was motivated by "racism." Some of them believe that there was also an element of not wishing to offend the white voters of Mississippi and the rest of the South or just generally of not wanting to upset the applecart.

A simple explanation is that Johnson was reluctant to exchange the support of long-time party regulars for a group that represented few actual voters. He did not care who was more moral or even who was loyal at that particular moment. He was also anxious to insure that his name would appear on the ballot in Mississippi as the Democratic nominee, rather than that of Goldwater. Prior to the convention, he had made a bargain with the regulars in which they agreed on this provided that they were seated.[86] For him, the FDP challenge must have been a vexing distraction and he was eager to get it out of the way with as little political loss as possible.

The motives of the FDP in refusing the compromise were widely speculated on among Northern liberals, who generally believed that the compromise should have been accepted. The liberals thought SNCC and the FDP guilty of an excessively moralistic approach to politics, an approach which was a serious impediment to genuine bargaining. SNCC did indeed resent the implication in all the compromises, even Representative Green's, that the FDP's standing was morally equivalent to that of the regulars and that the important point was to work out an arrangement which was at least minimally satisfactory to all parties concerned. SNCC members were also resentful of the fact that lack of party loyalty on the part of the regulars seemed to be considered a far more serious sin than the exclusion of black people from the franchise. The latter transgression was dealt with only in the rather vague promise concerning 1968, a promise that was almost meaningless because it specified that discrimination by the Democratic Party would be prohibited against "voters" only—and of course most Mississippi black people were not voters and at that time had little hope of becoming registered. The FDP, which felt its claims were so superior, did not even get equal treatment. Aaron Henry, the head of the FDP delegation, said at the convention that the Party would not have minded having none of its delegates seated, if the regulars had been treated the same way.[87] However, for those whose aim in the challenge was to put the Democratic Party on the spot or to demonstrate the futility of seeking help from powerful liberals, it is likely that no arrangement would have been acceptable short of complete exclusion of the regulars and full delegate status for the entire FDP delegation. To these militants, anything less was "tokenism." But even for those who would not have been so rigid, the two seats at large seemed meaningless because they failed to give recognition to the FDP's right to represent Mississippi, which was really the core of its demand. Moreover, everyone in SNCC and the FDP was indignant that the convention had specified which two FDP delegates were to be seated, because this implied that the FDP did not have the right to choose its own delegates.

The convention experience was profoundly disappointing and disillusioning for almost all of the FDP's grass-roots delegates and this disappointment made it extremely difficult for both the FDP and Mississippi SNCC to regain the momentum of organizing enthusiasm that had been created by the summer project. For all the delegates as well as all the SNCC members

51

present, the events in Atlantic City increased and deepened a feeling of resentment and distrust for the federal government and for liberals like Joseph Rauh. For some SNCC members, the challenge was only one of a long series of disillusioning experiences, and not necessarily the most important, but for many others, it was the turning point in the dashing of their hopes of help from non-radical groups. There were events before and after that contributed to their disaffection, but this one was mentioned spontaneously by SNCC members far more often than any other.

In spite of the general depression after the convention, SNCC decided to sponsor another Freedom Vote in the November 1964 elections, with white Northern volunteers, and another FDP challenge based on the Freedom Vote and aimed at the Mississippi delegation to the U.S. Congress. Almost no one in SNCC seems to have believed this second challenge had a chance for success, and it was undertaken mainly as an organizing device and against the wishes of most of the COFO staff.[88] The official reasons for this challenge were that the FDP had an even better legal case than it had had at the convention and that this was one more way of forcing the powers-that-be either to confront the injustice of the situation in Mississippi or else show their own moral bankruptcy. Considerable support from liberals was expected because most liberals had no great love for Mississippi's Congressmen. Still, there was far less enthusiasm in SNCC for this second challenge than there had been for the first.

The challenge was made on the opening day of Congress, January 4, 1965. In its original form, it had called for the unseating of the white Congressmen and the seating of the FDP Congresswomen in their place. However, the latter demand lacked the support of the NAACP, the Urban League, the Americans for Democratic Action and the AFL-CIO (although it had the support of SNCC, CORE and SCLC). In order to gain the backing of the more conservative (and more powerful) groups, the FDP finally asked only for the unseating of the regulars, who had been chosen in elections which excluded black people, until such time as the constitutional question of the validity of these elections could be decided. Almost a third of the House voted in favor of this, but the final decision of the House was to seat the regulars until the question could be decided, which would be the following September at the latest.

SNCC and the FDP spent the next eight months preparing for the September confrontation. They brought over 400 college students and others to Washington during the summer in week-long shifts in order to lobby for approval of the challenge. FDP lawyers collected about 600 depositions, mainly from Mississippi black people, giving evidence of illegal practices in the election of the five challenged Congressmen. Only under heavy pressure from the FDP did the Clerk of the House of Representatives, Ralph R. Roberts, print these depositions.

The main illegal practice attested to in the depositions was the exclusion of black people from voting. The FDP also based its case on the fact that the Mississippi secretary of state had refused independent nominating petitions for the challenging Congresswomen, Mmes. Fannie Lou Hamer, Annie Devine and Victoria Gray. Its lawyers pointed out that in forty-three cases between 1867 and 1901 similar challenges had led to the seating of black people or the calling of new elections. They also argued that a guarantee of free elections had been a precondition of Mississippi's re-entry into the Union after the Civil War and that the House has the duty to guarantee that elections of its members are free and fair.[89]

In the final week before the September challenge, the relatively conservative Leadership Conference on Civil Rights endorsed it, putting every major civil rights organization on the FDP side. The House Administration Committee, however, recommended that the challenge be rejected but that the House scrutinize all future elections. On September 17, 1965, it was indeed rejected, by a vote of 228-143.[90] Few SNCC members were surprised, but within the FDP, there was great disappointment and anger. Mrs. Fannie Lou Hamer said, "I had a bitterness I don't think I could ever express. I shook with sobs. I'm not crying for myself alone. I'm crying for America. Because it's later than you think."[91]

SNCC and the FDP never again undertook an important joint project and in fact SNCC never had another major project in Mississippi.

It is difficult to underestimate the importance of these two challenges in SNCC's history. They were part of a long-range trend toward increasing disillusionment with the federal government and with Northern liberals, a trend which these events accelerated. In both cases, SNCC felt that the FDP had both moral right and overwhelming legal weight on its side. In the first challenge, many SNCC and FDP people were shocked to find that moral and legal issues were negotiable only when transformed into the currency of hard political interest. They were particularly outraged to learn of the tight network of political obligation that tied together the Northern liberals (their supposed allies) and the white Mississippi politicians who were their most powerful enemies. They learned that this network was so powerful that even

53

serious acts of disloyalty or large numbers of "wrong" votes could not break it. Their conclusion from the failure of the two challenges was that the national Democratic Party and the majority of the House of Representatives were closer in interests and outlook to white-supremacist politicians than to civil-rights workers. If it came to a choice, they would choose the white supremacists. SNCC was therefore basically on its own.

One long-term SNCC man[92] believes that the convention challenge was definitely the most important turning point in SNCC's history. He thinks that SNCC had "morality, determination and good political thinking" on its side. "If that one event had gone the other way, the history of America could have been changed. But no, the calls went out from the White House . . ." SNCC really saw itself at a sort of crossroads in American history. It believed that a momentous decision had been made and that it was, irrevocably, the wrong decision.

SNCC was incapable of seeing the compromise offered as anything but a form of rejection. It could not accept the idea that the federal government can shift its commitments only very slowly. The partial commitment which it was prepared to give was seen as no commitment at all. SNCC members apparently preferred to retain what they saw as their moral purity than to take advantage of a partial commitment even from so powerful a potential ally as the U.S. government. SNCC's conviction that the U.S. government was not an acceptable ally was confirmed by subsequent developments in American foreign policy.

SNCC on Vietnam

On January 6, 1966, SNCC as an organization came out formally against U.S. policy in Vietnam. Before the rapid escalation of the war in early 1965, SNCC had been little concerned about U.S. foreign policy. Starting at about that time, SNCC began to see itself as one of many victims of U.S. power all over the world. As Howard Zinn, a SNCC adviser, put it in 1965,[93]

> Events in Vietnam became easier to understand in the light of recent experience in the South . . . Just as the white South finds it hard to believe that Southern Negroes are genuinely dissatisfied, and so attributes the Negro revolt to "outsiders," the U.S. finds it hard to believe that the Vietnamese peasant really is in revolt against the old way of life, and so blames the rebellion on "outsiders" from the Communist nations.

. . . in both cases there is a home-made uprising against an oppressive system . . . In both situations there is the use of special words that arouse hatred and distort reality . . . "nigger" [and] "Communist." The word is a blanket which smothers the true complexity of the world and the individuality of human beings.

In a less abstract way, SNCC people identified with poor, non-white people struggling against white Americans who showed little respect for their lives (the bombing of civilians seemed consistent with the non-punishment of murderers of Negroes) or their social order (the wholesale destruction of village life involved in "pacification" seemed consistent with the destruction of African culture among the slaves). To some Americans, this may seem like a distorted view of an attempt to protect a small country—but for SNCC members it seemed obvious that the threat to the Vietnamese peasant came not from native peasant guerrillas but from right-wing generals and heavily-armed foreigners.

Of course, SNCC as a civil-rights organization did not have to take a stand one way or the other. However, SNCC's fund-raisers in the North were often questioned about SNCC's views on the war and some Southern projects were exerting pressure, too. The McComb, Mississippi project had put out an anti-war pamphlet before SNCC as a whole took a stand.[94] The immediate event which touched off the SNCC statement on Vietnam policy was the murder of Sammy Younge, a SNCC worker and Tuskegee Institute student. Younge had lost a kidney while serving in Vietnam and then was killed by a white filling-station attendant for trying to use a white restroom. Another black man, who had been killed in Vietnam, had shortly before been denied burial in his native Alabama because the black cemetery was too crowded. SNCC felt it could remain silent no longer.[95] Moreover, SNCC saw no reason for remaining silent, since it had already been labelled "Red" and therefore dismissed as a legitimate group by almost all the people who supported the Vietnam war.

The Liberals Turn Against SNCC

Conservatives had of course never been supporters of SNCC—but SNCC had always relied heavily on liberals for funds, even after the Democratic Convention of 1964. The liberals generally defended SNCC in their publications before 1965. One exception was Theodore White, who in a

1963 *Life* magazine article[96] called SNCC an extremist organization which had twice attempted to convert peaceful demonstrations into "putsches" against government offices in Southern cities. In describing SNCC members, White used the words "lunatics" and "aliens."[97] He also said that SNCC had been "penetrated" by "unidentified" elements, with an implication that these were Communists.[98]

White was a lone voice at that time. A year later, though, SNCC was attacked by such liberals as Joseph Rauh (after he was dismissed as FDP counsel for advocating the compromise at the Convention); Roy Wilkins, the executive director of the NAACP (see Section C); Irving Howe, an old Socialist, who called SNCC a "bureaucratically deformed, manipulative and undemocratic" organization; James Wechsler, editor of the *New York Post*, who said the militants in SNCC were "staging an uprising against the major civil rights blocs . . . encouraged by a fragment of Communists"; and Rowland Evans and Robert Novak, the nationally syndicated columnists.[99] Evans and Novak attacked SNCC with particular zeal in a series of columns which appeared in late 1964 and the first few months of 1965. They described SNCC as "revolutionary" because some of its members had visited Guinea and because SNCC in general identified with African independence movements. They implied that SNCC was Chinese-Communist-oriented, giving as evidence the fact that Bob Moses had spoken at a *National Guardian* dinner. (The *Guardian* is not particularly Chinese oriented; it leans more toward the Soviet Union.) In a later column, they said, "There is no doubt whatever that SNCC is substantially infiltrated by beatniks, left-wing revolutionaries and—worst of all—by Communists." SNCC, they believed, was "taking over" the civil rights movement from Martin Luther King. In still another column, they stated that the Communist influence in SNCC was "infinitesimal" but credited it anyway with persuading SNCC not to accept the compromise offered at Atlantic City. Unlike most of those who attacked SNCC for harboring Communists, they actually named a name—Ella Baker—whom they cautiously called a "veteran leftist." Apparently, they were unaware that Miss Baker, who conceived the original idea of SNCC, had been an important influence on it all along and therefore could hardly be the cause of what they viewed as a recent turn in an ultra-leftist direction.

These liberal attackers were following the example of such conservatives as J. Edgar Hoover, the head of the Federal Bureau of Investigation, who said that SNCC, SCLC and the civil rights movement in general were pervaded by "Communist influence"[100] and Joseph Alsop, the syndicated columnist, who repeated Hoover's charge and added that "John Lewis, although not a Communist, quite frankly believes in quasi-insurrectionary tactics."[101] Ralph McGill, a Southern moderate who also has a nationally-syndicated column, went beyond the liberals by implying that SNCC had been taken over, and was being financed, in Havana.[102]

There seems to be little evidence for these accusations (see Chapter Five). The white volunteers who joined SNCC for the summer of 1964, and in some cases stayed on into 1965, probably included in their numbers some Communists, but it is doubtful that these young people had much influence on SNCC, since they had the double handicap of being white and new to the organization. SNCC as an organization had always had friendly relations with such "tainted" groups as the Southern Conference Educational Fund, the Highlander Folk School and the National Lawyers' Guild. Guild lawyers were sometimes used, but so were attorneys from the NAACP Legal Defense and Educational Fund, Inc., the Lawyers' Constitutional Defense Committee and the Lawyers' Committee on Civil Rights, all of which are completely acceptable to anti-Communist liberals. Bob Moses, in discussing the question whether individual volunteers should accept Guild lawyers, said, "The Mississippi staff has spent long hours discussing this matter. We have decided that we aren't going to let the politics of the '30s, '40s and '50s guide our movement in the '60s. It is irrelevant. Some of the best legal service we have received has come from the Guild. We have found the Guild willing to take cases that we could get none of the other lawyers to handle."[103]

Many liberal reporters visiting SNCC offices noticed that the *National Guardian*, a Communist-leaning weekly, was among the publications lying about or being perused. This in itself is not evidence that SNCC was Communist-leaning, since the *Guardian* was the only newspaper to publish regular detailed accounts of events in SNCC's history and was therefore used as a means of internal communication. Since the *Guardian* suited this purpose, SNCC members were not concerned if it shocked liberal reporters.

This view of the *Guardian* was consistent with SNCC's general attitude toward Communists, which was that it would accept help from anyone who cared to offer it. From the start, it had a policy of not excluding Communists, on the assumption that past political associations are irrelevant.

James Forman, SNCC's executive secretary, explained that SNCC was "revolutionary," that it did not require a "loyalty oath" of its members and that reports that it had been cut off from the rest of the civil-rights movement were false. (Some SNCC people had blamed "old-liners" in labor and civil rights for the Communist charges, saying they wanted to cause a split between SNCC and the rest of the movement.) Forman added, "I consider myself basically an agitator, seeking a nonviolent revolution in this country. Whether or not our opponents are successful in destroying SNCC, the thrust of the Southern movement will go on." Replying specifically to charges of alleged Communist influence, Forman said, "We have a positive program of nonviolent direct action. We stand on our affirmative program. We don't ask people what they are. We don't have a security check or a loyalty oath."[104]

What the SNCC leaders were saying, in a nutshell, was that they did not consider Communism an important issue. To SNCC members, a strong concern about Communist infiltration was a kind of neurosis that liberals shared with conservatives. Communism was not the enemy or even an ally of the enemy, which was poverty and racism. Communists, it was true, might have ends which did not coincide completely with SNCC's ends—but then so did liberals in power. The difference in ends between SNCC and powerful liberals had already become manifest; therefore, these same liberals were not taken very seriously when they warned of "Communist take-overs." Moreover, the warnings were not made in a friendly, private way but in the form of public attacks. In making such attacks, the liberals broadened the already deep gap between themselves and SNCC.

In dealing with Communists, SNCC never had to deal with another organization. The important point is that it assumed that any individual Communists who might join the organization would either be assimilated into SNCC's world view or would be left in very minor roles. As one SNCC member[105] put it, "When he gets mixed up with us, a Commie dies and a person develops." SNCC's confidence that it could deal with any person who actually joined it was in sharp contrast to its lack of confidence in dealing with other organizations.

Disillusionment with White Liberals Outside the Organization

SNCC has always been torn between its financial and political dependency on the good-will of white liberals and its psychological and social need to be free of them. This tension was not keenly felt by the rank and file until after the experiences of the challenges. In order for a group like SNCC to exist, it is necessary to reject the values of the rest of society, in terms of which the members of the group have low status, and to affirm a new set of values which give them higher status. If white America could be dismissed as "racist," it could more easily be rejected. But the existence of large numbers of white Americans who were not obviously racists made the task of rejection more difficult. Thus SNCC's search for identity was motivated by a mixture of organizational and racial drives. As Stokely Carmichael put it,

> Coalition's no good, 'cause what happens when a couple of Negroes join in with a bunch of whites? They get absorbed, that's what. They have to surrender too much to join . . . Black people got to act as a black community, and the Democratic and Republican Parties are completely irrelevant to them. I know we're gonna be on the outside now, we're gonna be on our own. But we've learned, in the past six years of trying to redeem the white man, that we don't have any alternatives now but to go this way.[106]

In short, cooperation was not possible without a loss of identity. It was necessary to withdraw from white society in order to maintain racial and organizational integrity.

Many SNCC members had at first assumed that if one only made a massive effort to inform white liberals in the North of the conditions of black people in the Deep South, they would come to see the matter from SNCC's point of view and would take strong action to correct the injustices, which would seem as unbearable to them as they did to SNCC members.[107] In its early publications and press releases, SNCC emphasized the most shocking aspects of its experience, in an effort to galvanize the rest of America into action which would wipe out the abuses. When tales of terror and murder were met mostly with $5 and $10 checks and government lawsuits, SNCC members began to see that most white Americans would never share their passion and urgency, even when they approved of their endeavor. Then, in Atlantic City and afterwards, SNCC members came to believe that in many respects liberals were not even on their side. Aware of its own helplessness, SNCC at first responded with anger: "If I can't sit with the white man at the table of American democracy, then I'll knock the legs off."[108] Soon the anger came to be turned specifically against the white liberals for whom SNCC formerly had had such high hopes. It was then that SNCC began to speak of racism pervading the American system, and, in some cases, of the consequent need to destroy that system. Such talk, of course, accelerated and exacerbated the attacks on SNCC by liberals described in the previous section.

59

"Don't use Mississippi as a moral lightning rod," said Bob Moses at an anti-war rally in April 1965. "Use it as a looking glass. Look into it and see what it tells you all about America."[109] SNCC members began to criticize middle-class liberal whites for their empty lives and their drinking[110] and for their pursuit of the dollar.[111] Other black-advancement groups had tried to secure for their clientele the privileges and amenities of the white middle class; SNCC rejected the middle-class life-style as empty and immoral.[112] Many of the white liberals who had seemed to offer the most hope of a shared world view and of substantial help (as well as many of the unassimilable whites within SNCC) had been Jewish. Therefore, some of SNCC's anti-white sentiment took the form of anti-Semitism.[113]

Thus, for a variety of reasons SNCC found it impossible to have dealings with whites outside the organization except on its own terms. Since it believed that its view of the world was wholly moral and reasonable, it expected that white liberals would come to accept that view and to act upon it. When they failed to do so, SNCC rejected all advice to work with these whites on their terms. To do this would have meant a denial of its unique experience as an organization, of the personal search for meaning of many individual members and of racial dignity. Its certainty of its own rightness and its bitter disappointment with whites outside the organization for not accepting its view of the nature of the problem led to increasingly harsh denunciations of the white liberals and of the society that they valued.

C. Relations with Other Civil Rights Organizations

The difference between a bargaining organization and a confrontation organization like SNCC becomes most apparent in the area of inter-organizational relations. In general, SNCC was capable of friendly relations only with other organizations oriented toward moral confrontation, like CORE in the South. It would have good relations with another organization only if there was real trust based on a similarity in ethos; a similarity in interests or goals was never enough. Stokely Carmichael had stated that SNCC will not ally itself with other groups because there are no groups with which to ally. By this he meant that there are no groups whose interests coincide one hundred percent with those of SNCC—and therefore SNCC is certain of being betrayed at the point where the coincidence of interest ends. Since SNCC has always been smaller and poorer and had less favorable press treatment than other groups, it feels it cannot help being the loser in any conflict with an allied organization.

Public attacks on rival organizations have never been used by SNCC as a means of organizational aggrandizement. In fact, SNCC has a policy, from which it rarely deviates, of never publicly attacking other black-led groups, in the interests of racial solidarity. Still, a high level of hostility and scorn for other organizations, especially those composed largely of non-activists, has served to raise morale among SNCC members.

COFO

SNCC's most direct contact with other civil-rights organizations was through the Council of Federated Organizations (COFO), of which it was a member. Technically, it was COFO rather than SNCC which sponsored the "Freedom Summer" of 1964. COFO was a Mississippi group that included the NAACP, SCLC, CORE, and several local organizations, as well as SNCC. It was founded in 1961 as an umbrella organization to obtain a meeting between civil rights workers in Mississippi and Governor Ross Barnett in order to negotiate the release from jail of the Freedom Riders. Among the organizers were two NAACP leaders—Aaron Henry, the Mississippi state chairman, and Medgar Evers, the Mississippi state executive secretary. After the meeting with Barnett in the spring of 1961, COFO became inactive.

In 1962, the private foundations which had decided to support financially a voter registration campaign in the South set up the Voter Education Project (VEP) through which to channel the money. The VEP was a subsidiary of the Southern Regional Council (SRC). It wished to distribute its money as equitably as possible among the organizations carrying on voter registration. Since there were several such organizations in Mississippi, it felt the need for an umbrella organization and COFO was reactivated to serve this purpose. Aaron Henry, who had been COFO's first president, was reelected, and Bob Moses of SNCC became program director. COFO sponsored the voter registration drives in Mississippi for the next few years and in 1963 it sponsored the "Freedom Vote" in which Henry ran for governor.

On COFO stationery, the highest names on the letterhead were those of NAACP people, but it was actually SNCC that did most of the work. The Freedom Summer (1964) was the peak of COFO activity. During that summer, SNCC provided all of the personnel in four out of Mississippi's five Congressional districts, ninety-five percent of the staff at the COFO state headquarters in Jackson and ninety to ninety-five percent of the money for the whole Mississippi program.[114] (The VEP had withdrawn its funds from COFO in early 1964 because it believed voter-registration efforts in Mississippi were futile.) CORE provided the personnel (about twenty field secretaries) in the remaining congressional district. SCLC sent two staff members and nominal financial contributions. The NAACP also gave some financial support, but SNCC members felt that it contributed almost nothing of importance.[115]

NAACP

SNCC's relations with the NAACP had always been bad. It suspected the NAACP of being a middle-class organization with very limited, conservative goals which would benefit mainly the black middle class. It resented what it considered the NAACP's habit of doing none of the work of organizing a confrontation but then stepping in and participating in negotiations and taking credit for whatever advances were made. The NAACP opposed direct-action campaigns in 1960, '61 and '62 (on the ground that they were ineffective) and in the negotiations was generally willing to settle for less than the more militant groups. SNCC suspected that this was in order to put an end to a type of activity it found embarrassing. (SNCC members never give the NAACP credit for leading the first sit-in campaign in Oklahoma City in 1958.)

NAACP leaders, on the other hand, made no secret of their distaste for SNCC. One Georgia NAACP official in 1962 said, "Let's face it. SNCC is a thorn in the side of the NAACP. It has no sense of responsibility."[116] Some people in SNCC believed that the NAACP was "out to kill SNCC in Mississippi."[117] Roy Wilkins was identified as a particularly determined enemy of SNCC; it was felt that the national NAACP actually opposed the existence of COFO, even though its Mississippi branch was formally a participant. On November 8, 1964, the Mississippi NAACP voted to withdraw from COFO. It issued a statement attacking SNCC for having "subversive" connections, among numerous other faults. By doing this, the NAACP touched off the Red-baiting campaign against SNCC by non-segregationists—a campaign in which it proved to be one of the most zealous participants.

The NAACP has always defended itself against charges of Communism by maintaining absolute purity within the organization and in its associations. Granted that the NAACP alliance with SNCC had hardly been a smooth one, it was nevertheless true that any person or group who could believe the NAACP to be sullied by Communism was probably very far from being its ally at all. SNCC was quite incapable of understanding an organization that would cater to the demands of its enemies and those who were at best indifferent to its aims at the expense of an ally, merely in order to insure its position. Moreover, those who were very much concerned about anti-Communism were mostly white and SNCC was mostly black. Therefore, to act in response to the desires of such groups could be interpreted by SNCC members only as McCarthyism or Uncle Tomism or both. For an organization like SNCC, the notion of sacrificing an ally's interests for a better bargaining position could be nothing but reprehensible.

From the start, SNCC's basic strategy had been different from that of the NAACP. It attracted those people who felt it was necessary to make a direct and moral confrontation with segregation. The NAACP did have a few militant members in Mississippi, like Amzie Moore. But mostly, it fought segregation through the courts in a legal and impersonal manner. Even the Mississippi state branch was directed by men considered relatively conservative by SNCC (Medgar Evers and then his brother Charles). The sit-ins were a more militant tactic; they attempted to bring the fight out in the open, to show every black and every white Southerner that the issue of the blacks' rights could not be evaded and that segregation was morally absurd. Was not every black man who walked to the back of the bus cooperating with segregation? The issue could not be evaded. Who could condone punishing a man for ordering a cup of coffee at a lunch counter? Segregation was morally absurd.

When SNCC turned away from pure direct action and went into voter registration, it entered the realm of the NAACP. But it soon went beyond the NAACP by doing voter registration in areas that the NAACP would not touch. (SNCC members assume that the NAACP by nature is reluctant to enter these areas; they seem to be unaware that two NAACP leaders were murdered during an NAACP voter registration campaign in Mississippi in 1955.) SNCC began to work in places where there was no NAACP and in fact no black middle class and therefore, it believed, little danger of future competition from that organization. As described earlier, this kind of work proved to be a dead end, and SNCC then went into political activity involving extensive white participation in the organization and the cooperation of white liberals and the federal government. The NAACP did not welcome the competition of a more militant group doing its own sort of work. It supported the FDP challenge in Atlantic City only with reluctance and it urged SNCC's leaders to accept the compromise when it was offered. In the congressional challenge, it refused to support the FDP until it was clear that the challenge called only for the removal of the white congressmen and not necessarily for the seating of the FDP congressmen. After both challenges failed, SNCC decided to turn back to the political organization of the "forgotten ones," those people who were neglected by the NAACP and similar groups. (COFO had by the end of 1965 faded out of existence.)

SNCC's black-power stance quickly earned it the hostility of the NAACP, whose executive director, Roy Wilkins, was one of the signers of a three-quarter-page advertisement in the *New York Times*[118] denouncing an exaggerated version of SNCC's position without mentioning SNCC. For the NAACP, this ad, like the Red-baiting campaign, was self-protection. For SNCC, it was another example of that organization's perfidy.

The other signers of the ad were Dorothy Height, the President of the National Council of Negro Women; A. Philip Randolph, the President of the Brotherhood of Sleeping Car Porters, AFL-CIO; Bayard Rustin, the Director of the A. Philip Randolph Institute; Whitney M. Young, Jr., the Executive Director of the National Urban League; and two leaders of black Masons and Elks. Conspicuously absent from the list of signatories were Floyd McKissick, the national director of CORE, and Martin Luther King, the head of the SCLC. SNCC has always gotten along fairly well with CORE.

SCLC

Good relations did not prevail, however, with SNCC's parent organization, the Southern Christian Leadership Conference (SCLC). Rather, there was a long history of conflict. SCLC had hoped at first that SNCC would become its student wing, but it soon became apparent that this was not possible. The young people in SNCC did not like the idea of being part of a "family," which might provide financial security but at the same time insist on making decisions for its offspring. By the spring of 1961, SNCC was ready to move in its own direction. Its members chafed at SCLC's "bureaucracy," sneered at the great pains it took to remain pure and respectable in its associations, were impatient at its insistence on nonviolence as a way of life and resented Martin Luther King's domination. SNCC's lack of hierarchy, its devil-may-care attitude toward the powers-that-be, its freedom from adult domination were among the most important qualities that attracted members in the early years. Even at the beginning SNCC was always willing to sacrifice reconciliation to justice; SCLC, on the other hand, consistently sought reconciliation as part of a religious vision. These qualities apparently distinguished SNCC sharply enough from SCLC so that it lost only a few members to the older group.

It did have a serious rivalry with SCLC in its organizational work, however. SCLC, unlike CORE, liked to enter "territory" which SNCC considered its own. SNCC's method of operation, except in the year 1964, was long, painstaking community organizing designed to build a movement that would not die when SNCC left and that would be a real force for the white community to contend with. SCLC also did community organizing—but its leaders believed that at a certain point a community could be given a lift by sending in Dr. King and thus getting national publicity and the direct aid of the federal government. This tactic angered SNCC because it seemed "cheap." Dr. King's appearance always caused a great uproar, but SNCC people felt that it had a bad effect because it reinforced in people a natural tendency to wait for leaders to solve their problems for them. It was successful in achieving immediate, spectacular gains, but SNCC believed that it did not leave behind in a community a lasting political force. SNCC was particularly angered when Dr. King entered a community where it had been working for months, or even years, with little concrete progress, and in a few days changed the entire balance of forces.

The first time this happened was in Albany, Georgia. SNCC began organizing that town, mainly around direct action, in October 1961. In December, Dr. King and the Reverend Ralph Abernathy were invited by the Albany Movement (the local activists) to lead a demonstration. They were arrested, tried and convicted for parading without a permit. Dr. King was sent to jail for this in July, 1962, but the federal government immediately secured his release, even though he wished to stay in jail as a sign of the sacrifice required of those in the struggle.[119] SNCC members resented this incident, particularly the attention given to Dr. King by the

65

press and the government after the blanket of silence surrounding several months of demonstrations and hundreds of arrests of ordinary people. One SNCC member even said that Dr. King "effectively destroyed the Albany Movement with his silk pajamas in jail"[120] although there is little evidence that this is true.

Later, in Selma, Alabama, a much more serious clash occurred between SNCC and SCLC, over much the same difference in tactics. SNCC had had a small number of organizers in Selma since February 1963 working on voter education and registration. White repression had succeeded in keeping civil rights activity to a minimum. During the last months of 1964, there was a state court injunction in effect against any activity by civil rights organizations and many other groups. After the injunction was finally lifted, SCLC (in January 1965) began a voter registration drive in Selma.[121] For the next two months, there was continuous minor irritation but no major clash between SNCC and SCLC workers.[122] Then, in March 1965, SCLC decided to sponsor a march from Selma to the state capital at Montgomery fifty miles away to demand voting rights for black people, in defiance of Governor George Wallace's order that they not do so. SNCC discussed the march in executive session and decided that it was only another of Dr. King's "tricks," that it would hurt people and that SNCC as an organization would not participate.[123] However, a number of SNCC members, including Chairman John Lewis, decided to participate as individuals.

A little over 500 black people set out from Selma on Sunday, March 9, led by Lewis and Hosea Williams, an SCLC leader. Dr. King himself was absent, a fact that SNCC members attributed to fear of violence and possible assassination. There was indeed violence. No sooner had the blacks crossed the little bridge leading out of Selma than they were attacked by Alabama state troopers and by Dallas County possemen led by Sheriff James Clark. The police, using whips, clubs, horses and tear gas, pursued the retreating nonviolent marchers back over the bridge. Many bones were broken and John Lewis himself was severely beaten and suffered a concussion.

Two days later, another march was held, this time led by Dr. King, in which the marchers went to about the same spot and then turned back again, this time without violence. This was according to a prior arrangement worked out between the SCLC leaders and the troopers, on the urging of President Johnson's representatives, who promised that a federal judge would enjoin Alabama officials from blocking a third march to be held that Thursday. However, SNCC was not informed about this agreement (possibly because it was not a formal participant in the march) and its members felt a great sense of anger and betrayal when the march turned back.[124] For years, they spoke angrily of Dr. King's "making secret deals with Jim Clark."

This third march was not actually begun until March 21, two weeks after the first one. Three thousand, two hundred persons participated, including hundreds of Northern whites; they were protected by almost 4,000 federal soldiers.[125] The march was an enormous success in that it succeeded in directing national attention to the denial of the franchise in the Deep South and in getting the Voting Rights Bill brought up before Congress.

In the two weeks between the first and last marches, there were numerous support demonstrations in Northern cities, most of which SNCC had a hand in. SNCC also took the opportunity to organize and direct a series of demonstrations in Washington, D.C.—including sit-ins in the corridors of the Justice Department, regular picketing of the White House, a sit-down that momentarily blocked traffic on Pennsylvania Avenue and an unplanned sit-down inside the White House. The purpose of the demonstrations was to pressure the president to provide federal protection for civil rights workers.

These demonstrations provoked an angry attack from the Reverend Jefferson Rogers, an SCLC leader, who called them "ill-timed" (just at the moment when the president was trying to push through the Voting Rights Bill) and pointless when not coordinated with the rest of the movement. Rogers also said he resented being "badgered" by SNCC to maintain a united front. He accused it of being more interested in "protest than achievement" and of demanding that all other civil rights workers pay "obeisance" to it.[126] (Top NAACP officials had at that time been making similar statements about SNCC.)

But top leaders of SCLC were apparently not interested in provoking a split with SNCC. Both Dr. King and his assistant, Andrew Young, made conciliatory statements shortly after the Rogers statement. Dr. King said, "SNCC is like a younger brother. You love 'em and you work with 'em, but they sure can be a pain in the neck."[127]

SCLC made considerable efforts to patch up relations with SNCC, and on April 30, 1965, Dr. King and Forman held a joint press conference in which they said they were in basic agreement on both goals and strategy. Dr. King took the opportunity to dismiss the charges of Communism then being made against SNCC, saying they were merely designed to sow the seeds of discord.[128]

The whole Selma episode illustrated perfectly the differences between SNCC and SCLC. SCLC wanted to bring about the kind of publicity and pressure that would result in a voting rights act and it was willing to cooperate with federal officials in order to do this. It wanted to obtain the kind of financial backing that would make possible the registration of large numbers of Alabama black voters—and it did not care if this meant that these voters would have to be registered as Democrats. Since the top leaders of SCLC refrained from attacking SNCC openly, it became much more important for SNCC to arouse internal suspicion and dislike of SCLC than of the NAACP. SNCC did this by claiming that it had laid the groundwork for the SCLC success in Selma by years of painstaking work in community organization. SCLC, SNCC members believed, then destroyed a great deal of the work SNCC had done, by bringing in Dr. King as a sort of *deus ex machina*.

In contrasting itself to SCLC, SNCC had to define its goals as "teaching people that they must act politically on their own behalf" rather than obtaining certain specific gains, such as the right to vote. No SNCC member ever admitted that a big, bureaucratic, bargaining-conscious organization like SCLC was far more effective in achieving concrete gains that SNCC could ever be. A number of them did, however, admit that SNCC was not very effective in this area. They felt that grass-roots personal-style politics were far more important. Starting as early as 1962, some people in SNCC became more aware that this political style was not the usual one in America; it followed that the very idea of SNCC as an organization was a challenge to the political process as it existed in the United States. Gradually, SNCC members came to see the main purpose of their organization as an alternative type of political activity—and they came to believe fervently that such a purpose was far more important than any incremental improvements that could be brought about by SCLC. This made it possible for SNCC members to maintain a belief in the special importance of their own group while at the same time acknowledging that it had less immediate effectiveness than other groups.

CORE

It was the special nature of SNCC as an organization described above, which made it possible for it to get along so well with the Congress of Racial Equality (CORE). SNCC's good relations with CORE are hard to explain in any other way. Like the NAACP and SCLC, CORE competed with SNCC for funds, following and personnel. Yet no SNCC member in this study ever expressed hostility to CORE in any form, even after prodding. SNCC members often spontaneously gave CORE credit for its achievements, such as initiating the Freedom Rides, whereas they never praised the NAACP or SCLC for anything. (The sole exception is James Bevel, an early SNCC leader who subsequently became an SCLC leader. When interviewed, he praised SCLC.) Southern CORE workers, such as Dave Dennis and Zev Aelony, were mentioned occasionally in interviews and frequently in SNCC literature, always in a positive light, often in the context of suffering bravely shared with SNCC members. Interestingly, though, CORE's national leaders, James Farmer and Floyd McKissick, were never mentioned, although Roy Wilkins and Martin Luther King, the national leaders of the NAACP and SCLC, often were.

SNCC members, when asked, did not perceive any major differences between CORE and their own organization. When asked why they joined SNCC rather than CORE, they usually said it was due to personal circumstances—SNCC was working in their town, they knew people in SNCC, etc. CORE is in fact different from SNCC, even though SNCC members did not perceive it as such. It is a nation-wide organization with chapters, a bureaucratic structure, and a long-standing ideological commitment to nonviolence. It is an established organization (founded in 1941) and it has a single outstanding national leader (Floyd McKissick and before him James Farmer) at its head. In all of these respects, it resembles the NAACP and SCLC more than SNCC.

Yet SNCC's perception *of the part of CORE with which it had contact* was not really inaccurate. CORE in the Deep South consisted of a number of isolated, fairly self-sufficient chapters. Although the organization was old, many of these chapters were new or newly reactivated. The sit-ins and Freedom Rides had stimulated not only the birth of SNCC but also the rebirth of CORE, which had long been moribund in many places. Unlike SNCC members, CORE workers generally lived and worked in their home communities. However, CORE chapters in the South often resembled SNCC

69

in the kind of total absorption and commitment given by their members. Although CORE chapters in the North had many white members, in the South almost all the members were black. Moreover, because of its nonviolent ideology, CORE placed the same emphasis on courageous confrontation as did SNCC. CORE members had approximately the same values and mood as SNCC workers in the early '60s.[129]

CORE and SNCC, instead of clashing, simply divided up the territory, SNCC concentrating in Mississippi, Alabama, Georgia, and Arkansas (with some direct-action projects in Maryland and Virginia), while CORE did most of its work in Louisiana, Florida and South Carolina. CORE was a member of COFO, but here too there was no direct clash. CORE simply took as its territory one of Mississippi's congressional districts, while SNCC took the other four. There was never a formal national agreement between SNCC and CORE to divide the territory. Leaders of the two organizations at the local and state levels were always on good enough terms so that this was unnecessary. Tacit or informal agreements were sufficient to avert conflict.

The trust necessary for such agreements was made possible by the fact that SNCC and CORE perceived each other as similar kinds of organizations with similar world outlooks. SNCC saw CORE as committed to the same kind of "alternative politics" as itself. As time passed, SNCC's belief in the importance of offering a new kind of politics strengthened and spread among the membership. Relations with SCLC and the NAACP grew worse as the commitment to alternative politics was reinforced, and at the same time relations with CORE continued to be friendly. CORE underwent the same kinds of shifts in mood and policy as SNCC and at about the same times.

By 1964, SNCC's view of itself as essentially like CORE and unlike the NAACP and SCLC was already quite strong. It was scornful of the latter organizations because their structure and policies were so much determined by concern with fund-raising and bargaining positions with regard to whites in power. The vast majority of political groups in America are concerned with such matters. The fact that SNCC was not set it apart from the norm. Its indifference to these matters arose from its very nature as an organization, a nature most clearly manifested in its unusual leadership and internal structure.

THREE

Leadership and Structure

The role played by leadership in SNCC was very different from that in other American political groups. Leaders in Atlanta never played an important part in planning SNCC's policies or programs on the local level. SNCC was always highly decentralized, relying on initiatives from its workers in the field. It had an ideological aversion to leadership, viewing it as a form of manipulation. This aversion was expressed in the line, "No more leaders over me," in one of its songs. The functions of the Atlanta office were to raise funds, provide publicity and maintain a relationship with the federal government in an effort to insure the safety of the workers in the field. Before 1964, policy decisions were made at periodic meetings of the entire staff plus adult advisers and all types of sympathizers. Since the staff was very small and very closely knit, it was difficult for any decision to be "railroaded" through at such a meeting. Decisions were arrived at not by voting but by hours of discussion aimed at arriving at a consensus or "sense of the meeting," Quaker style. The awareness of common danger created the kind of trust which made possible such a method of decision-making.

The smallness of the organization before the summer of 1964 was an important factor in influencing its nature and direction. The paid staff, consisting mainly of organizers called "field secretaries," fluctuated in size, being always much bigger in the summer (during school vacation). At all times, it was supplemented by a large number of local volunteers, some of them full time. All members of SNCC, whether paid or unpaid, were activists; most of them worked full time for it. In the summer of 1962, after a year of operation as a community-organizing cadre, SNCC had a paid staff of 40. The following summer, there was a staff of about 100, approximately a tenth of whom were in the office. By early 1964, this number had fallen to about 60 or 70, but shortly before the summer it had risen again to about 130, in preparation for the influx of volunteers. Thus, before the summer of 1964, the paid staff rarely rose above 100. There were never more than 20 or so whites among these. The staff members all knew each other and shared a sense of sacrifice and dedication.

The fact that the salaries were very low[1] and that so many of the workers were volunteers, receiving no salary at all, eliminated most of the influence the central office might have had through dispensing money. The central office hired people, usually on the recommendation of a project leader in the field, but before the summer of 1964 it never fired them. The central office did exercise some power through its control of money and cars for projects, but even this was minimal. Local projects took pride in their independence. A central belief was that the strongest projects were those that were supported to the greatest degree by the local people rather than by the SNCC office. Such projects, it was believed, could not be stopped by the imprisonment of "outside agitators." Local people tended to fear being put up to dangerous acts by outsiders and then deserted; it was easier to gain their trust if the role of outside aid was minimal from the start. Thus, it was clear to everyone that the leaders did not really have the power to make or break a program.

Many SNCC members said that what they liked best about SNCC was the fact that it was so decentralized. A person who had a new idea for organizing was able to try it out in the field; the organization's policy guidelines on both issues and tactic were so vague that almost anything was permissible, so long as it was within the SNCC spirit. To a great degree, "spirit" was what held the organization together—the feeling of camaraderie, the sense of a common commitment to a good cause. One long-term SNCC member said that he did not think SNCC had any broad goals nor that voter registration was particularly important but that he stayed in SNCC because he liked the people: their altruism, their concern about others.[2] Another one said that SNCC was like a big fraternity.[3] A white girl who joined SNCC in 1963 said that she thought she had deliberately been put in a position that would lead to her arrest shortly after she arrived in the Deep South. She believed that this had been done to remove any excessive fear of jail she might have.[4] Another explanation might be that her jailing was a kind of initiation into the SNCC fraternity.

But the great love, trust and confidence that SNCC people say thay had for each other in the early years seems to go beyond what fraternity members normally feel. Perhaps it is more comparable to the way members of a religious sect see each other. The white girl's jailing may have been something like a religious initiation, a proof of the genuineness of her conversion. SNCC certainly did possess many characteristics of a religious sect.[5] Like a sect, it thought of itself as an elect group with special enlightenment. Although it carried on a great deal of political and instrumental activity, there was a strong group in it which saw the personal perfection of each member as the most important goal. It was hostile to the rest of society and to the state; many of its members had joined it out of a revulsion against "secular" society. As in a sect, members could spontaneously express their commitment. In fact, there was a great emphasis on the possibility of spontaneity, both in expressing oneself at meetings and in initiating activity. Also, because of its isolation and to some extent insulation (through the adoption of the dress of the rural Southern black people) it possessed a total rather than segmental hold over its members.

Perhaps the most important point of resemblance between SNCC and a religious sect is the priesthood of all believers. Virtually all members of SNCC have been full-time staff members, devoted to spreading the organization's message. This fact has had an enormous influence on the organization's history, mainly in weakening the role of organizational leaders in general and particularly moderate leaders. In an organization of activists, it is very difficult for a leader to act on behalf of the "rank and file" unless all of them really desire that action. In SNCC in the early years, for example, no one person spoke to the press. If a reporter visited the SNCC office, any member who happened to be around might take it on himself to speak for the organization and no one else would deny his right to do so. (After all, he had probably been to jail for SNCC.) Moreover, in an organization like this, in case of a conflict between the leadership and the activists, the leader has no bloc of inactive members for whom he can claim to speak. There were a few older advisers, like Howard Zinn and Ella Baker, but their influence waned as more people who did not know them personally joined the organization. There were also the Northern donors, mostly white liberals, but no SNCC leader would admit that he was swayed by them, since this would be defined as "selling out."

Until this point I have been using the word "leaders" to refer only to leadership from the national office in Atlanta. The influence of these leaders remained minimal so long as the organization was loosely structured and oriented around local action projects. Leadership did play an important role in SNCC, but on the regional level. In each geographic area where SNCC sustained a program for several years, there was a single capable and charismatic leader who was able to surround himself with organizing talent. In Southwest Georgia, that leader was Charles Sherrod. In Arkansas, it was Bill Hansen. In Mississippi, it was Bob Moses. Largely because of Moses' leadership role, the Mississippi project was for a long time the nucleus of SNCC's program and outlook, serving as a focus and model for national SNCC, often setting precedents and priorities. After Moses left the state in January 1965, Mississippi quickly waned as a center of SNCC activity. The Arkansas project continued to be quite active in 1965 and 1966, but Arkansas never played the symbolic role of Mississippi. This was partly because Ben Grinage, who succeeded Bill Hansen as Arkansas project leader in August 1964, was not particularly charismatic.

Some of the same factors that weakened leadership from Atlanta tended to enhance project leadership. In an organization of activists, the successful organizer of action, not the man sitting at a desk, receives respect and trust. The man who makes the immediate decisions about action, not the one who talks to the press, is best known to activist members. In SNCC before 1964, there was a high turnover in membership. Many members worked for only a semester or a summer. Then, being young and restless, they moved on to other jobs or went back to school. Also, the physical and psychological wear and tear of SNCC work took their toll. The result of the high turnover was that each leader in the field was able to recruit and socialize his own assistants on a continuous basis. Since the national office paid such low salaries, his charisma was the major factor keeping his people in the organization. Their short tenure guaranteed, he did not need to worry about major challenges to his power from them.

The nature of the work also tended to reinforce charismatic leadership in the field. There was a great deal of danger and therefore a continual need to make decisions involving high risks. Such decisions required a leader whose judgment and courage one could trust completely. Without leadership, the natural tendency of groups to flee in the face of danger would quickly have dispersed SNCC. Like the lead singer in a spiritual, the SNCC leader could make possible that "spirit" which was so vital in holding the organization together. The singing of spirituals, of which the most famous was "We Shall Overcome," was common in SNCC before the winter of 1964-65; after that the practice seems to have died out. This coincided with the departure from SNCC of a number of the long-time major leaders.

The role of SNCC's leadership in the field bears certain resemblances to the role of field officers in an army, who also keep their men together in the face of danger. The average age of SNCC members (about twenty-one) is about the same as that of soldiers in combat. One writer[6] has compared

SNCC to a seasoned infantry unit, in that there are many inside jokes and a disdain for outsiders.

But the personal style of SNCC's important leaders was neither military nor evangelistic (although some SNCC leaders did use the techniques of pentecostal preachers to arouse people at meetings in churches). The major field leaders of the early period were quiet and introspective, gentle and serious in demeanor. A reporter at a SNCC fundraising meeting in New York described the speaker's style as "low key," "unimpassioned," "unauthoritarian."[7] The speaker in question was Charley Cobb, one of the most militant of SNCC's leaders. In the early years, SNCC's style was not one of open anger. Great bitterness there was, but it was generally concealed behind a stoical front. SNCC members did not hesitate to speak of their beatings and jailings, but their tones were monotonous when they did.[8] The "mixture of humor and coolness" that made up the style of many SNCC workers [provided] a means of facing the danger courageously."[9] SNCC sought workers and leaders not for the flamboyance of their personalities but for their righteousness and above all their courage.

Ability to bargain with the opposition was also not a desired quality in leaders. In fact, any leader who made concessions to someone outside SNCC was regarded as somewhat suspect. The purpose of the organization was to create a certain kind of community feeling among its followers, which would stimulate them to confront institutions that were seen as bad. For this purpose the ability to bargain had no value. Many people were SNCC leaders while they were very young and then left SNCC to join bargaining institutions (like SCLC) when they felt the need to make more permanent organizational commitments. Thus, the youth of SNCC's membership was a built-in-mechanism for the renewal of militancy and purity.

Formal Structure

As long as SNCC remained a small organization in which everyone knew and trusted everyone else, there was little attention paid to formal structure. Informal means of setting policy and distributing resources within the organization proved satisfactory. In late 1963 the formal structure still consisted of two representatives from the campus-based sit-in movement of each Southern state (the "coordinating committee"), plus an "executive committee" which carried on the day-to-day work of the organization. There were staff conferences once or twice a year at which the staff gave its recommendations on broad policy questions. There was a chairman, whose main job was to represent the organization to the press and at conferences with other groups—a post held by John Lewis, an early sit-in leader. There was also an executive secretary, James Forman, who had held his job since the fall of 1961, when SNCC first became a community organizing cadre. He was formally in charge of the Atlanta office, the Northern offices and of fund-raising in general and, by virtue of his personal qualities, actually had considerable influence in other areas as well.

This formal structure bore very little relationship to the actual SNCC of late 1963. The campus groups which theoretically comprised the coordinating committee had actually ceased to exist during the period 1961-1963. At the same time the staff had grown to about sixty people, plus a large number of full-time volunteers. In December 1963, the staff demanded a vote as well as a voice on the coordinating committee. At the spring 1964 staff conference, a constitutional amendment was passed, granting the staff six voting representatives on the executive committee, at least three of whom had to be state project heads, plus representation on the coordinating committee.

Shortly afterwards, the staff approximately doubled in size in order to handle the influx of white volunteers expected during the summer of 1964. After the summer, a large number of the volunteers stayed on to work for SNCC, almost all in Mississippi. By October of 1964, the organization had close to 200 staff members, about half of whom were white. In the spring of 1965, it still had more than 150 members. The old SNCC held together by trust and camaraderie was no longer possible, particularly since almost all of the staff consisted of neophytes whose integrity and loyalty to SNCC had not yet been tested.

SNCC began to think in terms of devoting a considerable amount of its organizational resources to staff education. This forced the leaders to think about *what* should be taught concerning SNCC and its environment. The intellectual ferment occurring in SNCC at that time (see Chapter Five) had important implications for SNCC's structure. For instance a staff bulletin in November 1964 raised the questions, What does "One Man, One Vote" (SNCC's main slogan of the previous two years) mean? Is true democracy possible in this country or are there natural limits to democracy? Then, a little farther on, Should SNCC itself operate on the principle of One Man, One Vote? Can true democracy be achieved within SNCC?

A proposal made in the fall of 1964 to hold another summer project, this time covering the entire Black Belt, was the occasion for a radical challenge to the formal structure. There were a great many people in SNCC who were very unhappy about what had happened during the summer of 1964. They now began to ask how the decision to have the summer project had been made, and thus the general question of decision-making in SNCC arose. The staff in Arkansas, Alabama and Southwest Georgia felt that their projects were not receiving a fair share of the resources (money, cars, etc.), now that the Mississippi project had become so large. They began to ask who decided where resources went and it soon became apparent that the decisions were made unsystematically on the basis of whether the people in the office liked and trusted the person who made the request. The people in the office, in turn, were worried about the careless use of resources in the field. There was no system for checking on the spending of money, but word had drifted back to the office that a lot of people on the payroll were not working very hard, a lot of cars were being driven rather recklessly, etc.

In the fall of 1964, SNCC's two long-simmering problems—whites and structure—came to a head. The fact that both problems became acute simultaneously prevented the solution of either one. If SNCC had had a clear, strong and practical structure, it could have fired the whites who were causing the greatest difficulty and placed the others in an auxiliary and subordinate role. Conversely, if there had not been so many whites, it would have been much easier to agree on a structure; in fact, structure problems might not even have arisen, since the earlier informal method of decision-making would have continued to be satisfactory. Instead, SNCC was wracked for months by a bitter and complex dispute. There was a staff meeting, lasting a week to ten days, almost every month in the fall of 1964 and the winter of 1965. The sessions were highly emotional and lasted late into the night. The two basic problems, whites and structure, were complicated by power struggles, by personality conflicts and by a cultural gulf between Southern blacks (who tended to be uneducated or poorly educated) and all Northerners. The entire crisis debilitated SNCC by preventing it from developing new programs and strategies to replace those that had been exhausted or discredited by the events of the summer.

The large number of whites exacerbated the structure dispute in several ways. The tripling in size of any organization in a short period of time is bound to create severe problems. The newcomers must be trained and socialized, even if they are of the same general background as the original group. Many long-time SNCC workers found that as the organization grew, the nature of their work had changed rapidly, so that they were no longer sure of their role. The work of initiating and administering programs seemed to be displacing the work of direct organizing. And for the first time, it became apparent that the leaders in the Atlanta office were capable of making decisions that would radically affect the way organizing was done on the local level.

The increase in size was thus traumatic for many SNCC members. But it was the fact that the organization as a whole had decided to send large numbers of *whites* into Mississippi that most disturbed the black workers in the field there. These white people resisted socialization and assimilation into SNCC's old way of doing things. One reason was that it was very difficult to communicate with them. During the structure dispute, many native Southern black people walked out of staff meetings because the discussion was being carried on in terms that were meaningless to them. It was not only the whites but also the black Northerners who inhabited a universe of discourse from which the Southern black people were excluded. The whites discussed such matters as whether SNCC favored "reform" or "revolution"; the question had never occurred to the Southern black people if only because they were not familiar with the words. And yet it was the black Southerners who had been the core of SNCC until 1964. This problem caused Jesse Morris to suggest that only people with no more than a high-school education (who in SNCC were all Southerners) be permitted to serve on the executive committee. The suggestion was supported by Bob Moses and therefore seriously debated—but never adopted.

Much of the debate over structure was centered around the question whether SNCC should have "tight" or "loose" structure. The Southern black people tended to favor tight structure. They valued SNCC in itself as an organization and they also valued concrete accomplishment, concrete advances in the conditions of the people among whom they had spent their lives. SNCC as an organization gave them a sense of identity; they wanted it to have an impressive office and powerful spokesman of whom they could be proud. More important, they feared that without formal procedures, the articulate Northern minority on staff would come to dominate the organization—that SNCC, which they had created, would slip through their fingers and be transformed by strangers into something quite different.

One fear was that the newcomers would draw SNCC away from the political organizing which had occupied it since 1961. There was a group within SNCC, composed largely of whites, which said that the organization should support a certain number of people for thinking and exploring new ways of life. These people were derisively nicknamed the "Freedom High" group implying that they were "high" on the experience of freedom itself or on the thrill of awakening a taste for freedom in others. Some of these people also got high on drugs such as marijuana. All of them spent many hours discussing the ultimate goals of SNCC, the beauty of the "black folk" of the Deep South, the meaning of life, the difficulty of finding personal meaning, etc. The Freedom High people favored loose structure, so that people would have leeway to do this kind of exploration. Most of this group, although white, were not newcomers to SNCC, but people who had been working in the Deep South for a few years. Many of them had come with great expectations of rapid and dramatic change. They had worked for SNCC and become discouraged when change did not come. Some of their critics said that they were "burnt out," or that they were suffering from battle fatigue. Other people said that everyone who worked for SNCC for a long period of time needed to go through a phase of retreat and self-exploration from time to time in order to be renewed, and that the organization should be flexible enough to permit this. The difficulty was that a large number of people seemed to require a rest simultaneously in the fall of 1964.

Those who needed a rest were not all white. The corollary to the whites in Freedom High was the "floaters," mostly Northern black men who travelled about from one project to another, never staying long enough to do any real work, apparently also searching for some meaningful kind of activity. There were other black people in SNCC who reacted to the crisis by indulging in a considerable amount of reckless driving, drunkenness, sexual activity, etc.

All of this contributed to a strongly-felt need for tight structure, not only among black Southerners in the field but among almost all the people who worked in the office in Atlanta. These people had a commitment to running an organization which they saw as seriously threatened. They felt that one could not "make the new world and live in it, too." Moreover, they saw their own power challenged by the sudden growth of the Mississippi project. During the summer of 1964, national SNCC had opened an office in Mississippi and conducted much of its work from there, at the insistence of Bob Moses and other people who worked in Mississippi. For a while during the summer, it almost seemed that Moses, who was Mississippi project director, had more power than James Forman, who was executive secretary of national SNCC. Moses' charisma and organizational talent gave him enormous influence, and he was not entirely trusted, because he was closely associated with the Freedom High group. There was some feeling that a lot of people who resented the power wielded by Forman were using the anarchistic ideas popularized in SNCC by Moses to oppose him.

The above account should give some notion of the complexity of the issues that tormented SNCC that fall and winter. There is no simple correlation among these issues. There were many whites who favored tight structure and there were office people who favored tight structure and there were office people who favored loose structure. To most people it never became clear exactly what was at stake in each issue in the debate. It was difficult to make decisions through parliamentary procedure and orderly voting because some people did not understand how they worked and many of those who did understand rejected such systems on philosophic grounds. This meant that much of the time the meetings were in an uproar. The problems were never really resolved and eventually helped to destroy SNCC.

Although the problems were not resolved, some actions were taken. The entire staff was made the coordinating committee, a change that resolved the original structure problem without dealing with the basic loose-tight problem. The executive committee was expanded to twenty-one members, with enough seats set aside for field staff, both project directors and "less visible" members, to vest control in them. A "call committee" was established in order to keep contact with any college groups that might develop and with the Friends of SNCC chapters in the North. A program secretary, Cleve Sellers, was chosen, with the function of providing a link among the various projects and between field and office, so that eventually decisions might be made rationally about the discarding of old projects and the creation of new ones.

In the spring of 1965, a purge of the staff was conducted by the Atlanta office. Every member of the staff was asked to give an accounting of his recent activities or be taken off the payroll. A few people were actually dismissed; many more drifted out of the organization. Most of these were whites, both newcomers and long-time workers; others were blacks who liked working with whites or who objected to their harassment. It seemed that the tight-structure people had won, but it was a pyrrhic victory, since much of SNCC's best organizing talent were casualties of the conflict.

Since the spring of 1965, the changes in SNCC's formal structure have been minor. The name of the executive committee was changed to "central committee" and it was reduced in size from twenty-one to ten members. The program secretary became program chairman, with a whole department under him. A few other unimportant adjustments were made.

But the effect of the crisis of 1964-1965 on SNCC's leadership has been drastic.

Leadership

SNCC has always been ambivalent about the idea of leadership. On the one hand it would seem that the purpose of the organization is leadership—to lead the poor black people of the Black Belt to a sense of the possibilities of improving their own lives, or, put somewhat differently, to lead them into developing leadership. On the other hand, a large number of SNCC members, when asked about leadership in the organization, denied that there was any such thing. "Leadership" to them implied manipulation and exploitation; it was seen not as a prerequisite but as a substitute for political participation. To them, leadership was the sort of thing that the NAACP and SCLC indulged in because they were hopelessly removed from the great mass of black people. They claimed there were no leaders in SNCC, only helpers.

This was by no means a universal attitude within SNCC. The organization held several "leadership conferences," so there must have been some people within it who saw leadership as something desirable.

The first leadership conference, held in 1961, was for the explicit purpose of transforming the sit-in leaders into well-informed and professional political organizers. Timothy Jenkins, a black man who was national-affairs vice-president of the National Student Association (NSA), had been a central figure in the negotiations with the federal government and the foundations for support of a voter registration effort by SNCC. He looked to the best of the sit-in leaders to carry out this effort, but he was concerned about "their lack of comprehension of the institutional world and the way in which their program had to plug in and manipulate those forces in the institutional world in order to succeed."[10] He persuaded NSA and the New World Foundation to sponsor a Civil Rights Leadership Institute to make up this lack. About twenty SNCC leaders attended all or some of the sessions, which ran from July 16 to August 11, 1961, in Nashville, Tennessee. There were seminars and discussion groups on such topics as "The Negro in American History," "Southern History," "Personal and Psychological Effects of

Discrimination," "Southern Economics," "Southern Education and School Desegregation," "Southern Politics in State and Nation," "How Communities Work," "Other Freedom Movements," "The Movement in the North after the Legal Barriers are Gone," plus how to run freedom schools, community centers, voter registration drives, etc. Most of the faculty were civil rights leaders and faculty members from black colleges. Jenkins envisaged a group of trained, full-time political organizers and this was exactly what SNCC was to become.

Another leadership conference was held on Thanksgiving weekend, 1963, in Washington, D.C., this one under the sponsorship of SNCC itself. This second conference was more oriented toward providing practical information on how to bring about change in the Deep South. It had speakers from the Manpower Development and Training Agency, the Migrant Health Section of the U.S. Department of Health, Education and Welfare, the National Sharecroppers Fund and the AFL-CIO. In addition, Norman Thomas and Bob Moses spoke on the political and economic background. At least part of the purpose of this conference was to stimulate morale: there was a great deal of group singing.

This conference took place at what was probably the peak of the old-style SNCC leadership. These were the people who had originally been leaders of direct-action demonstrations against segregation. They possessed a certain magnetism because of their courage and their inner forcefulness, which was in many of them inspired by religion. A number of them possessed an individual mystique, with which they attracted a coterie of followers. In some cases, they encouraged this mystique by developing certain mannerisms which their followers could imitate. They also inspired a love akin to worship among the local black people. In one black home in the Mississippi Delta, a magazine photo of Bob Moses hung beside a picture of Jesus.[11] The courage involved in nonviolent confrontation was at the core of the appeal of this leadership.

A black native of Mississippi who worked for SNCC told me,

> The movement was a kind of magic—like Moses, like Jesus. Here's a guy not afraid to get his head beat and tell the cop he loves him. You want to get involved with that human being, because he must be special to be able to do that. The SNCC organizer was a hero; he was loved, he was given food, cars, everything. Then there was a transition. These people became part of the community; no longer Jesuses and Moseses. And they found themselves without those personal rewards. Then they began to worry about money. Guys

began to go back to school and to go to the North to raise money. Only then did people sit down and think about the problem of how to organize. When you were a magician, all you had to do to gather a crowd was to walk down the street. You had charisma.[12]

This loss of charisma by field leaders was very damaging to SNCC. There is evidence that a single powerful and appealing leader is essential to organize a Southern black community around any issue. For example, in Natchez, Mississippi in 1965, there was a struggle between the NAACP and the FDP over who would organize the town. The NAACP was far more successful, largely because it had an outstanding leader, Charles Evers, the brother of the martyred Medgar Evers.[13]

Between 1963 and early 1965, a large number of SNCC's most active early members left the organization. Among them were James Bevel, his wife the former Diane Nash, Bernard Lafayette, Charles Jones, Charles Sherrod, Charles McDew (who had been chairman from 1961 to 1963) and finally Bob Moses. Most of them left for a combination of personal reasons and a belief that their talents could be used better elsewhere.

The case of Bob Moses was a special one. He left in January 1965 during the crisis over structure and white participation. He had been closely identified both with the cause of loose structure and with the presence of whites in the organization. He had been one of those who strongly urged the importation of large numbers of whites in the summer of 1964, and many of the whites in SNCC had looked to him as their leader and mentor.

Moses had a great deal to do with the success of SNCC's project in Mississippi. He had gone to McComb, Mississippi, in 1961 to start a voter registration project there. When the McComb project fell apart a few months later, he went to other towns in Mississippi and created more successful projects there. It was in Mississippi that SNCC first began to develop a statewide political program not aimed at winning isolated offices but based on a long-range plan to try to attain certain kinds of power. Moses was the mastermind of this plan, which set forth a four- or five-year program for winning offices at the municipal, state, congressional and party-delegate level. Moses also possessed a vision of a future political order based on his readings of Camus and other philosophers. (He had an M.A. in philosophy from Harvard.)

His success was based partly on his intellectual and organizational capacities but perhaps even more on his personality. He is a quiet, pensive man who gives an impression of great wisdom and understanding. Many people who worked with him speak of him in awestruck tones. He seems to have combined great withdrawal and introspection with a real concern about people, a concern that he was able to communicate to them. People who did not know how to type would type when he asked them to—because he believed in them.[14] They felt that he knew and understood things that were beyond them. This was true both of uneducated local black people and of highly educated whites, the two groups who constituted Moses' most loyal followers.

Moses apparently also had great influence on educated black people. He is credited with an important role in preserving SNCC's commitment to nonviolence. At a meeting in August 1964, Stokely Carmichael is said to have been ready to make the decision to put physical pressure on non-cooperating black people and to answer white violence with violence. He left the meeting "to get the mandate from Bob" (who was head of the summer project) and came back, after a long time, saying quietly, "What I think we ought to do is work harder on freedom registration forms."[15]

Moses was not present at that meeting. If he had been, it would probably never have reached the point that it did. He had a great deal of influence on people and he could shape the course of a meeting by his mere presence. He had a talent for waiting without saying a word for the point when a debate had reached an impasse and then standing up and in one clear statement saying precisely what most of the people in the room wanted said and resolving the issue. After a while he became disturbed by the power that this ability gave him and he stopped speaking at meetings. He still had enormous influence because people tried to guess what he was thinking and to do what they thought he would want on the basis of their guess. He is said to have left the state when he did (in January 1965) largely because he was disturbed by the dependency implied in such respect. (Apparently the Selective Service was also in pursuit of him at the time.) Moses was haunted too by a feeling of responsibility for the deaths of Schwerner, Chaney and Goodman, because he had been so important in bringing about the summer project.[16]

His departure was probably also directly connected to the crisis that followed it. In January 1965 the values of the loose-structure wing seemed to have been rejected. The need for discipline and standard procedures and an accounting of work seemed to have been accepted by most of the organization. Also, the feelings of rejection of whites which came to the surface during the crisis doubtless disturbed Moses, who was closely identified with the leading whites in SNCC. Most of these leading whites left Mississippi in the months after Moses did. An interesting sidelight is that Moses changed his name (to Parris) at the time he left Mississippi. This seems to confirm the theory that he was rejecting the role of legendary leader—though perhaps he was just avoiding the draft.

Moses, a black man from Harlem, may also have been ambivalent in his feelings toward whites. He is said to have refused to have anything to do with them later on. This pattern with regard to whites was followed by a number of other Northern black people in SNCC. In many cases, they had gone to high schools and/or colleges that were predominantly white, where they had had exclusively or almost exclusively white friendships. (This was true of both Moses and Carmichael. Moses attended Stuyvesant High School in New York City and Hamilton College. Carmichael went to the Bronx High School of Science.) They all came to have doubts as to the sincerity of these friendships and to feel that it was never possible to be certain that there was not an element of exploitation in any relationship with a white person. Some of these people, all of them black Northerners, later became the most bitterly anti-white faction in SNCC. (Carmichael himself did not belong to that faction.)

Moses was the last of the early major leaders to leave SNCC before the May, 1966, election through which Stokely Carmichael became chairman. The interval between his departure, in January 1965, and the election was a low period for SNCC. It was helping the FDP with its Congressional challenge, which was finally defeated in September 1965, but it had only one lively, ongoing project of its own. This was the one that was begun in Lowndes County, Alabama, by Stokely Carmichael in the spring of 1965. By May 1966, the Lowndes County Project was approaching its climax, which was to take place at the elections in November 1966. Carmichael, in short, was the only successful local project leader at that time. His election as chairman was therefore not particularly surprising, but the circumstances of that election, which were a little unusual, shed some light on the nature of the leadership shift.

The election occurred at the end of a week-long staff conference in Nashville, Tennessee. John Lewis, who as chairman had been largely a figurehead and spokesman, was running for reelection. The office of chairman promised to take on new importance because the very powerful executive secretary, James Forman, had announced that he was resigning that office. A number of candidates for chairman had been nominated. John Lewis had handed over the meeting to a temporary chairman, who announced that there would be a run-off between the two top candidates in the first ballot. John Lewis won the first ballot, sixty to twenty-two.[17] The candidate with the second largest number of votes was Stokely Carmichael, but Lewis' margin of victory was so large that no run-off was held. At that point, Lewis took over the chair and some people left the meeting, since it was close to midnight. The election was then challenged by Worth Long, who had worked with SNCC for years but was not technically on staff. At about 5:30 A.M., after much discussion, a new election was held. In the meantime, Carmichael had been offered the post of executive secretary, which Forman was resigning, and had refused it. In the second election, Carmichael won, sixty to twelve.[18] The following day, there was a motion to hold still a third election, which was voted on and defeated. These are the bare facts, agreed on by all, but explanations of the strange reversal vary.

John Lewis believes that the election was unfair. He thinks that most of the people in SNCC wanted him to be chairman, but that Forman and other powerful people wanted to have him dropped. The first election, according to Lewis, reflected the true desires of SNCC. After that election, a lot of people left the meeting and went to bed, since it was late at night, and others left Nashville to return to their projects. Lewis says that the people who spoke in the discussion between the two elections aroused the emotions of the other SNCC members against him by accusing him of not being able or willing to "tell off" President Johnson and Martin Luther King. (Lewis was then a member of the board of SCLC, Dr. King's organization.) Lewis' integrity is universally respected within SNCC and it is unlikely that his story is deliberately false.

Worth Long, who presented the challenge, offers a different explanation.[19] He says that he believed the huge vote for Lewis on the first ballot was mainly a vote of thanks for his courage and leadership and that many of those who voted for him intended all along to vote for Carmichael on the second ballot. They wanted Carmichael because he was a dynamic leader who would carry out SNCC's new dynamic and aggressive program. Others perhaps did have their minds changed during the discussion. There had been no discussion of the candidates before the first election. During the discussion after the first election, Forman asked people to vote for a candidate not on the basis of personality but on the basis of how well he would carry out SNCC's program. According to Long, no more than five people left the meeting right after the first election to go to bed, and Lewis had these people awakened before the second election. There were, after all, a similar number of people voting in the two elections. (However, many people abstained in the first election, so there may not have been a similar number present.) Long believes that since Carmichael's victory was so overwhelming, very few people thought the second election was unfair.

There is probably a good deal of truth in both stories. Lewis had been travelling for a month or two before the meeting and he may well have been correct in believing that there was a "plot" to deprive him of the chairmanship. However, he probably underestimated the lack of support among SNCC's membership for what he stood for. Lewis was and still is a supporter of nonviolence as a way of life and in this he was probably almost alone in SNCC by May 1966. Most of the people in the organization were committed to nonviolence only as a tactic, and for some even this commitment was rather weak. Perhaps even more important, Lewis was a strong believer in working together with the government. He had great faith in marches and other tactics for enlisting the aid of the powers-that-be. During the discussion preceding the second election, it became clear that Lewis was determined to attend the White House Conference on Civil Rights, "To Secure These Rights," which was to take place shortly afterward. He had participated in the planning sessions for it and he apparently took it very seriously. Lewis has a framed photograph in his home of himself shaking hands with President Johnson. Most of the members of SNCC by May 1966 felt that Johnson's handshake with the civil rights movement was less than sincere. They voted that night to boycott the White House Conference because they believed that while the murderers of civil-rights works were still free and the U.S. continued its "aggression" abroad, the government could not be sincere in its desire to aid civil rights. This belief was further confirmed by what SNCC believed to be an undue emphasis at the conference on the black family instead of on white exploitation.

There was a great deal of anti-white and black nationalist sentiment expressed at the SNCC staff conference. There were proposals to ban white reporters from all future SNCC conferences and to provide scholarships to train black people in nuclear physics so they could build a bomb and blow up America.[20] (This last suggestion probably was not serious, but it reveals something of the sentiment at the conference.) It was at this conference that the decisions were made to deemphasize the role of whites within SNCC and to concentrate on third-party rather than Democratic politics.

In general it seems clear that Lewis lost the chairmanship of SNCC because he was closely identified with an earlier phase in the organization's history, a phase which was already in decline even when he was first elected chairman (in June 1963). Most SNCC members probably still had great affection and respect for Lewis, but when new leadership came along, it was hard to resist it. SNCC was in a period of stagnation, and Carmichael was the leader of one of the few active projects (in Lowndes County, Alabama). Lewis had been a member of the Nashville movement, which was closely associated with the theory of nonviolent confrontation. As a direct-action leader, he had been arrested and beaten many times. But by the end of 1963, direct action was already no longer a major SNCC strategy, and the wonder is that Lewis stayed in power as long as he did. Stokely Carmichael did not kill the old nonviolent, reformist SNCC; it had died gradually long before he became chairman.

The predecessor to the slogan "Black Power" was "Freedom Now." That too had a decidedly militant ring. It was no longer satisfactory for SNCC because it had been adopted by the other groups on the Meredith March, some of which were merely moderate pressure groups. SNCC had to be beyond those who were merely bargaining with the Establishment.

Carmichael's views and personality were in accord with the general mood of black militancy in 1966 both in and out of SNCC. Moderate strategies no longer seemed to be relevant; SNCC had tried a succession of them with little success. The message of Malcolm X had already spread to a large portion of the black community—and to SNCC too. Actually, SNCC's mood had been militant for several years. Even while it was sponsoring moderate programs, its members sounded militant. SNCC's more moderate leaders had been unable for months to find an attractive program around which to rally the staff and other black people. SNCC's members did not know that Stokely Carmichael was to become a nationally famous figure. It was not until the following month (June 1966) that his cry of Black Power during the Meredith March through Mississippi was to bring him instant national fame. If they had known what would happen to SNCC under Carmichael, perhaps they would not have voted for him (but they might well have done so anyway).

Carmichael's fame did have some immediate negative effects on SNCC. Contributions from whites declined drastically and they were never replaced by black money (as had been hoped). Membership also declined, from about 120 in the winter of 1966 to well under 100 in the winter of 1967.

(However, the biggest decline had been from a peak of almost 200 in the spring and summer of 1965.) Integrationists like Lewis and Ben Grinage, the chairman of the Arkansas project, resigned after the Meredith March. Whites, feeling unwelcome, drifted out. The black candidates lost in the November election in Lowndes County and SNCC left that area. Since then it has been unable to start any really successful project. It lost its old freedom from reliance on central leadership; for the first time, by far the most important figure in SNCC was the chairman. For the first time too, the central office dominated the organization.

However, Carmichael did bring fame and importance for SNCC far beyond what it had known in its more moderate days. He directed SNCC toward the Northern ghettoes, which are in the long run more important than the Black Belt. He brought SNCC more in line with the mood of black ghetto youth and at the same time caught the imagination of black college students. And he brought about a greater (if perhaps distorted) awareness in SNCC of the institutional and world context of its problems.

There certainly was a major shift in leadership in SNCC between 1961 and 1966. The early sit-in leaders were largely Southern, nonviolent, integrationist, and conventional in life-style, religion and political views. The leadership conference of 1961 was a step in the direction of transforming them into sophisticated political organizers. Their experience in the next few years went further in this direction, but left them ill-prepared to deal with the influx of whites into the organization in 1964. By this time SNCC had many more Northern black people, who were generally more articulate and less conventional than the Southerners. In the fall of 1964 and winter of 1965, the tensions among these three groups—whites, Southern blacks, Northern blacks—came to the surface and the organization was rocked by the resultant crisis. By the end of the crisis, many of the original charismatic Southern leaders were no longer in SNCC. The whites began their gradual drift out and the people who were left continued to grope for a direction and focus that would restore the earlier vitality of the organization. John Lewis was kept on for a while as chairman, in recognition of his role in SNCC's earliest dynamic phase. But when it appeared that Stokely Carmichael might be able to revitalize SNCC he was elected chairman. It should be stressed that, except for his (partly fortuitous) issuance of the Black Power slogan, the advent of Carmichael was less the cause than the expression of the fundamental changes that had occurred in SNCC.

The decentralization and informality of SNCC's organizational structure and the nature of its internal conflicts over structure and leadership were to some extent a function of the sort of people who were members of SNCC. The sociological background and the psychological outlook of SNCC members are the subjects of the next chapter.

FOUR

Background of Members

To the sheriffs of the Deep South, the typical white SNCC worker was a "New York Jewish Communist atheist beatnik" who was dedicated to egging on the "niggers" (or "nigrahs") into creating trouble and friction. To these sheriffs, given the character of SNCC workers, there was no need for an elaborate analysis of SNCC's organizational structure or the pressures it faced in order to explain its radicalization.

Perhaps this is a caricature of the views of the typical Southern sheriff—but, in any case, the assumption that the social background of SNCC's members had something to do with the way SNCC developed is certainly a valid one. The difficulty with such explanations of SNCC's radicalization is that the background of SNCC people, in terms of age, class, race, region, religion and educational level, was probably not very different in 1966 than in 1961. Unfortunately, there are no statistics available to demonstrate this, but it is significant that no SNCC worker interviewed in this study saw a major change in the type of person in SNCC during the period he worked for it. The only exception is in the matter of race: the number of whites rose rapidly starting in early 1964 and then declined in 1965. In all other periods, there were only a handful of whites in SNCC, most of whom did not at all fit the hypothetical sheriff's stereotype.

Perhaps the most striking fact about SNCC workers is their age. Almost all are very young. In late 1963, Howard Zinn took a survey of Mississippi SNCC, which was at that time about one-third of the total SNCC force in the Deep South. Of the forty-four Mississippi SNCC workers, twenty-nine were between the ages of fifteen and twenty-two; twelve were between twenty-two and twenty-nine; and there was one person each in his 30's, 40's, and 50's.[1] This pattern was repeated throughout SNCC and has not changed since that time. James Forman, who is now about forty, has always been far older than almost all other SNCC workers. The oldest and the youngest SNCC members have usually been local people who were recruited to the staff. It was almost exclusively between the ages of eighteen and twenty-five that people had the freedom, the idealism and the physical stamina to leave their own communities and undertake the hardships and dangers of the life of a SNCC field secretary. This youngness of the membership tended to perpetuate itself. Many people who were interviewed said they were attracted to SNCC because of the youthfulness of its members, especially the leaders. They did not want to be held back by the bureaucratic slowness or mature restraint of the NAACP or even SCLC. SNCC had more appeal than, for example, an NAACP Youth Council, because the policy decisions were made by one's contemporaries, who were both more accessible than older leaders and more similar in outlook.

Many people joined SNCC quite frankly in search of themselves.[2] To a fair extent, the changes in the tone of SNCC can be explained by the fact that a young black person trying to find himself or his place in society in the 1960s was likely to move from an integrationist outlook to an increasingly angry and militant stance, if he were in tune with the *Zeitgeist*. Of course, such a statement really begs the question of why the *Zeitgeist* was what it was. Some of the other chapters indirectly give answers to this question.

The youthfulness of SNCC members helps explain a number of the organization's characteristics. For example, SNCC was shaped by the young people's orientation toward action and their strong feelings of impatience and frustration when quick successes failed to come.[3] Young people often see with unforgiving eyes the injustices of the world adults created. Their time perspective on correcting these injustices is far shorter than that of adults, even of those adults who still see that all is not as it should be. The importance attached to complete freedom of action (see Chapter Three) is also related to the adolescent character of SNCC's membership.

One SNCC veteran, still a member, says[4]

> The uniqueness of SNCC is that very few of us have worked in institutions or within the establishment (jobs, etc.) where you are carefully taught that in order to survive "you have to go along. If you want that paycheck, promotion or raise, you better follow the rules of the game." That's why people are frightened by us—because those rules are meaningless to us, and therefore we cannot be bought or controlled.

SNCC members were indeed difficult to control. They possessed the burning moral anger of youth, with none of the resignation, lethargy or caution with which adults approach injustice. As one of them put it, "It was very clear and simple to me—a fight between the clearly bad guys (the crackers) and the clearly good guys (SNCC) and I very simplistically wanted to fight with the good guys."[5] SNCC's young members wanted action; they did not want to bargain with the devil or with anyone who was willing to tolerate the devil. To them, SNCC was the "most truth-telling, dynamic, reality-oriented, uncompromising group around."[6] Thus, SNCC's anti-ideological, activist, moralistic stance stemmed directly from the youthfulness of its members. SNCC's members have always been exceptionally young, and SNCC has always been activist and moralistic.

Its moral stance, while attracting many members, caused some rather unattractive psychological twists. It was probably at the root of a "he-who-is-not-with-us-is-against-us" mentality. A sympathetic observer of SNCC noted that, while love and friendship between members was strong, so were animosities. He added that many members felt more resentment toward their families than the families' disapproval seemed to warrant. He concluded that, "While most SNCC workers can meet love with love, and trust with trust, many meet partial love and trust with suspicion and sometimes meet enmity with hatred."[7] This may help explain why SNCC reacted so negatively to the partial commitment of white liberals.

It has been suggested that SNCC's suspicion of white liberals arose from a kind of paranoia. Working in an environment (the Deep South) that really did persecute it, perhaps SNCC came to believe in a persecuting world. Yet, before 1966, at least, SNCC did not have other symptoms of political paranoia. Rather than being over-heated, over-aggressive or grandiose, SNCC leaders usually had a low-key style and limited goals. Nor did they have unreasonable beliefs about the powers or intentions of those who opposed them. Their enemies were not seen at first as all-powerful and unremittingly evil and in fact SNCC at first tried to make a moral conversion of its most obvious enemies, the white segregationists. As for the white liberals, SNCC for a long time behaved like a disillusioned lover[8] rather than like a psychotic afflicted with paranoia. It kept trying to renew the affair on the liberals' terms, even after successive rebuffs.

The youthfulness of SNCC's members was an important source of cohesion within the organization. The shared subculture of youth, added to shared danger, made SNCC very tight-knit. Before 1964, the members all knew each other well and knew exactly what they could ask of each other.[9] The closeness of the organization was further reinforced by similarities in sociological background. At first, almost all of SNCC's members had been Southern blacks (and a few Southern whites) from non-middle-class backgrounds who had attended Southern colleges. There was a slowly increasing number of Northerners of both races between 1961 and 1964, but these people were few enough so that they could be assimilated into SNCC's Southern ethos. The Northerners in this period learned to play down their intellectuality, their impatience, their eagerness to attack new targets.

Thus, the unity of SNCC's moral world-view was not threatened. After 1964, there were, however, several threats to that unity raised by the entrance of people with a different social background from the earlier members. It is my view that, although the percentage of Northern blacks in SNCC increased slightly between 1964 and 1966, by far the most important challenge from within to SNCC's world-view was brought about by the entrance of large numbers of whites. These whites had almost all drifted out of SNCC by the fall of 1965, but they left a legacy of shock and fear that remains to this day.

The theory that there was a Northern black take-over has a good deal of plausibility and attraction, especially for white journalists. Let me deal with it in some detail. The first problem with the theory is that it is not clear who qualifies as a Northern black. Is a West Indian who has lived in New York for a long time a Northern black? (Stokely Carmichael, Courtland Cox and Ivanhoe Donaldson, three very important leaders during the Black Power phase, are all West Indians.) Is someone who spent his early childhood in Mississippi but was educated in Chicago a Northerner? (This is the case with James Forman, who was SNCC's executive secretary from 1961 to 1966 and is still very powerful in the organization.) What do you call someone who was born and raised in the North but attended a Southern college and is generally identified with Southerners? (Diane Nash, the head of the direct-action wing, and Charles McDew, chairman from 1961 to 1963, both fit this description.) How do you categorize people who come from Baltimore? Or St. Louis? Or Cairo, Illinois?

The assumption behind the Northern-takeover theory is that Northerners tend to be more militant and anti-white and less concerned about the moral nature of the struggle. Yet the most eloquent spokesman of the early SNCC which welcomed whites in the organization and was concerned about moral and religious principles was Bob Moses—by any definition a Northerner. And Stokely Carmichael's executive secretary, who had been an important power in SNCC from the beginning and had been anti-white for years, was Ruby Doris Smith Robinson—a Southerner born and bred. Rap Brown, the chairman between May 1967 and May 1968, who is extremely militant and anti-white, is also a Southerner. When Stokely Carmichael succeeded John Lewis, a Southerner, as chairman, it looked on the surface as if the militant Northerners were taking over from the pro-white Southerners. In fact, though, Lewis had never had much power within SNCC. While he was chairman, the power in Atlanta rested in the hands of James Forman, the executive secretary, who was Northern-bred.

Below the top leadership, also, the attitudes of Northerners and Southerners toward whites cannot be simply contrasted as anti- and pro- respectively. Some Southerners, like John Lewis and Fannie Lou Hamer, were clearly "white-lovers" and dedicated to integration. It was a Southerner, Charles Sherrod, who first integrated a SNCC project as a matter of policy. Most Southerners, though, were suspicious of whites in the organization. Having grown up in a strictly segregated society, they were uncomfortable with whites, and they were probably the first to realize that whites had special, perhaps insurmountable, problems in organizing black Southerners. Southern black people also tended to lack confidence in their own abilities and to be much more fearful about whites taking over their jobs. At least two members of the black nationalist Atlanta Project in 1965 were Southerners (Bill Ware and Gwen Robinson).

By contrast, many of the black Northerners in SNCC were even more self-confident than the whites about their organizing (and other) abilities (and for this reason tended to have similar destructive effects on the development of local black leadership). Also, many of them had had white friends in the North and for this reason they were not fearful of or uncomfortable with whites. It was a black Northerner, Bob Moses, who pushed through the idea of the 1964 Summer Project, against the opposition of almost all the black Southerners in the organization.

Black Northerners also had a lot in common with whites. Like the whites, they tended to be educated, articulate, aggressive. They were interested in the philosophic implications of what they were doing and they were also interested in the underlying causes of American racism—as were the whites. Southern blacks, on the other hand, tended to see their group's problems as isolated and relatively simple.

Many of the black Northerners found it difficult to settle down in one project and become immersed in the life of a Southern town. Instead, they liked to move around from one project to another. For this reason, they often favored loose structure, a preference they shared with the whites. When they became anti-white, their reasons for the change were well-thought-out and profound: they saw the insincerity of many inter-racial friendships; they realized that all whites were "trapped within the racist institutions of their culture"; they became aware of the ineffectiveness of whites in organizing in black communities; they saw the need for the black man to shape his destiny separately. Because of their past close association with whites and white views, they found it necessary to affirm their blackness with particular vehemence. The Southerners too changed in their attitudes over the years, in large part because of the tensions of working with whites and because of other frustrations. Thus both Northerners and Southerners became opposed to whites as SNCC workers, each for a different reason.

The direct-action, anti-segregation movement of the early '60s was very much a Southern phenomenon. Almost all of its leaders and participants were Southern. The Northerners participated only in sympathy demonstrations and in special events, like the Freedom Rides. By 1963, however, most SNCC projects were primarily devoted to voter registration and many Northerners were working on them. It is not clear that since that time there has been an increase in the number of Northerners in SNCC.

This question is complicated by the fact that it is hard to define the words "in SNCC." If one defines them narrowly as meaning "on staff" (receiving a paycheck), then the percentage of Northerners would be much higher than if one defines them broadly to mean anyone who works for SNCC, full- or part-time. Local people from the communities always did a great deal of SNCC's work, and there were generally more of these volunteers than there were SNCC staff members. In the early years, the volunteers attended staff conferences and did not necessarily have less of a voice than the regular staff members. Only after the staff became the coordinating committee and acquired a vote (in late 1964) did SNCC people become very concerned about who was in the organization technically and who was not. This was partly because there were many whites in the organization who came from the North and worked full time but were not paid because they did not need the money. The new concern about whether or not one was "on staff" was a way of expressing hostility against these whites and particularly suspicion about the depth of their commitment to SNCC. Many people were disturbed that even if these whites were not welcome in the organization, there was no way of getting rid of them because they were not paid anyway. (As it turned out, whites did leave when it became clear that they were not welcome.)

Thus, the rather vague nature of SNCC membership makes it very difficult to get accurate figures at any given time on the size of SNCC or the percentage of any group within it. Most people, however, do seem to believe that the percentage of Northerners, however defined, has remained about the same since 1963. From all of this, it seems safe to conclude that one cannot explain the changes in SNCC's orientation since the summer of 1964 in terms of a Northern take-over.

There was, however, an important shift in the background of SNCC members which had a major impact on the direction of the organization. This was the influx of white members which occurred in the spring and summer of 1964. Although most of the whites had left SNCC by the fall of the following year, their earlier presence had a lasting impact on the organization. Most black SNCC members had opposed the Mississippi Summer Project before it took place. It was only after much persuasion by Bob Moses and with extreme reluctance that the staff consented to the introduction of so many whites. SNCC almost had no choice. Its activities were at a low ebb, and the NAACP was planning to sponsor a similar project even if SNCC did not participate.[10] When between 100 and 200 whites stayed on in Mississippi after the summer, many black people who had been SNCC field secretaries there for several years became alarmed about white participation and power.

There had been a handful of whites working in Mississippi for several years, but these whites were of unquestioned dedication and also possessed a great deal of sensitivity about their position. The new whites tended to lack awareness of the fact that they had a special role. Virtually all of them had attended college and they tended to be highly capable and self-confident in organizing skills such as typing, putting out newsletters, speaking at meetings, etc. They began to take over a number of these functions from black people, who had been doing them for the previous few years but were not as skilled or as self-assertive. Even more serious, whites who had no organizing experience began to take over from experienced black organizers the prerogative of making day-to-day and week-to-week decisions in organizing. Many black people felt that this demonstrated an unconscious feeling of racial superiority on the part of the whites. They began to question the motives of the whites for coming South.

It turned out that the whites had a great variety of motives for coming, almost none of which seemed to the blacks to be legitimate ones. Among them were: to learn about life in the Deep South, to learn about themselves, to help the poor benighted black people and earn their gratitude ("noblesse oblige"), to act on an ideology, to satisfy a need for engagement or for "meaningful" activity, to play the political game, etc. Some came out of guilt for their own color-consciousness and their own sins of omission. One summer volunteer said, "It is a pilgrimage to a foreign country; traveling there, I can leave my guilt behind and atone for someone else's."[11] Others came to escape themselves by becoming black, rural and poor. And still others came to "find themselves," having failed to do so on college campuses.[12]

Some of the doubts cast on the white students' motives seem quite unfair. Many black students had strikingly similar reasons for joining SNCC.[13] It is possible to find fault behind the motivation of any human action. What appears to be altruism may be dismissed as either self-love or self-hate. Dedication to a cause may be interpreted as "politics" or "ideology." In someone who helps others, a desire to understand them and to see the world from their point of view may be seen as self-rejection or a selfish desire for personal education; but a lack of such desire could equally well be seen as "noblesse oblige," implying snobbery and condescension.

It is my belief that it was not the nature of the whites' motives but the depth of their commitment that was really under question. The motives of those whites who stayed in SNCC for two years or more were never questioned, although they may have been just as political or as psychologically aberrant. The questioning of the motives of the whites who entered in 1964 was a way of expressing doubt as to whether they could ever be assimilated into the SNCC moral universe, which required a total and long-term commitment. The whites, when they were not seen as psychologically disturbed, were believed to be excessively intellectual and ideological. Even if they had been more "spirit"-motivated, the whites could never be "soul brothers."

Black people's attitudes toward whites, also acquired in a racist society, were the other side of the coin of the difficulties of race relations within SNCC. Black SNCC members found it difficult to work with whites because of their own feelings of insecurity about skills and education, because of deep-rooted anti-white feelings that went back to racial incidents in early childhood and because in many cases they had simply grown up hating and distrusting white people. Work in an integrated SNCC caused tensions between an impulse to hate all whites and the necessity to distinguish between good and bad whites in order to cooperate with the good ones. Emotionally, it was simpler to work in an all-black organization.

Black people also felt that the presence of whites made it impossible for them to get over their obsession with the standards and expectations of white people. They felt that it was important for black people to trust black leaders and that as long as whites were highly visible it would be harder for this self-confidence to grow. They feared that local blacks who saw white people in the central and field offices would assume that whites were in charge. The reaction of both whites and blacks to the discovery of negative attitudes toward the other race further exacerbated the tensions.[14]

Moreover, the whites presented enormous problems in organizing. Their conspicuousness and frequent lack of caution often increased the danger of organizing among black people. In the Mississippi Delta it was almost impossible for them to visit the homes of sharecroppers, because most of these were set far back from the road with a long, flat view and the white owners had the right to shoot trespassers on sight. A white person who did visit a black person and urge him to register to vote was likely to receive the reply "yessir, boss." Since SNCC's goal was to inspire black people to initiate and sustain their own political activity, this was hardly the sort of response desired. Whites were, however, used fairly effectively to teach remedial reading in Selma, Alabama, Cambridge, Maryland and other places and also to run "Freedom Schools" and community centers during the Mississippi Summer Project. These educational activities were, however, on the periphery of SNCC's interest.

At meetings, whites had a tendency to express their ideas eagerly and forcefully, thus obviating the need for the local black people to have ideas. (Some black SNCC organizers did this too, however.) When whites became more sensitive, they learned to wait until the end of the meeting, when they would express their ideas only if the black people had not come up with a good solution to the problem at hand. The black people, however, soon became aware that the whites were doing this and so there was no pressure for them to solve the problems themselves. Some of the local black people noticed that white organizers were very eager to give credit to black people even where it was not deserved. Some whites would put their own ideas into the mouths of black people, for example, by using a black person as a spokesman at a meeting. This created enormous resentment among the blacks, who felt that they were being manipulated. Some of the more sensitive black people were angered by the implication that white organizers believed black people were likely to do unquestioningly anything suggested by whites. In short, whether the white people were sensitive or insensitive to the situation, their very presence brought to the surface a great deal of the pathology of black-white relations in America.

Whites were also resented because even when they joined SNCC their white skin protected them in many ways. White males were less likely to be beaten than black males, white females than black females. Whites were more likely to be bailed out of jail by their parents, even if they did not want to be. The FBI gave more protection where there were whites, especially white girls. The press was far more likely to run stories on whites. Probably most important of all, whites had a sanctuary, a refuge. They could always return to the North and forget about the problems of the blacks. A white student might spend this summer in Mississippi—and next summer in Paris. He might even consider himself morally superior to the black SNCC worker because he chose to work in SNCC even though other options were open to him. To the black SNCC worker, all this was infuriating. He suspected that the problems which were profoundly real and inescapable for him were for a white SNCC worker merely a source of adventure or an educational experience.

Black SNCC workers felt that even those whites who joined SNCC shared many of the racist attitudes common in the rest of white America. Many white SNCC members, for example, seemed to believe that, although black people were not very intelligent, they had "soul" and were sexually liberated.[15] Regardless of the actual behavior of a white girl, she would be suspected by both white and black Southerners of having a perverse sexual interest in black men.[16] In those cases where white girls did establish liaisons with black men, it turned out almost invariably that the relationship was insincere and exploitative. This caused deep hostilities between the partners. The existence of such relationships also created antagonism in white men toward black men and black girls toward white girls (jealousy), and in black men toward white men (resentment when the white girls turned to the white men with their troubles). White-black sexual relationships were also very bad for public relations; they were deeply resented by both the whites and the blacks in the Deep South.

For many black Southerners, SNCC in 1964 provided a first experience of integration that was deeply disillusioning. They observed the inability of many of the local black people to stop calling the whites "sir" and "Miss Ann" and they themselves suffered the sting of condescension. Paternalism, *noblesse oblige*, the "Bwana complex,"[17] the missionary complex,[18] the White African Queen complex[19]—all were words applied (with some justice) to whites who came South essentially to lead and help their inferiors.

Other whites seemed to think of black people as a species of noble savage. They romanticized the black way of life and tried to adopt it themselves. They seemed to desire to be black. (This phenomenon was not unique to whites. There was a corresponding glorification by some black Northerners of the Southern rural black life-style.) According to Bob Moses, some of these whites kept their whiteness while attempting to live like black people and became objects of amusement (and also suspicion as to their motives). Others were able to transcend race and to live together with black people as human beings.[20]

Whites within SNCC seemed to have similar motives to white liberals outside SNCC who claimed to be allies. As SNCC became suspicious of help from outside white liberals, it was natural that it should have similar suspicions about its own white members. To some extent, these suspicions were unfair. Whites in SNCC were not less militant in their demands on those in power than were blacks, and in fact it was whites who popularized in SNCC the notion that its problems were caused by factors endemic to American institutions. Still, SNCC's anger at white America in general was inevitably transferred to a great extent to its white members, who were often said to be products of their environment.[21] The direct confrontation with white America implicit in the convention and congressional challenges coincided in time precisely with the period when SNCC had a large number of white members. The one disillusionment came to be very much associated with the other.

Both disillusionments together had a profound effect on SNCC, making it both more impatient and more anti-white. The level of activity in SNCC after the whites left in 1965 was not lower, and probably a little higher, than it had been in late 1963. But, having once been part of something very much larger and very much more famous, SNCC members were not able to return to the slow, obscure, unrewarding toil of earlier years. The whites had made possible the challenges and a vastly increased organizing effort in 1964; many of them had also raised hopes by their own enthusiasm and optimism. Moreover, they had made SNCC see its problems in a broader focus, which made a return to small-town organizing much more difficult to face. The whites, and the challenges made possible by them, showed SNCC the rest of America and in doing so made it sharply conscious of its own powerless, minority status.

It was at the same meeting, in May 1966, where Stokely Carmichael was elected chairman, that it was decided that whites should not be permitted to be SNCC organizers. The whites remaining in the organization did not leave immediately, but within a year there were no whites on SNCC's payroll. A few whites still, at this writing (April 1968), consider themselves to be "in SNCC" in the sense that they have never broken with it and are still trusted by its members, but no whites are actually doing any form of work for SNCC.

This exclusion of *all* whites, even those who had served SNCC well for several years, was not caused by the difficulties encountered by whites in their organizing work among black people, but rather by the demands of the doctrine of Black Power. A small number of whites, such as Bob Zellner and Bill Hansen, are generally acknowledged to have been effective organizers even by black people. Others performed valuable auxiliary roles in fund-raising and office work. Thus, the exclusion of all whites without exception does not seem to have been motivated by purely practical considerations. It was the atmosphere of Black Power that necessitated this exclusion. Interestingly, the whites themselves were so much imbued with this atmosphere that they did not object to their own exclusion. Not one of the white SNCC members interviewed in any way questioned the white exclusion policy, possibly because to do so would have further alienated them from black people.

The whites themselves had contributed in major ways to the creation of the Black Power atmosphere. For example, it was the whites who caused SNCC to drop almost all thought of integration as an organizational goal or strategy.

In early 1964, before the influx of whites, SNCC was still engaged in direct action for integration in a number of places. As late as March of that year, SNCC workers were approaching performers to participate in a cultural boycott of segregated facilities.[22] The experience of the summer of 1964 and its aftermath changed all that.

If integration within SNCC, a voluntary association, had not worked, how could it work for America at large? SNCC members do not completely rule out integration as an ultimate goal. They merely say that it has to be postponed until America is no longer a "racist society." The presence of whites in SNCC heightened black SNCC members' awareness not only of subtle forms of white racism but also of the more destructive side of middle-class American life. Most blacks in SNCC were from non-middle-class backgrounds, and their contact with white donors and white members of SNCC showed them what they assumed was the best of the middle class. The smugness and emptiness of the middle-class life style that they saw irritated them.[23] This rejection of the middle class served to turn them against integration, which implies an acceptance of middle-class standards.

From the beginning, SNCC's following had always come mainly from non-middle-class groups. In Mississippi at least, SNCC tended to reject any offers of aid from the middle class. (In Southwest Georgia, it did direct its efforts toward the black "community" as whole.) Much of its hostility to the NAACP, especially in Mississippi, was based on its view of that organization as being concerned chiefly with advantages for the black middle class. James Forman believes that "if you're going to have any kind of profound change you must get people whom some would call the lower class."[24] The influx of middle-class whites coincided with the infusion of some Marxist beliefs, including a rejection of the "bourgeoisie" on far more systematic grounds than SNCC had ever developed. Because these ideas were in accord with SNCC's anti-middle-class bias, they were readily accepted.

The importance of the fact that SNCC's early members and following were mostly non middle class in background should not be exaggerated. The nature of the organization probably had more to do with its rejection of standard American values than did the backgrounds of the members. Since SNCC membership required a renunciation of wealth and social standing, everyone who joined it, regardless of social background, had to reject the usual American life-style. The atmosphere of the organization, in which non-activists were generally despised, reinforced this rejection. After a few weeks in the Deep South, SNCC members from all social classes generally shared the rest of the group's profound alienation from the rest of American society.

In general, the social background of the members merely reinforced the trends created by the political environment and the nature of the organization. The members' youthfulness was probably more important than either class or race. But class and race did serve as unifying factors in the early years and then, with the advent of whites, as barriers that helped to divide the organization. The exclusion of whites in 1966 was a reaction to a profound shock to SNCC's moral world-view. This world-view could not be sustained in a large and heterogeneous organization. SNCC therefore moved to expel a threat to its existence.

FIVE

The Mind of SNCC

SNCC was not founded on the basis of someone's critique of ideology in any sense: not in the Marxist sense of a set of beliefs propounded by the ruling class to maintain its hegemony, nor in the sense of a clear vision of a future order of society, nor even in the broad sense of a set of ideas that explain the world and offer some broad prescription for political conduct. My interviews with SNCC members yielded few insights that could be classed as "ideological." I have had to rely heavily on inference and on secondary sources for my discussion of the mind of SNCC.

Although SNCC was not founded on the basis of an intellectual rejection of the "ideology" (in the Marxist sense) of American society, it certainly did not share the prevailing political assumptions in America. However, it was not intellectual analysis that eroded these assumptions but rather the nature of SNCC as an organization. All SNCC members were isolated from most of American life, and their immediate experiences showed them only the ugliest part of it. Most SNCC members were not intellectuals and were admirers above all of the non-intellectual virtues of courage and charisma. Even the courageous and charismatic intellectual, Bob Moses, seems to have had little ideological influence on the black members of SNCC, although he was the only SNCC member in the early period to develop a set of ideas concerning SNCC and its goals. The whites who entered SNCC in large numbers in 1964 were in many cases intellectuals, but they were eventually rejected by SNCC, partly because of their intellectuality. The whites had a habit of discussing at great length the philosophical significance and ultimate meaning of all activities and events, a habit that irritated many of the black members, whose style was action-oriented.

Although the whites were finally rejected, many of thesir ideas, usually in a slightly altered form, did go into the set of beliefs generally associated with Black Power. SNCC's actual experiences, as well as the earlier experiences of its members, were, however, much more important than ideas in the creation of Black Power. The set of beliefs associated with Black Power was developed mainly *after* the enunciation of the slogan and the appearance of the psychological and institutional characteristics of Black Power. Ideology buttressed rather than brought about both black nationalism and the strategy known as "freedom organization."

When SNCC was founded in 1960, it inherited from its parent organization, SCLC, an ideology (in the broad sense of "a set of ideas") centered around nonviolence as a way of life. This part of SNCC's inheritance was lost soon after the end of the sit-in movement, when nonviolence came to be thought of as a tactic rather than as the central tenet of a philosophy. SNCC gradually abandoned nonviolence even as a tactic, but its reasons for doing so had more to do with the conditions of organizing in the Deep South than with ideology, and they are discussed in the present work under that heading.

Because of the unimportance of the role of ideology, SNCC has often been called pragmatic by its friends. However, its pragmatism was based not so much on a principled rejection of ideology in any form as on the absence of clearly defined long-range goals. SNCC has never had a program. It has used one organizing device after another, depending on what the circumstances seemed to call for. None of these strategies was ever elevated to the sphere of ideological truth even in the narrowest sense; all were seen merely as means for attacking "symptoms."[1] Although SNCC members came to view these "symptoms" as reflecting an underlying malady, SNCC never, until Black Power, adopted a systematic description of that malady.

SNCC did not have an ideology in any sense; what it did have was a vague world-view derived from the immediate experiences of its workers in the field. These people believed deeply in their own moral rightness; it was that belief that sustained them in a hostile environment. They came to believe that their job and their way of doing it were both more moral and more valuable than those of others who led safer and more comfortable lives. Specifically, they came to place high values on both community and freedom; they sought a coherent community in which each individual was free to carry on his life as he saw fit. Such a community, rather than the nation-state, was envisaged as the basic unit of political life. In this sense SNCC was fundamentally anarchist. Its members came to believe that the American political system was antithetical to such a community, although before 1964 few of them could have articulated such a diagnosis of the system, mainly because few of them ever thought about the system in such broad terms. Their beliefs constituted not so much an ideology (in any sense) as an ethos.

One who did think in broad terms was Bob Moses. An important exponent of anarchist ideas, he was until 1965 the guiding spirit behind Mississippi SNCC. Since Moses was a beloved leader, his ideas influenced SNCC although in a somewhat diluted form. SNCC later came to be influenced also by some of the ideas of Marx, Lenin, Frantz Fanon, Mao Tse-tung and Malcolm X. SNCC never adopted any system *in toto* but rather plucked ideas from here and there in an effort to piece together a picture of its political environment which accorded with its own mood and experience. In general, the infusion of ideas that came after 1964 had the effect of making SNCC examine underlying and broader causes of its difficulties. Although its earlier anarchist ideas conflicted with some later Marxist notions, the effect of both ideologies was to arouse in SNCC the conviction that its problem arose out of the capitalist, industrial system rather than any person or institution. Before 1964, there had been a strong tendency to focus attention on particulars—Police Chief Pritchett, Attorney General Kennedy, the FBI, etc.

The anarchist strain developed as a reaction to what was seen as the unresponsiveness of the American state to SNCC and to the people among whom it worked. The forerunner to this anarchism was the philosophy of nonviolent confrontation that underlay the sit-ins. The direct-action wing of SNCC, with its strong emphasis on moral confrontation, had always been anti-political in the same way that anarchism is. One could say that its purpose had been to replace impersonal, amoral political bargaining, in which the stronger side always won, with a kind of face-to-face encounter between two human beings in which the right side would ultimately win. Thus, like anarchism, the nonviolent direct-action wing relied on an appeal to community rather than on the intervention of state power. Belief in the possibility for success of this kind of face-to-face appeal died early in SNCC. Although direct action continued, it came to be seen as a political tactic rather than as a form of moral action. Voter registration was, of course, even more explicitly political. But SNCC did develop a theory of "alternative politics"[2] (see page 68), which contained a vision of a "moral social order" in place of the vision offered by the adherents of philosophic nonviolence.

Bob Moses, who had been deeply influenced by Albert Camus and other existentialist philosophers, was largely responsible for developing this theory. He is credited by some people with originating the concept of "participatory democracy," which was adopted by other New Left organizations, notably the Students for a Democratic Society (SDS). He derived this concept in large part from the thought of Camus. Moses was deeply concerned about the question how one could cease to be a victim of society without becoming an exploiter. With Camus in *The Rebel*, he concluded that the answer lay in recognizing that each individual man had rights only insofar as he recognized that every other individual had the same rights. Unless all men are sacred and are therefore ends in themselves, no man can claim the right to be treated as sacred. Moses therefore felt that in every community each man must be a full participant in making all the decisions that can affect his life. Otherwise, the community will act upon him rather than through him, which is to say, will treat him as less than an end in himself. Participation through voting is not a satisfactory arrangement, since voting is only the final and possibly the least important step in the long process by which policies are made and since those who lose on any given vote are simply sacrificed to the majority. It was for this reason that Moses and his friends were deeply committed to the kind of small and intimate community in which decisions are made by long discussions that include everyone and that eventually result in a "sense of the meeting." SNCC somewhat approximated this before the summer of 1964. After the summer, it became too large, but the Moses group fought for the old ideals in the long controversy that paralyzed SNCC that winter. They wanted participatory democracy not merely because they believed that it was the right structure for SNCC, but because they believed that SNCC must be a model of the just future order.

The new order was to be brought about by the creation of a series of model institutions paralleling in form and purpose the established institutions while remaining small, open, and democratic. The Mississippi Freedom Democratic Party (FDP), which SNCC founded, was just such a parallel institution, corresponding in its activities, structure, and procedure to the regular Democratic Party of Mississippi. The experience of the FDP illustrates the basic dilemma of "alternative politics"; while it may offer sustenance to those who believe in it, it often interferes with the carrying out of instrumental goals in a bureaucratic, impersonal society. In the first few years of SNCC's existence, the dilemma did not become apparent because there were so many other factors interfering with the attainment of concrete goals. The FDP brought about the first real manifestation of this dilemma. It was a parallel institution and at the same time a vehicle for achieving a concrete reform (fair representation for black people at a national party convention). As a parallel institution it was not really intended to be an effective competitor with large, powerful, "regular" institutions. Few SNCC members really expected the FDP to be seated at the Democratic National Convention. Its purpose was simply to present an alternative way of doing things which was on a more human scale than most American institutions and bore a more direct relationship to certain abstract goals, such as genuine self-government in the anarchist sense. The dilemma became apparent because most of the black Mississippians who were members of the FDP did not know this, and a good deal of the FDP's initial organizing success was based on a real hope among these people that the black delegates would be seated. When the compromise was offered, Aaron Henry and at least some of the others were watched carefully by SNCC leaders so that they could not be cornered and persuaded by NAACP people or other moderates who advocated accepting the compromise.[3] It was the SNCC people behind the FDP who absolutely insisted on the rejection of the compromise. To give up the integrity of their parallel institution in exchange for a trifling two seats which did not even formally represent Mississippi was completely unthinkable to them. The compromise was rejected and most of the FDP members left the convention downhearted and disappointed. It was still possible to organize them for the congressional challenge the following January, but that effort completely lacked the excitement and enthusiasm of the convention challenge.

Moreover, the events in Atlantic City were an important cause of the crisis faced by SNCC in late 1964 and 1965. At that time, the anarchist current in SNCC surfaced in the Freedom High movement, which came into bitter conflict with the advocates of tight structure. The latter wanted an organization that could be effective in tackling immediate problems, even at the expense of radical internal democracy, although they too had a radical, perhaps even anarchist vision of the future society. But SNCC's anarchist vision, when applied to SNCC itself, did serious damage to its effectiveness and unity.

SNCC's instrumental goals could not be dropped, because a belief in the importance of furthering them was part of SNCC's moral ethos and it was this ethos that bound SNCC together as a community. On the other hand, the requirements of the vision of alternative politics conflicted seriously with immediate effectiveness in a manner that became increasingly apparent after the summer of 1964. SNCC could not maintain the purity of its parallel institutions while at the same time taking advantage of the American system's capacity for reform. After 1964, as the situation eased somewhat in the Deep South, it became more apparent to SNCC's clientele, the black poor of the rural Deep South, that SNCC was too radical in outlook to take advantage of the new possibilities for reform. It would never dilute its program in order to gain federal cooperation.

One of the assumptions behind the theory of alienation politics was that, if left to themselves, people would spontaneously choose such values as freedom, respect for the individual personality, a better social order, over values like personal gain, social standing, and so on. SNCC believed that those people who had been least "brainwashed" by middle-class white American values, the poor blacks of Mississippi, could be counted on to make the right choice.

But SNCC organizers soon learned that the poor blacks of the Deep South had mainly very concrete, narrow desires (for jobs, better housing, educational opportunities, etc.) and that they felt no particular need to be part of an alternative political order. Having not yet gained the right to participate in standard, two-party politics, they were hardly in a position to reject it. Since they did not share the organizational ethos of SNCC, they began to drift away from it when the demands of that ethos came into conflict with their material needs. In many cases, they joined more moderate groups like the NAACP. This is why the Voting Rights Act of 1965 and the introduction of the poverty program in Mississippi were seen as threats to SNCC rather than as welcome assistance. Although SNCC had led its people out of the "slavery" of political exclusion and through the "wilderness" of rebellion, it could not lead them into the "promised land" of full participation in the American political system. By the time such participation began to be granted (for example, through the Voting Rights Act), SNCC no longer saw it as desirable; it had a more demanding vision of democracy than the American system could fulfill.

SNCC's anarchist strain reached its maximum strength in the "Freedom High" group, which was prepared to subordinate, completely, instrumental goals to anarchist values. At about the same time, a second intellectual strain began to influence SNCC: Marxism in several variants, most notably a modified Maoism that really boiled down to anti-colonialism.

Late 1964 and early 1965, the period when SNCC first became interested in Marxism, was generally a period of intellectual ferment. Ambitious study programs were planned for the staff, at which such writers as E. Franklin Frazier, W. E. B. DuBois, John Hope Franklin, etc., were to be read.[4] It is significant that not classical Marxists but black intellectuals were seen as the appropriate writers to study.

110

Marxist ideas were introduced in SNCC mainly by the new white members; the black people in SNCC accepted those ideas that fit into their world view and rejected the others, including those most central to Marx's philosophy. For example, Marx's belief in the fundamental importance of economic institutions does not seem to have taken hold in SNCC, which still placed primary emphasis on political organizing. It is true that, like the Marxists, SNCC came to see the American system as bearing the responsibility for the problems of black people—but it identified it as "the American racist system" rather than "the American capitalist system." Probably, the most appealing part of Marxist teaching for SNCC was the notion that "the system" exploits people in underdeveloped countries all over the world for the same sorts of reasons that it excludes and exploits blacks at home. This idea, derived from Lenin's theory of proletarian nations, fit very well with the ideas about international black unity then being expounded by Malcolm X.

Malcolm's trip to Africa in the spring of 1964 was an inspiring event for many SNCC members. Some of them saw a connection between his assassination, the murder of Lumumba and the overthrow of Nkrumah, all of which they believed to be the work directly or indirectly of elements within the U.S. government.[5] But SNCC members had had a broad interest in Africa from the beginning. Africans visited Southwest Georgia as early as 1961 to speak at SNCC-sponsored direct-action mass meetings.[6] Classes on African culture and history were offered in many of SNCC's freedom schools. After the summer of 1964, ten or twelve SNCC members, including John Lewis, Bob Moses and Fannie Lou Hamer, visited Africa. Lewis extended his visit for about six months. His home is decorated with African handicrafts and a "Zambia Independence" poster. On the political side, SNCC has sponsored demonstrations in this country against South Africa and U.S. economic involvement with it. SNCC now has an international office which tries to establish links with developing nations. Thus the focus on the developing nations, which was somewhat misleadingly identified as "Maoism" by most Americans, actually had a good deal more to do with black consciousness than with events in China.

Marxism also reinforced and made more conscious SNCC's policy of concentrating on developing the right kind of organization rather than on obtaining specific small reforms. Lenin had said in his famous pamphlet "What Is To Be Done?" that to concentrate on satisfying the bread-and-butter demands of the workers was mere "tailism." The important task was to build the right kind of party. Although it is unlikely that any SNCC members read "What Is To Be Done?", the message filtered down to them through Marxists in the organization and Marxist publications.

In general, however, Marxist thinking was appealing to SNCC members only insofar as it coincided with and verified the teachings of men like Malcolm X. The influence of Malcolm on SNCC cannot be exaggerated. A poster showing his portrait today hangs in the home of almost every SNCC member. His emphasis on black pride and self-reliance was particularly in tune with SNCC's mood in 1964 and 1965. So was his angry militant tone. It seems fair to say that his ideas were admired less for their intrinsic worth than because his personal style aroused a responsive chord in SNCC members. SNCC had just suffered a stinging rejection from its friends in Washington (or so the denial of the convention challenge was perceived) and it was having acute difficulties with its white members. Its mood was "We're through begging from the white man" and, even beyond that, "We don't want any help from the white man even if he wants desperately to give it."

SNCC's reasons for this total rejection of white aid were related to a growing belief that as long as white people belonged to it, it could not be the kind of organization in which all members were equal and were therefore ends in themselves. The white people, no matter how well-meaning and liberal, came to SNCC with some of the attitudes toward black people characteristic of American culture at large. For example, most of them soon revealed that they expected blacks to be wonderful people (with "soul") but not particularly intelligent.[7] A very high percentage of the white volunteers (many SNCC members say all of them) had similar unconscious attitudes which were interpreted by black SNCC members as racist (see pages 99-101). Clearly, racism is incompatible with a society in which each person is sacred. Thus, SNCC's rejection of whites could be seen as an effort to secure the kind of community Bob Moses had envisioned. Moses himself, at the time he was in SNCC, had not regarded the presence of whites as an obstacle to a fully humane community, but afterwards he did cut himself off completely from contact with whites for a time.

In SNCC there was a growing belief that black Americans were alone, that they could not rely on white help, not only because white help would never give them the full measure of their desires but also because they could not be men in Camus' sense as long as the meaning of a black man's life was not the same as the meaning of a white man's life.

SNCC was nevertheless in a dilemma. To cut itself off from whites at its particular time in history meant the loss of all its allies who possessed power or wealth. Such a loss would make it even more a victim of white society than it had been. The solution was to seek a new context: the context of all the non-white people in the world. The theories of Mao, as well as Malcolm X's trip to Africa, pointed in this direction. In 1966 SNCC found a philosopher who expressed brilliantly and forcefully the need for the unity of all the world's non-whites. This was Frantz Fanon, a black psychiatrist born in Martinique. Fanon's major work[8] has an introduction by Jean-Paul Sartre and thus is linked to SNCC's Existentialist tradition. In its anti-colonial emphasis, it is compatible with Maoism, but, unlike SNCC's thinking, is almost completely devoid of orthodox Marxist ideas.

The Wretched of the Earth is not about the American black man but about Algeria under colonial rule. SNCC members reading it substituted the words "black man" for "native" and "white man" for "colonialist" or "settler." They assumed that the position of the black man in America is analogous to that of the natives in a colony. (Incidentally, this was not the first time that black Americans had borrowed ideas from national independence movements in the non-white world. Both CORE and SCLC, especially in their earlier years, had drawn inspiration from the theory of non-violent resistance developed by Gandhi during the struggle for India's independence.)

Fanon, however, was far from nonviolent. In the opening paragraph of The Wretched of the Earth, he says that "decolonisation is always a violent phenomenon." Later, he says, "Liberation must, and can only, be achieved by force."[9] "The practice of violence binds them (the independence fighters) together . . . , since each individual forms a violent link in the great chain, a part of the great organism of violence."[10] "Violence alone, violence committed by the people, violence organized and educated by its leaders, makes it possible for the masses to understand social truths."[11] SNCC itself has, of course, never advocated violence so unequivocally. In fact, its leaders have often been quoted as saying that the strategy of Black Power is a substitute for the violence that would otherwise surely erupt.

In other areas, though, Fanon's analysis appears quite relevant to the problems that SNCC faced. His description of the conditions in which the Algerians live, the violence they commit against each other, the decay of their traditional culture, etc., sounds all too familiar to an American reader. Fanon analyzes the role of the native intellectual who is at first attracted to Western culture, but then learns that the European is prepared to do limitless violence in order to maintain that culture's supremacy. This native intellectual comes to see that the European has no interest in coexisting with the native except as a superior. He then joins the liberation struggle and through contact with his own people sees the emptiness of the foreign culture. He learns to take his cue from the common people. "They do not *say* they represent the truth, for they *are* the truth."[12] The intellectuals must lead the independence struggle instead of seeking status in the European community. The independence movement should approach first those elements of the native population who are least influenced or "pampered" by the Europeans: the rural masses and the urban "lumpenproletariat." These people "have no intention of standing by and watching individuals increase their chance of success. What they demand is not the settler's position of status but the setter's place."[13] Unlike the intellectuals, they cannot be taken in by the colonialist's false concessions. They know that a few seats for natives in the legislature are not a real concession but rather must be paid for by a much greater sacrifice on the part of the natives: their own culture, their own political order, their own way of thinking. For if the colonialists abandon their more brutal methods, it is only to use other methods which will make their control more complete.

All of this seemed to SNCC's members in 1966 and later to be an accurate, forceful and sympathetic description of the course that SNCC was taking. The chapter on the native intellectuals might almost have been written with the SNCC leaders in mind (although in fact it was based mainly on the Algerian independence movement).

The Wretched of the Earth, which has been called "the Bible of SNCC," contains many of the ideas behind Black Power. It never uses the phrase "black power," which is of uncertain origin. There are at least two books called *Black Power*, one by Richard Wright about Ghana, the other by W. E. B. DuBois about the United States. The titles may have inspired the slogan. Another book by DuBois, *The Souls of Black Folk*,[14] inspired some of the thought behind Black Power. DuBois wrote,

> . . . the Negro is a sort of seventh son, born with a veil, and gifted with second sight in this America—a world which yields him no true self-consciousness, but only lets him see himself through the revelation of the other world. It is a peculiar sensation, this double-consciousness, this sense of always looking at one's self through the eyes of others, of measuring one's soul by the tape of a world that looks on in amused contempt and pity.

Black Power combined an acute consciousness of the above condition with a variation of the "alternative politics" described earlier. Although it has been compared with the ethnic politics of the Irish, Italians, etc., in the nineteenth and early twentieth century, there are several important ways in which it differs. One is in the intensity of its nationalism. SNCC's leaders believed that the black man in America could not guide his own life in the political sphere until he came to see that he had a culture and a people worth preserving. Otherwise, even those black men who were successful in the white world were so only on other men's terms. Their self-government was therefore largely illusory and consisted only in details. The immigrants who engaged in ethnic politics accepted these assumptions too; they too wanted to govern whole cities, not just have a few token representatives who looked primarily to the Anglo-Saxons in power. But, since they did not have to overcome such a powerful tendency to look at themselves always "through the eyes of others," their nationalism was less vehement.

The other difference is that the SNCC leaders are much more pessimistic than the immigrants were, probably with good reasons. Most immigrant politicians knew that there were many hurdles to full acceptance, but they never believed the system was hopelessly stacked against them. Therefore they did not become radical; they did not try to invent new forms that would give them a chance denied them by the old forms. They never questioned the basic structure of politics.[15]

Black power does do that. It aims to start at the very lowest level of political organization and reform the system from the bottom up. This explains the paradox of a group that identifies the source of the problem as a small elite at the top of a few powerful governing hierarchies and then goes about solving the problem by trying to take over a few very small, poor units. It is only the smallest units—rural counties in the Deep South, local school boards in Harlem—that SNCC feels it can offer a real alternative, because only the smallest units can be completely taken over and radically changed. SNCC leaders hope that such units can provide a power base, and at the same time a model, for the eventual radical alteration of the system. (Some of them think this alteration will only occur through a violent revolution, but they usually claim that not they but the white man will fire the first shots.) In the meantime, the small units will provide certain kinds of specific relief—a fairer allocation of tax monies, the selection of more effective teachers, and so on. SNCC's new forms turn out to be not particularly striking after all (they are "people's boards of education," tenants'

115

unions, reformed county governments, etc.); what is different about them is that they are intended to derive directly from the people whose lives they affect in immediate ways.

Thus, Black Power incorporates the basic tenets of SNCC's earlier anarchist thinking. But in doing so it runs into the old problem of anarchism's incompatibility with the furthering of instrumental goals. Freedom organizations renounce the effort to control any significant portion of America's wealth. But a massive infusion of wealth, such as has been demanded by Bayard Rustin and A. Philip Randolph, is necessary to transform the ghettoes—and only bargaining organizations can obtain it. As the bargaining organizations begin to achieve even minor successes in obtaining this wealth, they will attract SNCC's potential following. SNCC leaders tend to deny the possibility that its followers can be tempted to give up their self-governing freedom organizations and their manly right to self-defense by small concrete reforms and the trappings of power. If they can be, that would mean that one cannot rely on the people to make the "right" kinds of decisions about their lives. SNCC would then be forced to become the usual "manipulative" kind of organization. It has already seen some of its most excluded followers "bought off" by the poverty program in Mississippi. Yet its leaders do not seem particularly worried about the gap between what the people really need (in their view) and what the people think they want. They believe the gap can be bridged by their own educative role.[16]

The other problem in the theory of Black Power—a problem arising with any anarchistic theory—is the difference between taking over local institutions (at which SNCC has still not had a clear success) and fundamentally changing the system. To put it succinctly, if the problem lies with vast governing institutions, what good does it do to control Lowndes County, Alabama? In a sense, the problem with SNCC ideology is that no one has ever woven together its Marxist and anarchist strands. The Marxist influence teaches SNCC to see the source of trouble in the underlying economic institutions of the society. (Since its Marxism is not very orthodox, SNCC also attributes fundamental importance to social institutions.) Hence, racism is seen as inseparable from the workings of the American system and only the direct overthrow of the system can eliminate it. The anarchist influence, on the other hand, leads SNCC to approach the problem through the reform of primary political groups by acting essentially as if society were already an anarchist utopia.[17] The two strands, which were both part of Black Power, became distinct as far back as the 1840s when Herzen and

Proudhon challenged Marx on the grounds that all large organizations were evil, even those controlled by the working class.

The nineteenth-century anarchist program for overthrowing vast institutions and replacing them with small democratic communes was violence, specifically political assassination. SNCC has never advocated this particular form of violence, and Stokely Carmichael at least does not seem to believe in the absolute necessity for a violent revolution; he still holds out Black Power programs as a substitute for race war. He may do this only to assuage the fears of whites; sometimes, he sounds as if Black Power programs are part of the preparation for revolution. In any case, he is not burning his bridges. Even after he became chairman, SNCC continued to use calls for integration and voter registration as an organizing device. And as late as January, 1968, there were rumors of a new alliance between SNCC and white radicals. Like its idol, Malcolm X, SNCC may finally have arrived at the conclusion that not all white people are necessarily enemies of black people.

Whatever the fragmentary intellectual contributions to SNCC of Camus, Marx, Mao and Fanon, it is important to reiterate that SNCC is and had always been an anti-ideological organization in every sense. It was not the ideas of Camus that made SNCC value small, democratic groups; it was its own experience both internally and in relation to other organizations. Only a small group within SNCC was even aware of the writings of Camus. Other SNCC members became familiar with these ideas mainly second-hand from this group. The same is true of Marx. SNCC members became skeptical about the extent to which the American system could reform not because of any understanding of the ins and outs of Marxian analysis. Again, only a small group had even read Marx. Warmed-over Marxist ideas merely buttressed the distrust of "white liberal capitalist institutions" that SNCC acquired from its experiences. Very much the same is true of Fanon and Malcolm, although here there was an added dimension. Being black men, these thinkers were appropriate symbols for SNCC and therefore their actual intellectual influence may be exaggerated by many SNCC members. Several SNCC members who cited Fanon as an influence admitted that they had not yet gotten around to reading any of his works. Malcolm especially was admired more for being a dynamic and outspoken black leader (and a martyr besides) than for his ideas.

The main change in the mind of SNCC since its founding was the one toward an increasingly broad view of the nature of the problems faced. At first the problem was seen as the local segregationists in power in the little towns where SNCC worked; then the whole Southern "power structure" came to be blamed. And, finally, the American government and political system came to be seen as the underlying cause of the trouble.[18] This last step came quite late. In late 1964, many if not most SNCC members still believed with a part of their minds that the American dream could be realized.[19] Moreover, during and after the period when there were many whites in SNCC, the black members came to believe that the problems affected not only black Americans but also whites. A long-time black SNCC member[19] says,

> . . . the blacks are a demonstrable example of what happens . . . when the political instrument functions poorly, ineffectively, when it becomes more concerned with its own perpetuation than with the service of the people, of the polis from which it comes . . . The blacks aren't the only ones who suffer from this. The poor aren't the only ones who suffer from it . . . But the blacks could make the argument and at least have it seem clear what they were arguing about, providing a kind of basis so that people across the nation and the world could say, "That's where I'm at . . . I've got the same problems, only I've got money, I've got a house, I've got a job, I've got the instruments of the bureaucracy at my command, and so forth, but still I feel that I'm being misused and abused too . . ." Just recently is the society beginning to recognize that the question is not one of blackness, really. What's wrong with the structures that are killing people and how do you change them?

This radical view of American society became prevalent in SNCC partly through the influence of anarchist and Marxist ideas but mainly because the weariness of those who stayed in SNCC for several years came to express itself in this way, and they in turn attracted new members who were similarly alienated. The people who viewed SNCC's goal as simply to make possible the full participation of rural Southern black people in the two-party system generally drifted out of SNCC before 1964 and went to work for some conventional group in the field of black advancement. One of them[21] called SNCC a group of "destructionists" who performed the essential purpose of tearing down institutions but who left SNCC when they felt the need to do constructive work. The ones who stayed in SNCC were those who did not see the possibility of meaningful, constructive work outside it. For them SNCC's communities were either havens from or models for the rest of society (sometimes both). In their own enclaves black people could perhaps live as "humans."

The word "human" is an important one in the SNCC vocabulary. A black Mississippi woman who worked for SNCC[22] said that she felt that SNCC's great success was to make people with little or no education see themselves as human. SNCC members say that SNCC's goal now is not civil rights but "human rights." To be human, for SNCC, meant above all to be able to control the basic decisions affecting one's own life. Participation in a vast governing bureaucracy was not considered a meaningful way of exercising such control. SNCC knows that the American system cannot provide the kind of political environment from which its members will not be alienated—yet it has only the vaguest notions about the causes of the evils it sees and the sort of system that would provide a better environment. In 1968 it is really still as anti-ideological as it was in 1961. It concentrates on action against specific evils rather than on political theorizing.

Staughton Lynd, a SNCC adviser during the summer of 1964, sees this lack of ideology (in the sense of a clear vision of a future order of society) as the major difficulty with SNCC. He believes that "the penalty for non-ideological thinking is an undercurrent of despair; a tendency to restrict the focus of vision to the next, and the next, and the next tactical action; and a failure to make contact with groups who might be partners in a more broadly conceived movement."[23] Lynd may be right—but it was not really in SNCC's power to become a standard radical ideological group. SNCC was bound together as an organization, not by ideology, but by a shared moral ethos.

SIX

Conclusions

SNCC changed in six years from a small committee formed to coordinate a social movement with moderate demands into a somewhat larger committee oriented toward radical political action. In undergoing this change it rejected several opportunities to become a conventional pressure group, preferring to maintain a stance of moral purity and complete independence. By 1966, SNCC was a radical organization; it believed that it could not achieve success without a fundamental change in American institutions. Yet SNCC's history is far from that of a typical American radical organization. SNCC differed from most other radical groups, foreign and American, in its nature as an organization. And it is this nature that is the most important factor in explaining why it became radical in the way it did.

Many radical organizations resemble non-radical political groups, in that they are bureaucratic and non-pervasive, that is to say, the organization touches on only a small part of the members' lives. Often, the only requirement for membership is acceptance of a set of principles, or ideology, and payment of a small fee (dues). The fee is necessary to support the organization's leaders, who carry out most of the organization's activities. The leaders possess almost all the authority in the organization; rank-and-file members rarely challenge them. The organization is often sustained by a bureaucratic hierarchy operating impersonally. Usually, most of the members do not know each other. Since their likes and dislikes do not have much influence on policy, which is formed and executed at the top, the organization is free to form any alliances it believes to be in its interests. Even if most of the rank and file have nothing in common with the rank and file of the allied group, the top leaders may find the alliance to be expedient. Although there is generally a certain amount of social satisfaction derived from the activities of the chapters, the force that holds the organization together is the members' belief in the ideology and the importance of furthering it. Therefore most radical organizations may be called "ideological" organizations.

Both the Socialist and the Communist Parties in America follow this pattern. For the Socialist Party in its heyday, the organization itself and its activities were relatively unimportant in terms of the real meaning of socialism, which consisted in its millennial goals and teachings.[1] When for a variety of reasons its ideological teachings came into doubt, the organization and its activities declined rapidly. Ideology had held the party together.

For the American Communist Party before the 1960s the role of ideology was even more apparent. The Soviet Communist Party was acknowledged to be the only party with a right to interpret Marxist ideology, and therefore every decision of the Soviet Party was followed by the American Party—even if the decision meant a drastic change in the Party's size, atmosphere, leadership, recruitment policies (and therefore character of membership) and type of activity. Such changes occurred on the occasions of the beginning of the Popular Front in 1934, the Hitler-Stalin Pact in 1939, the Soviet entry into World War II in 1941, and the beginning of the Cold War in 1946.[2] These periodic changes insured that it was not atmosphere, individual leaders, or character of membership, that held the members to the Party, but rather devotion to the Marxist ideological vision (as interpreted by the Soviet party), which was the only unchanging factor.

SNCC could never have survived such a change in its membership, leadership and so on. As Staughton Lynd pointed out, it had no ideology to sustain it. There was no set of formal beliefs to which all members adhered. There was no bureaucracy that would work to further the ideology regardless of any changes in the size or character of the membership. Authority was scattered throughout the organization, sometimes in the central office, sometimes in the hands of the state project director and occasionally in the hands of people with no formal position at all. Moreover, authority was weak; a great many individual members made decisions for the organization on their own. All the members worked full time at carrying out the organization's work. They were bound together by their shared way of life and outlook. The only way to prove that one was a member was by participation over a period of time in SNCC's most distinctive activities. People who had once so participated were considered to be still "in SNCC" if they still shared the basic outlook. Those who did not share it might join the organization (there was very little screening), but would not remain members for long. The only way to become a leader was by outstanding ability or commitment to the organization's activities or way of life.

The basic outlook was derived directly from this way of life; no person who had not shared in the way of life could be assumed to share in the organization's code or ethos. This ethos consisted of a set of shared beliefs about politics, social customs and, in fact, all matters considered important by the SNCC members. This set of beliefs was never made explicit; no particular belief was essential to SNCC membership. Nowhere was it specified which beliefs are more important than the others. (See Chapter Five for a description of some of these beliefs.) The beliefs were not held lightly; they became a lasting part of the outlook of every person who worked for SNCC for more than a year. Almost every person interviewed who had left SNCC after more than a year reported great difficulty in making a readjustment to "civilian" life.

The beliefs of SNCC members were analogous to "moral" beliefs in that a SNCC member who acted contrary to them would feel guilt. He was responsible to all other SNCC members for right action in terms of the SNCC beliefs, in the same sense that most people are responsible first to their parents and then to themselves (or God or all mankind) for right action in terms of moral beliefs. For this reason, SNCC may be called a "moralist organization" (a category suggested to me by James Q. Wilson) and its basic outlook may be called its "moral ethos." "Moralist" is here distinguished from "ideological." In ideological radical organizations, the ideology provides the basis for the rejection of established institutions that every radical organization makes; in moralist organizations, it is the moral ethos that provides the basis for that rejection. The radical moralist organization strives to be itself a microcosm of the new society it seeks to build, as well as the instrument for bringing it about. (SNCC did not, however, have more than a vague picture of the kind of society it wanted to see eventually.) The moralist organization need not, however, be radical at all; so long as it is isolated or insulated from the rest of society. The U.S. Army's Special Forces, or "Green Berets," seem to have been a moralist organization in many respects during the Kennedy administration. In the role played by leadership, they differed sharply from other military units, which are highly bureaucratic. The soldiers seemed to have their first loyalty to the Green Berets as a unit and to the values of physical courage and independence from non-military standards that they represent. Field officers sometimes defied men of higher rank.[3] Yet the Green Berets are, of course, hardly radical.[4]

The best example of a non-radical moralist organization is SNCC itself before 1965. SNCC has always been held together by its moral ethos, but

123

it did not reject the possibility of success without fundamental institutional changes until after the failure of the challenges.

Moralist political organizations are in many ways analogous to religious sects (as distinguished from churches, in the works of Ernst Troeltsch and others). The analogy should not be overdrawn because moralist organizations are purposive—that is, they are oriented toward the accomplishment of a purpose that transcends the organization itself—whereas religious sects are oriented mainly to the salvation of their own members.[5]

Moralist organizations are like religious sects and unlike most political groups in that they possess a total rather than segmental hold over their members. Virtually all SNCC members were totally absorbed in SNCC work at all times. In sects, spirituality or grace is something to be lived or at least sought at every moment, not merely occasionally or one day a week.[6] In the same way, the SNCC moral ethos pervaded the lives of SNCC members at all times. Just as SNCC's ethos was never expressed in a formal ideology, in sects there is often no clear doctrine. This is because the sect often arises in reaction to the excessive theologizing of the churches and is sustained by anger against the churches.[7] In the same way, many people joined SNCC because of their moral revulsion against "secular" society, a revulsion that was reinforced by the moralist atmosphere of SNCC. It was moral anger, not ideas, that bound the organization together. The moral ethos of SNCC played a role analogous to that of faith or "inner light" in sects; the members considered it superior to mere doctrine. For SNCC, moral impatience took the place of a systematic body of ideas, just as for sects millennialism takes the place of theology.

A moralist organization need not be politically radical, provided that, like the Green Berets or the early SNCC, it is isolated or insulated from society in some way. Conversely, even a very radical organization whose members are barred from full participation in society (and thus insulated) need not become a moralist organization. This is demonstrated by the history of the Industrial Workers of the World (IWW), also known as the Wobblies.[8] In the period 1905-1920, the IWW challenged the conservative, bread-and-butter trade unions of the day by being radical and visionary, just as SNCC challenged the existing civil-rights groups. The IWW was intended to be one big union, including all the workers in all industries, which would eventually bring about a proletarian revolution. It organized mainly the poorest and weakest of the American workers—recent immigrants, itinerant laborers, and miners in the far West. These men were resented by the conservative unions, partly because they were thought to "give labor a bad name" by being frequently violent and dirty. Similarly, SNCC organized the poorest and weakest black people, the ones who benefited little from the NAACP's lawsuits and were often shunned socially by members of the more conservative civil-rights groups. Also like SNCC, the IWW never had much direct political influence, but caught the imagination and won the sympathy of a large section of the American public by its songs, such as "Casey Jones," and by the brutality of the police during some of its strikes. The IWW fought not so much for specific advances as for the very right to organize—another similarity to SNCC.

The Wobblies also resembled SNCC in that they tried both to build the "new society" and to be a microcosm of it. They envisaged an undying struggle between the workers and the bosses until the wage system was abolished—just as SNCC today sees no possibility of integration with the white man until race-consciousness is abolished. The IWW was racked continually with factional fights—over very much the same issues as SNCC. For example, one faction within it favored political action, whereas another faction favored direct action (strikes), claiming that political action would lead only to reform whereas direct action was necessary to bring about the new society. This quarrel sounds very much like the dispute in 1961 between the voter-registration and direct-action wings of SNCC.

The IWW shared SNCC's hostility to the idea of leadership; in 1906, the year after it was founded, it abolished the office of president, on the ground that "we are all leaders." IWW members preferred to view themselves as advisers of other workers rather than as their leaders. After 1910, the IWW split into two factions with regard to structure, one favoring centralization, the other favoring more autonomy for local branches. These factions bear an obvious resemblance to SNCC's tight- and loose-structure groups.

In spite of its many similarities to SNCC, however, the IWW was not a moralist organization. It was bureaucratic and large, with a peak membership of about 100,000. Its disputes over strategy and structure were fought out among the top leaders in the language of European radical ideologies, like Marxism and syndicalism, whereas SNCC's disputes directly involved the whole organization and had little to do with any radical ideologies. The IWW had to be large because its ideology called for the inclusion of all the workers. However, it could generally support only one strike at a time; this meant that most of the time the majority of its members had no activist role. It was therefore run by the leaders at the top, in spite of the anti-leader ideology. Moreover, although the IWW had quarrels over structure, the faction favoring a loose structure probably envisaged a more bureaucratic organization than SNCC's tight-structure wing. A basic assumption of all SNCC members was that SNCC would be energized mainly from below; the tight-structuralists only wanted a few curbs on the worst abuses caused by decentralization. In the IWW, on the other hand, it was assumed by the members of both factions that the organization would be sustained by its bureaucracy; the loose-structuralists merely wanted to mitigate the worst abuses caused by centralization.

The bureaucracy operated on the basis of an ideology which could be (and was) summarized into a few sentences or expounded at length. All the members of the organization were aware of and presumably in agreement with the organization's purposes as set forth in the ideology. It was the ideology that induced them to stay in the IWW rather than join bread-and-butter unions. Since the organization had members all over the United States, from the Anglo-Saxon miners of Montana to the immigrant mill-hands of Massachusetts, it certainly could not have been bound together by a moral ethos. Within individual locals there were doubtless strong solidary and even moralist incentives—but the organization as a whole was run by its bureaucracy and held together by its ideology.

In the way it sustained itself and carried on its functions, SNCC was basically different not only from other radical groups like the IWW but from most other organizations. People who share a moral ethos do not usually find it necessary to join an organization to further it. Significantly, SNCC seems most similar to a radical group that was not in fact an organization: the Russian populists of the "Going to the People."[9] These were young men and women from the middle and upper classes who between 1872 and 1874 left their homes by the hundreds, perhaps thousands, to go out and live among the peasants and workers in order to educate them and to bring them a message of political emancipation. Like the SNCC volunteers of 1964, they romanticized the common people's way of life and rejected more intellectual or ideological prescriptions for curing Russia's ills. Meeting with harassment by the police and incomprehension and rejection by the common people, they became deeply discouraged and turned to more radical solutions, in particular organized terrorism. The early populists did not have a central organization; rather, the "Going to the People" was a spontaneous outpouring of political energy inspired by the broader promise implied in the emancipation of the serfs in 1861. In the same way, SNCC was founded and sustained through its first few years very largely by the political energy released by the Supreme Court's 1954 decision outlawing school desegregation. Yet by 1964 it had become enough of a conventional organization to resist going out of existence when its initial energy began to wane.

One of the most striking ways in which moralist organizations differ from ideological organizations is in their relations with other groups. Moralist organizations seem to be in continual conflict with all other groups, the only exception being other moralist organizations with a similar moral ethos. Radical ideological groups are capable of getting along with many groups—forming, for example, a "Popular Front"—though they may be very hostile to non-radical groups whose activities impinge on theirs and to radical groups with similar ideologies. Non-radical groups that are not moralist generally get along with any organization whose activities they see as beneficial to their own.

Moralist organizations, whether radical or not, seem to thrive on conflict. Even before it became radical, SNCC gravitated to a hostile environment, the Deep South. When it began to shift its center of activity to the North, it insured by its rhetoric and actions that it would receive a hostile reception there, too. Today it considers pointless any demonstration conducted with a permit; only an action that is resisted by the authorities is seen as truly exerting pressure. The continual state of beleaguerment resulting from such policies serves to hold the organization together—especially in the absence of concrete gains for members or clientele.

Characteristically, moralist organizations despise not only non-radical groups but also radical ideological groups with similar goals. They tend to see the latter as immoral and the former as amoral. The only groups they respect are other moralist organizations that have similar goals deriving from a similar moral ethos. In this regard, moralist organizations are unlike radical ideological organizations, which characteristically denounce as heretical any organization with similar goals derived from similar ideologies. Such groups are viewed by radical ideological organizations as an even worse threat than non-radical organizations with similar goals.

To a moralist organization, the worst threat is posed not by a similar moralist organization but by a group that has similar goals, implying a similar moral ethos, but which is actually not moralist in stance. Such a group threatens the sanctity of the moral ethos by acting amorally or immorally in its behalf. Only another moralist organization can be relied on always to act

127

in accord with the moral ethos. This explains why the only group SNCC trusted was CORE, which at least in the South was a moralist organization, and why so much hostility was directed against SCLC and the NAACP, non-moralist (and non-radical) organizations with similar goals to SNCC. Such groups are often seen as participating in a sinister effort to strengthen those in power by contributing to the belief that they can bring about basic reforms. They present the greatest threat to radical groups like SNCC precisely when they are most successful in achieving concrete gains. This would explain why so many SNCC members criticized SCLC (a non-radical group) most bitterly for the Selma-Montgomery March, which was its most strikingly successful endeavor. The immediate rewards offered by the way of life of a moralist organization, like the long-term promise offered by the ideology of a radical ideological organization, must compete continually with the temptations presented by the success of non-radical groups.

However, radical ideological organizations may on occasion form alliances with groups that do not share their ideology, sometimes even with non-radical groups—always justifying such behavior on ideological grounds, of course. In this respect, their behavior differs strikingly from that of moralist organizations.

For example, the Communist and Socialist Parties, since they were ideological organizations, were able to cooperate with other radical groups and even with liberals at various points in their history, despite the fact that their ideology defined many of these groups as counter-revolutionary. But SNCC, as a moralist organization, was almost completely incapable of smooth cooperation with groups that did not share its world view. In both the VEP and COFO, its cooperation was almost entirely on paper, except with CORE. SNCC members, including the leaders who had arranged the alliances, did not change their negative views of SCLC, the NAACP and other moderate civil-rights groups during these periods of cooperation; if anything, the antagonism was enhanced. It is true that rank-and-file Socialists continued to loathe Communists during the Popular Front period in the late 1930s and were in turn despised by individual Communists—but the two Parties cooperated with each other, and the leaders at least sounded as if they were firmly convinced of the absence of basic reasons for antipathy. In this respect, the Communist and Socialist Parties were more similar to non-radical groups like the NAACP than to SNCC.

Most non-radical groups are capable of having friendly relations with any organization whose operations they see as beneficial to their own. Differences in ideology or structure may cause hostility but are not the primary determinant of the warmth of the relationship.[10] An exception would be the relationship of non-radical American groups with the Communist Party; they invariably shun it because association with it makes them so vulnerable to attack. In general, however, non-radical organizations do try to minimize conflict with other groups.

In sum, most non-radical organizations try to have good relations with almost all other organizations. Radical ideological organizations are generally in conflict with non-radical organizations in their field and with radical organizations with similar ideologies but are capable on occasion of forming alliances with any group. Moralist organizations, even when they are not radical, are incapable of getting along with any other groups except other moralist organizations with a similar moral ethos.

Not only in its relations with other organizations but in every other respect, SNCC seems unlike an ideological organization. The interviews in this study make clear that SNCC had no ideology, at least before 1966. In discussing the nature of SNCC, members never defined it in terms of its beliefs. In fact, SNCC's beliefs about the world outside small towns in the Deep South were rarely referred to by members. When pressed to define SNCC's goals, members either answered in terms of *methods* (to organize poor people, to stimulate political action where none had existed before) or gave extremely vague answers (to end injustice or to end the exclusion of black people from American society). The fact that the same answer was rarely given twice is strong evidence that SNCC had no ideological creed. Further evidence is that none of SNCC's literature discusses the ultimate purpose or meaning of the organization. It is all centered around a description of the organization's current activities. The very fact that SNCC members were ardent followers of such diverse thinkers as Albert Camus, Frantz Fanon, and Karl Marx indicates its lack of an ideology. Malcolm X, not through his ideas but through his life and his martyrdom, had more of an influence than all of them.

SNCC's structure, too, sets it off from ideological organizations. The most important leaders were not necessarily at the top in SNCC. James Forman was balanced by Bob Moses and Fannie Lou Hamer. In fact, the most important locus of leadership was at the project level, where a highly personal, morally-oriented approach was most effective. In the early years, the informal exercise of power worked well, but it was inevitable that a large increase in size would rock the organization. SNCC members stress the fact that their organization was held together by ties that could bind only a small, homogeneous, united group. SNCC was rent by factional conflict during the whole period when it had over 150 members (1964 and 1965). It was able to resolve the conflict only by excluding most of the whites and becoming a very small organization again. It is important to note that none of the conflicts within SNCC about size and structure were argued in ideological terms. Most SNCC members had no knowledge of earlier debates in other radical organizations and no awareness of the underlying questions implied in the debates.

Leaders, like structure, were never chosen for ideological or bureaucratic reasons. Until the election of May 1966, neither the beliefs nor the formal qualifications of leaders was considered particularly important. What mattered was a proven commitment to the way of life and the moral ethos of SNCC, which could be demonstrated only by leadership in the field. Even Stokely Carmichael, whose beliefs did play a role in his selection, would never have been chosen if he had not been a successful field leader.

A moralist organization must be homogeneous in membership. Only if most of the members share a social background can they be as totally absorbed in the organization's world-view as full membership requires. A small number of people with different social backgrounds from the majority may be assimilated if they happen to have similar beliefs and a similar psychological outlook. This explains why most of SNCC's following was never admitted to membership and why it was impossible for SNCC to absorb more than a few whites.

Thus, SNCC's basic nature as a moralist organization was reflected in its external relations, in its ideology (or rather lack of it), in its structure and leadership and in the nature of its membership. The fact that SNCC was a moralist organization also directly affected the nature of its development into a radical organization.

There is an internal mechanism at work in moralist organizations and not in other organizations, which tends to move them toward an unconventional and often a radical moral stance even if they begin (as SNCC did) with a fairly conventional one. Thus, a moralist organization is rarely "moral" in the conventional sense. Moralist organizations have a fairly simplistic view of the world. It is easy to judge, in their view, who shares the moral ethos and any organization which does not share it is seen as "the enemy." The great majority of American organizations, on the other hand, judge other organizations pragmatically, on the basis of their actions, which may be helpful one day and harmful the next. For moralist organizations, which emphasize values, there is often a "he-who-is-not-with-us-is-against-us" mindset. Therefore, although a moralist organization may begin by affirming its own rightness and only incidentally pointing out the moral wrongness of all others, it will often end by stressing the moral wrongness of others.

This change occurs in the following manner. Since a moralist organization usually seeks a hostile environment, it is usually persecuted by other groups. In the normal course of political events, it is also opposed or only partially supported by still other groups—and, because of its black-or-white mindset, it views these other groups as persecutors as well. For this to happen, the individual members need not be particularly paranoid, as they were not in SNCC before 1966. (They may have become so after that date.) In SNCC in fact, most members had a personal style that was the very opposite of the grandiose manner of paranoids. It is the organization's internal dynamics that caused the "paranoia"—by its standards, it is persecuted by everyone.

The perception of the world as persecutory leads to an increasing emphasis on the moral wrongness of others rather than on one's own rightness. Finally, the moralist organization tells its chief enemies that since they are utterly amoral or immoral, every act is justifiable against them. Thus, SNCC's early persecution by segregationists caused it gradually to de-emphasize its stance in favor of nonviolence. And the later criticism by liberal groups, which was viewed by SNCC as persecution, caused it to emphasize increasingly the wrongness of its enemies until it began to justify violence and even, finally, violent revolution.

The resort to revolution by at least some SNCC members followed from the organization's growing "paranoia," which caused it to see its enemies as an increasingly large group. For at least some people in SNCC, that group eventually became all white Americans. It was in this way that SNCC moved from a world-view that was acceptable to most Americans and in which Gandhi and Camus were admired to an ethos that permitted the admiration of Frantz Fanon, who to most Americans seems quite immoral.

In its relationships with Southern segregationists, SNCC did not behave irrationally; its belief that it was being persecuted was accurate. It was in SNCC's relations with Northerners or representatives of the nation as a whole that it became clear where its practical demands and its tactics left off and its moralist vision began. When, at the Democratic Convention, its tactical move (calling for acceptance of Representative Green's compromise) was met with another tactical move that was not entirely unreasonable (the proffered compromise), it became clear that SNCC was less interested in concrete advances than in recognition of its moral position. Similarly, when SNCC's demands for federal registrars were met through the Voting Rights Act, it became clear that SNCC really wanted something other than the right to vote; it wanted a new political system based on a new moral code—one which it felt it exemplified. The sending of federal registrars to the Deep South, which would seem to be a beneficial act in SNCC's terms, was instead interpreted (correctly) as a threat to the organization. It was yet another temptation offered by practical politics that would lead members to defect.

To most Americans, who were not aware of the moralist context, SNCC's behavior became increasingly repugnant. But SNCC did have some success in the period before it became a symbol of black militancy. This success was not in the form of concrete achievements or insightful ideological prescriptions but, appropriately, in the form of a moral critique based on its ethos. The SNCC way of life itself entailed certain criticisms of the way of life of the rest of America. In the late 1950s, just before the founding of SNCC, American society appeared particularly smug and blind to its failures. Its political system was largely amoral and unideological; it seemed to function almost entirely on the basis of power relationships, with the result that the weak were not only excluded but often ignored. When the "end of ideology" was announced by Daniel Bell, most Americans welcomed it; they had no desire to listen to ideological analyses of what was wrong with their society. The liberals dismissed such analyses as irrelevant; the conservatives dismissed them as Communistic.

What SNCC tried to do was to bypass ideology by appealing directly to America's conscience. To this end, it mobilized the young and the dispossessed into a group that challenged directly first conservatives and then liberals and finally all those who were not dissatisfied with the status quo. By its activism and self-sacrifice, it rebuked those who saw some evils but contented themselves with passive and untaxing remedies. By its impatience, it challenged those comfortable ones who piously called for patience on the part of the excluded. By its scorn for both the trappings and the reality of power and success, it criticized those who had respect only for power and success.

The nation at large apparently was prepared to hear SNCC's reproach: there was a new wave of interest in civil rights and poverty. The young people particularly were ready to listen. A COFO summer volunteer named Mario Savio founded the Berkeley Free Speech Movement. Tom Hayden, who had worked for SNCC, became one of the founders of the Students for a Democratic Society (SDS). Other SNCC members, like Abbie Hoffman, became leaders among the hippies, who also seek an alternative life-style and world view. This is not to give SNCC the credit or blame for founding any of these movements or trends; the most that can be said is that it was among their forerunners.

Ironically, SNCC's influence on black people before 1966[11] is perhaps the most tenuous. CORE, the Black Muslims, the much-reviled SCLC—all were very active in stimulating black militancy in the same period as SNCC. In this area, SNCC was only one of several easily identifiable influences. SNCC, then, is of interest as one of the earliest manifestations of a new self-examination on the part of Americans in the 1960s.

Appendices

ONE

Some Provisions for Federal Prosecution in Civil Rights

From Title 18 U.S. Code

FBI Arrests—18 U.S. Code, Section 3052: The Director, Associate Director, Assistant to the Director, Assistant Directors, inspectors, and agents of the Federal Bureau of Investigation of the Department of Justice may carry firearms, serve warrants and subpoena issued under the authority of the United States and make arrests without warrant for any offense against the United States committed in their presence, or for any felony cognizable under the laws of the U.S. if they have reasonable grounds to believe that the person to be arrested has committed or is committing such felony.

Interference with the Vote—18 U.S. Code, Section 594: Whoever intimidates, threatens, coerces, or attempts to intimidate, threaten or coerce, any person for the purpose of interfering with the right of such other person to vote or to vote as he may choose, or of causing such other person to vote for, or not vote for, any candidate for the office of President, Vice President, Presidential elector, Member of the Senate, or Member of the House of Representatives, Delegates or Commissioners of the Territories or Possessions, at any election held solely or in part for the purpose of electing such candidate, shall be fined not more than $1000 or imprisoned not more than one year or both.

Deprivation of Constitutional Rights—18 U.S. Code, Section 242: Whoever, under color of any law, statute, ordinance, regulation, or custom, willfully

137

subjects any inhabitant of any state, territory, or district to the deprivation of any rights, privileges or immunities secured or protected by the Constitution or laws of the United States (or to different punishments, pains, or penalties, on account of such inhabitant being an alien, or by reason of his color, or race, than are prescribed for the punishment of citizens), shall be fined not more than $1,000 or imprisoned not more than one year, or both.

TWO

Interviewees

Ella Baker
Marion Barry
James Bevel
Unita Blackwell
Willie Blue
Julian Bond
Barbara Brandt
Miriam Cohen
Margaret Dammond Day
Ivanhoe Donaldson
Archie Epps
Sylvia Fisher
Charles Fishman
Barney Frank
Betty Garman
Fannie Lou Hamer
William Hansen
Donald Harris
Curtis Hayes
William Higgs
Timothy Jenkins
Charles Jones
James Jones
Bernard Lafayette
John Lewis
Worth Long

Allard Lowenstein
Pattye Mapp
James Marshall
Charles McDew
Lester McKinnie
Gerald McWorter
Francis Mitchell
Jesse Morris
John O'Neal
John Perdew
Edward Pincus
Cordell Reagon
Reggie Robinson
Michael Sayer
Donald Shaw
Nancy Stoller Shaw
Charles Sherrod
Frank Smith
Joseph Spieler
Jane Stembridge
Elizabeth Sutherland
Mary Varela
Claude Weaver
Robert Zellner
Howard Zinn

Selected Interviews

A Note on
the Transcripts

The interviews on which this dissertation was based were carried out in 1966 and 1967. They were not undertaken with a view to publication or even permanent documentation, but rather as sources for Dr. Stoper's research. We include a sampling here because of the richness of the material and because these now twenty-year-old interviews provide a picture of SNCC that is literally no longer available to us in any other form.

The interviews are divided into two groups—full transcriptions of tapes and publication of "snippets" of transcriptions that Dr. Stoper made immediately after the interviews. The first group is composed of interviews with Donald Harris, John Lewis, Charles Jones and Jane Stembridge. The reader will note that in all of these cases the transcriptions do not contain the complete discussion between the subject and Dr. Stoper. The omitted portions of the interviews do not occur on the tapes as they presently exist.

The second group is composed of interviews with Ella Baker, James Bevel, Julian Bond, Barney Frank, Betty Garman, and Fannie Lou Hamer. Tapes do not presently exist for these interviews and these transcriptions were not necessarily made (and thus are not published here) in the order that the interview occurred.

We found these materials fascinating and trust the reader will, as well.

Ralph Carlson
Carlson Publishing

Donald Harris

ES: When did you first join SNCC?

DH: I first went down south during the summer of 1962. I had been working in New York and in New Jersey on civil rights projects, fund-raising, with supportive kinds of things, rallies, speaking engagements, raising money.

ES: Why were you attracted to SNCC rather than some other organization?

DH: Primarily because I knew a number of people in SNCC, knew them from various college meetings, campus conferences, these kinds of things. At that point I didn't see where any of the other groups were really doing anything outside of local protest groups in particular cities, in particular areas. No other national group was involved as extensively at that time.

ES: What was SNCC doing then? What were its basic goals?

DH: At that time SNCC had two projects mainly; a voter registration program in McComb and the direct action program in Southwest Georgia. During that summer, however, I think we got involved in a couple of other counties in Mississippi, and in Southwest Georgia we were operating in three counties: Daugherty County, which was Albany, Terrell County and Lee County.

ES: What was behind the various different kinds of activities? Did they all have a very similar ultimate goal? Voter registration? Direct action?

DH: Essentially the voter registration plan was that working to assist people to register and vote and encourage them to register and vote provided the broadest Constitutional protections for civil rights workers as well as those people who were actually engaging in registration and voting. The direct action campaign was testing the new ICC ruling, barring discrimination in interstate transport as well as the facilities: bus depots, train stations, so on.

ES: What I was driving at is, did these two very different kinds of things, voter registration and direct action, have the same end? How did it come that they were in the same organization? Were there two branches of the organization?

DH: There were two factions in SNCC at that time. One believed that attacking voter registration would bring the most meaningful gains, and another feeling that attacking the ICC ruling would bring the most gains. So essentially what happened, I guess Bob Moses went to Mississippi and that was ostensibly the voter registration program. Sherrod came to Southwest Georgia. What in fact happened was almost the reverse. The Albany group got involved in bus station activity as well as voter registration in Terrell and Lee County, and the group in McComb did some—well, the first activities involved demonstrations in school, in a number of schools, as a matter of fact, in McComb.

ES: Where were you working at this time?

DH: When I went down in the beginning of that summer I went to Albany. Well, actually I went to Lee County and worked on voter registration. Matter of fact, most of the time I was in Lee County and for a while in Terrell County. I didn't get involved very much with anything that was going on in Albany. Martin King was down there that summer leading and participating in demonstrations and when there was a plan for a demonstration in Albany or there was going to be a mass meeting, generally the people in the counties would come into Albany and bring some of the county people into the mass meeting. But during the day our actual work was out in the counties talking to people in the fields.

ES: What sorts of problems did you run into?

DH: The biggest difficulty in the counties was that both Lee and Terrell Counties are just completely rural, not even a hint of a town. I guess Leesburg, which is the county seat, must have a population of a couple of hundred but they're spread out. Dawson, county seat in Terrell County, had a few more but it was a much more hard-core county. Actually both counties then were hard-core. But the problem was just getting to people and transporting them to Leesburg so that they could attempt to register. The primary difficulty was transportation. The second difficulty was communication. The phones in both counties were party lines. More often than not there was a white somewhere on the party line and they were constantly listening in and calling up and intimidating people that they knew had been involved with us or with whom we had talked.

ES: So you sort of had this double problem: the white intimidation plus the pure physical difficulties of getting to people.

DH: Right. They were very difficult counties to work because, as I said, they were both very, very hostile counties, in the first place. Terrell County has a long history of lynchings and murders, beatings and so forth. That summer the house we were staying in in Lee County was shot into a number of times. The house we stayed in at Terrell County was shot into four, five, six times. On one occasion people were hit. Workers were constantly being beaten as they traveled about in these rural areas. There was no protection at all offered by any officials. As a matter of fact, officials were the ones who were carrying out most of the intimidation. The sheriff in neighboring counties, one in particular, Sumter County where we eventually moved in about a year or so later, the sheriff used to come down and come into mass meetings, just generally intimidate people on back roads and things like that.

ES: How did the program develop? How did you deal with this kind of thing as time passed?

DH: Well, the workers themselves lived in the communities in somebody's house so that at least in each county there was one central base of operation and this was a local person's house. If on occasion there were too many people for that one house, other people would offer their homes. Their friends would come by, we'd talk to them. . . . We held weekly mass meetings at local churches. That was the summer, also, that three churches in Southwest Georgia were bombed.

ES: How long did you work there in Southwest Georgia?

DH: Well, I worked in Southwest Georgia most of the time I was in SNCC. I worked in Mississippi for a while. I was in Alabama for a little while, but those were only periodic things, if there was a particular crisis or just a special project for a limited period of time. I worked in Southwest Georgia until I quit, which was March '65.

ES: So you're really sort of well-qualified to tell me how it developed. Did it pick up momentum as it moved along? Did you try new types of techniques as time passed?

DH: Well, prior to June of '62 there had been only three people working in Southwest Georgia. Sherrod, Cordell Reagon and Charlie Jones. The summer of '62 maybe ten or fifteen students from the north—some from the north, some from the south—but several students came down, ten or fifteen. This increased the publicity of what was going on in Southwest Georgia from SNCC's point of view. People in their respective home towns and colleges heard about the Southwest Georgia project. Martin King was down there that summer and prior to that summer. That added greatly to the publicity.

ES: SNCC welcomed King at that point?

147

DH: Yes, by and large.

ES: Were there any sort of tensions between SNCC and SCLC?

DH: Well, there were a lot of tensions. There always were, I guess, but they certainly weren't on the magnitude that they have been more recently, as the split has been more recently. It didn't really affect the operations going on within the community at all. There were just tensions in terms of what to do and when and these were worked out. Also, by the summer of '62 the Albany movement had solidified to the extent that probably it was the strongest local movement in the country at that time. William Anderson was president of the Albany movement. He was a local doctor. Slater King was vice president or at least an officer. He was a local real estate and insurance broker. C. B. King, the only black lawyer in Southwest Georgia, was involved. This was significant to the extent that not only was this movement encompassing professional people, not only was it strongly community-oriented and based, this was probably the one community at that time that had a lawyer right on the scene to involve himself to a hundred percent of his time of dealing with the local arrests, dealing with kids being thrown out of schools and whatever happened. This was significant to that extent. Albany was significant also in that Albany State Teacher's College was there. The Albany State students actually were the first people to get involved in any action or activity in Albany. The students were the ones who first started attempting to desegregate the bus station. Prior to that summer also there were city-run buses in Albany that were segregated and it was a combination of Albany State students, and primarily the black domestic workers, the women, who put the city buses out of operation in Albany because they formed a car pool. Probably this was the foundation of the Albany movement, something very similar to the movement in Montgomery. That it came out of a bus boycott. That the foundations were developed through the organization of car pools to get these domestics to work and back every day. To the best of my knowledge the car pool is still operating. There still are no buses in Albany. The car pool is operating to a minimal extent. It's clearly not as strong as it was at one time. But there are no city buses.

ES: What were the achievements of the Albany movement?

DH: The achievements or goals?

ES: Well, the achievements.

DH: When? Now?

ES: Over all. Over the whole time it's been in existence. It didn't desegregate the buses. What did it do?

DH: I think the goals and therefore the achievements have changed over a four or five-year period. I think initially the goals were to desegregate the city buses, to desegregate public facilities and accommodations, to desegregate public schools, and voter registration. Although, the gamut was probably as wide as you can go, the immediate goal in late '61, beginning of '62 was desegregate the buses. At this point I think the goals have changed to the extent that they are just to build up a strong community-wide organization that can meet, discuss, decide and ultimately act on problems and situations that are of interest and concern to the black community. This would go from block voting for a particular candidate and running their own candidates to establishing a black-owned bank, to acquiring real estate, to building up the economic strength of the community.

ES: How would you evaluate the success in achieving both of these types of goals that you mentioned?

DH: Well, it's difficult to evaluate a community kind of organization because you can say if it didn't meet each and every one of its aforestated goals then it in some measure failed. I don't think this is necessarily true.

ES: And if it met some you could say it succeeded?

DH: Yes, right. I think it has met some. It has failed in a great number, but the effort generally did a tremendous amount for the city of Albany, especially for the black citizens. I think the attitude of people, probably not the entire black community (and certainly not the entire white community), but their attitude toward whites has changed significantly.

ES: In what way?

DH: The black community can and does, as a community and as individuals, respect themselves more. They are less frightened individually and community-wise of intimidation and retaliation from the white community. The white community at the same time is more respectful of the black community in terms of anything they do. At one time the pervasive attitude of most blacks in Albany, certainly a majority of them, was obviously nonviolent. I don't think that same attitude prevails today and if you want to measure it as a gain or an achievement, I don't know, but the white community is certainly more reluctant to engage in any sort of activities that would either bring harm or certainly be injurious to the black community. In the development of the whole Albany movement—I think the Albany movement is significant in a number of ways, also. A lot of things grew out of the Albany movement. C. B. King ran for Congress in 19 —

ES: '62, was it? '63?

DH: It must be '63. It couldn't be that. '64.

ES: I can check that. Zinn's book would have that.

DH: Okay. I'm not sure whether at that time if we had started running black candidates across the board, people like Mrs. Boynton, for example, although I guess some basic work had been done on Fannie Lou Hamer's campaign in Mississippi. But this was certainly an important step for Southwest Georgia as a whole. In the campaign he ran, I think, fourth out of six candidates. Maybe there were twenty thousand votes. Maybe he got nine or eleven [thousand] or something like that, but I mean it was a fairly impressive number of votes compared to the situation, budget, just the whole total operation. Not only was this man trying to wage a campaign on practically no funds at all. All his work was volunteer, all his time was in addition to his practicing law. All of the people who worked on the campaign were volunteers. There wasn't one paid person on his so-called campaign staff. This was significant. After that more and more blacks started to run for office in Albany itself; from outside of the Albany movement also.

ES: I notice that most of the time you do mention Albany as the place where these gains were made, psychological gains and political gains. Does that imply that the more rural counties were less successful?

DH: Simply in terms of geography Albany is a city of maybe fifty, sixty thousand people and a center, if you want to call it that, in Southwest Georgia. There are two military bases. Immediately outside of Albany there's a state college. There's heavy industry in Albany. You had a C. B. King in Albany. You had a Slater King. You had a strong local organization with a nucleus of local people but also a nucleus of professional people who could add professional kinds of competence in terms of legal, real estate kinds of assistance. You had money people who could put up bonds, which was crucial. You also had college students. Even though at one time we tried to get away from having it the center of the Southwest Georgia project, it in fact always remained the central office in Southwest Georgia because it was central to just about every place we were working and the necessities to run any operation were there. SNCC had, and if it has any friends left, they probably will be in Albany, in Southwest Georgia.

ES: Does SNCC now actually have a project there?

DH: I doubt it very much. I don't think they do.

ES: Sherrod is still down there.

DH: Right. Right. Well, he's not in Albany. He's in Baker county. He's in Newton, which is thirty miles south, almost due south. But in Albany also in the last couple of years more and more blacks have been hired in the companies, large companies. A great deal of business, heavy industry is moving into the Albany area.

ES: In decent jobs. Not just janitor and stuff?

DH: I wouldn't say decent jobs. Factory kind of jobs, assembly line, parts, small —

ES: Jobs formerly held by white men, though?

DH: These industries are hiring people all the time now. I learned about a week ago that a couple of the factories, people in the factories have formed unions. About two weeks ago there was a big strike at Bob's Candy Company, which is a nationally known producer.

ES: I never heard of it.

DH: Nobody else ever heard of it either.

ES: If it's so nationally known . . . ?

DH: It is. It is. They do a hell of a lot of business. So the whole labor aspect of it got hooked into Albany because of once again, a strong community organization in Albany. Also, growing out of the Albany movement and the civil rights—or not the Civil Rights Act but the Anti-Poverty Bill in '64 or whenever it was.

ES: You think that some of this hiring of Negroes in these jobs has to do with the fact that Albany is now a united black community, is that what you're saying?

DH: Not so much hiring, but whereas ten years ago a Negro maybe working out at Bob's Candy Company. He gets fired for what he thinks is an unjust cause and he's just fired and they get somebody else. Two years ago he gets fired, he goes into C. B. King's office. C. B. King says, "Okay." He calls up somebody, the manager, supervisor of Bob's Candy Company and says, "We are ready to sue unless you give this man a hearing." Bob's Candy Company, not wanting to go through a potential suit or not wanting the Albany movement to request or the other people at Bob's Candy Company to organize and form a strike, will hear these grievances. Whereas, without this kind of community solidarity, this kind of pressure couldn't have been brought to bear. This kind of thing. Similarly, if there was a particular situation involving the police or local government, they would be much more hesitant to act if at a trial, or at a hearing, or at a conference there were 800 people out in the street awaiting the decision of whatever the body was, than if nobody was there at all and there was no evidence that the community would be concerned one way or the other. I think the power, latent or in fact, that was created by the formation and relative stable organization of the Albany movement contributed to a significant extent of change in Albany.

ES: Do you remember how you and other people in the Albany movement felt about the Mississippi Summer Project at the time it was proposed? This is '64.

DH: '63.

ES: Oh, the big one in '64.

DH: I tend to think not. I would tend to think that also probably much of the planning —

ES: About what?

DH: I tend to think that much of the planning that was done for that was done with people working in Mississippi and was brought up at an all-SNCC conference just for informational purposes or supportive purposes more than anything else.

ES: How did you feel about it as it was actually taking place?

DH: I don't know. SNCC got to be so cumbersome around that time, cumbersome in terms of its size and its number of people, the number of places where we had projects, so that contact with other areas diminished. I would tend to think that most people got rather self-conscious about what they were doing themselves and not too much involved.

ES: Did you feel neglected?

DH: Oh, there were constant complaints by people in Arkansas, people in Alabama and people in Southwest Georgia that their areas were being neglected for Mississippi. At that time Mississippi could bring much more press and publicity than any of the other three areas could, or any other area: Danville, Cambridge, Maryland, so forth. There was a lot of bitching and griping going on by the staff. I think the problem was when they had the big summer project that had—I've forgotten the number—maybe a thousand, eight hundred students going into Mississippi, it was damn near impossible to know anybody of that eight hundred, especially if you were working in another state. Therefore, you became somewhat detached from those people. They didn't know who the hell you were; you didn't know who they were. I tend to suspect that some of us, anyway, who had been around felt that these people didn't know what the hell they were doing and were about to botch things up, which many of them did. But I think the organization disintegrated a great deal that summer.

ES: That summer?

DH: Yes, simply because when I first started working with SNCC, and when I first went south in the summer of '62, by the end of that summer I knew every person on the staff of SNCC, knew them well.

ES: How many people was that?

DH: Probably about forty at that time. I knew them well enough to have some faith and confidence (or lack of same) in them in a crisis situation. Presuming I didn't have the faith and confidence in one person that I might have in another, I knew him well enough to know what his strengths were and that if I was calling on him in a situation which he could handle best or deal with, I could count on him or her entirely. Whereas, during the Mississippi Freedom Summer you could call maybe three, four, five different areas on the telephone one right after another and ask for anybody in that project and maybe you wouldn't know a name. We were calling from another state and may have been involved in SNCC for a year, two years.

ES: What was the significance of that? Did that have a significance in the decision-making process of SNCC, you couldn't trust the other people who were going to make decisions?

DH: Well, it was significant, at least for Southwest Georgia, in a number of ways. Personally, from my own point of view I think it helped our own project a great deal in that —

ES: You probably had less money.

DH: Yes, than we needed. We certainly got a lot less attention than we wanted or thought we should have had. All of us—that is, all of the workers, "outside agitators"—were forced to develop for ourselves our own resources. In terms of transportation, we didn't have cars or the cars we had were broken or not enough, not adequate. We had to make our own contacts in terms of getting out news releases and news stories to the press. By and large we made our own decisions on where to go, that is, what counties to go into; what we were going to do in those counties. We sort of ran our own show. Personally, I think for me that was probably the most rewarding or certainly among the most rewarding periods of time that I was down there. This was while we were in Americus, or Americus was developing. Except for a couple of crucial—Well, let's say that two or three months prior to the arrest of Ralph, John and myself—

ES: Ralph who?

DH: Ralph Allen, John Perdew and I, along with Daniels and Sally May of Americus were the first to start organizing in Sumter County. Our organization, the Sumter County movement, was operating solely upon its own initiative, its own inspiration, its own ideas. It had no support whatsoever from SNCC. It had no outside assistance of any kind and I think that is why the developments up to the first part of August in Americus were practically—well, they were in fact unstoppable by the local authorities simply because all the power was in the hands of the local people. They were using their own resources, their own ideas entirely and there was nothing that could be cut off from the community that was vital to the movement. The only thing that was vital to the movement was the citizens of Americus and Sumter County.

ES: Switching back to something we were talking about before, what was the purpose of the voter registration campaign in Southwest Georgia? Was there a real hope of being able to take over actual office or was there another purpose?

DH: You mean back as far as 62, '61?

ES: Yes. Discuss the history of it. If the purpose has changed over time I'd like to hear about that.

DH: Well, I think that at that point, although we were talking about registering the number of . . . In Lee County there were more blacks than whites eligible to vote. In Terrell County there were more blacks than whites eligible to vote. I think primarily we were thinking in terms more of controlling what happened in a county politically. That is, by using the vote to vote for a white—and I say this is probably what we were thinking—using the vote to vote for a white person that would take into account the wishes and concerns of blacks as well as whites, rather than the more recent concept of running a black slate, i.e., the Black Panther movement in Alabama.

ES: Why is that so since you did have a majority? Why content yourself with that?

DH: Well, personally, I would say—and this is strictly a personal view of my own impression, we weren't sophisticated—I wasn't, anyway—to the point of political activity and political organization in this country. I don't think actually that we ever had the idea that we would register a majority in Lee County or Terrell County. We were aiming for the significant minority that could swing a vote. Possibly we were aiming for it, but it was subconscious in that the difficulties at that particular time and the handicaps under which we were operating were just too great to conceive of registering two thousand people.

ES: You were thinking mainly in terms of filling county offices or Congressional seats rather than statewide offices?

DH: I wouldn't even take in those seats. I think we were thinking more of things like sheriff, police chief, registrar, alderman or city council or what have you, rather than even statewide offices. Bear in mind that at this time we were operating literally on a shoestring. If somebody wanted to come north to fund-raise, that person probably would have to get out and sell SNCC buttons or sell the first record album that SNCC had and raise his carfare north. We weren't operating as SNCC has operated in the recent past in terms of some people having credit cards and expense accounts and people flying not only all over this country, but to other countries. Certainly nobody was flying.

ES: I read somewhere that you made a trip to Africa with John Lewis.

DH: Right, that was in '64, later in the game. I guess the original concept of what we wanted to do in Southwest Georgia involved spreading out—and this goes back to something you asked before—spreading out from Albany, as once again the core or the central base in Southwest Georgia, into the surrounding counties. Up to February, '63 we were operating in just Lee County and Terrell County. In February, '63 we moved down into Sumter County, the county seat being Americus, and sometime after that—I guess it was when C. B. King ran for office—we moved out into the entire, I believe it's second Congressional District and we were operating at one point in twenty-two counties in that district. We had offices in Thomasville, and in Moultrie, in Cuthbert, Cordele, all over the place.

ES: It's about as exotic to me as Samarkand.

DH: Not quite.

ES: Strange names. It strikes me that your political plan there had a certain consistency and it made a certain amount of sense. It seems strange that SNCC is still thinking very much on the county level in terms of county field organizations and that sort of thing, and yet at the same time SNCC's broader philosophy has changed so that it realizes now or thinks now that it's the broad institutional structures in American society, a very broad attitude, that has to be changed and attacked. Do you have any explanation for the inconsistency between SNCC's practical targets and its sort of long-range definition of its problem now?

DH: I would first of all venture to say that SNCC provided a significant education for a great number of the people involved in the movement. That is, people who were involved in the movement for two, three years. I would venture to guess that when most of us got involved we knew very, very little about community organization or probably nothing. We knew very little about the political institutions in this country. We knew very little about the development of political power or economic power in this country.

DH: But as far back as '61 and the early part of '62, all those people who were going into field operations, specifically into new field operations, there was maybe a three or four page sheet of questions about a community. Population; racial composition; percent; what is the main economic foundation of that city, of the county; what industries; what kind of resources in terms of the local community and the black community; is it significant Klan country; what is the historical background in attitudes of whites towards blacks? All this kind of thing. Basically it would probably take two weeks to find out all that information, but by the time an individual got that information, he probably knew as much about the community when he or she began to work as anybody else there. Well, not as much, obviously, as somebody who had lived there all their life. I don't recall that this was done after the summer of '62, say. Students from the North, students from urban areas in the South went into communities that they knew nothing about. If they were just summer volunteers or summer workers, they left the community after three months knowing perhaps very little more than they knew when they came in. They knew ten people. They had been to mass meetings and they had seen a cop beat on some Negroes, but that may have been the extent of it. What I'm getting to is there was no preparation in terms of somebody doing any significant amount of work. Similarly, there was very little mental preparation of the first students —

ES: Why did it change? Why did SNCC's technique get worse, as you seem to imply?

DH: SNCC, being dynamic and almost loose organizationally to its own destruction, as more and more people came onto the staff, as the organization itself became more wealthy, there wasn't, once again, the personal confidence and confrontation among individuals. There wasn't the communication, the sharing of information of what had gone on in Greenwood with people from Arkansas or Alabama. There wasn't that sort of a bond, a binding camaraderie between the individuals as much as there had been in the early days. Of course, when they first started out there were only sixteen people and subsequent to that maybe forty or fifty. In '62, even the early part of '63 —

ES: Did this have something to do with the character of those people who were coming in?

DH: Well, yes. They were a very different kind of people. In '63, '64 civil rights work, voter registration work became a fad for college students. And white college students came pouring out of all over the place just to be in the South for every possible reason. Although, the very first group of SNCC students were there for every reason also, the danger was much more imminent than it was in '63, '64, '65 than now. Personal, physical confrontation with a bullet, with a club.

ES: The danger was greater three years ago then now?

DH: Right. So I couldn't afford to work with somebody who didn't know at least as much as I knew about a community. I couldn't afford to send somebody out in a community to do a job, to involve themselves with other people who were basically putting their trust in us. Send a person out there who was going to misuse the trust of these people. When we had eight hundred kids going into Mississippi we didn't know who we could trust in the sense of trust their judgment and abilities or competence because there was no way to get to know eight hundred people—even though there was training before they went into the field. These kinds of things.

ES: What was your attitude and the general attitude of people in your project toward the federal government? Again, if this changed over time I'd like to hear how it changed.

DH: Our contact with the federal government basically involved FBI agents. There was no respect for FBI agents simply because at that time, and probably it continues, agents are hired from a particular area to work in that area. In other words, they're hired to work in their local community. They may leave to be trained, but eventually a Georgia boy is going to end up being an FBI agent some place in Georgia. Further, that agent from Georgia will represent the ideas and the attitudes of people from Georgia from his local community, which was invariably racist. Other than that our contacts were very little. The FBI gave us no support. Very often they did their best to work against us. They had close contact, of course, with local officials.

ES: What significance did you attach to or hope did you put in federal laws of various kinds?

DH: I think it was just a constantly declining faith and belief that the federal government would or could—well, not could—but, really help. We all thought the federal government could do something if they wanted to, but there clearly was never an effort by them.

ES: To what did you attribute their reluctance to help?

DH: Primarily I would say the attitudes of the local agents and their inability to view the situation objectively, or their unwillingness to want to judge the situation objectively. By and large all our contact with the government was FBI, and as I say, the longer somebody stayed there the less respect they had for the FBI generally, as well as the individual agents.

ES: Were you by any chance in Atlantic City in August, '64?

DH: I wasn't.

ES: What did you think of what happened there?

DH: I don't even remember. I think I was in jail at the time. One of those years I was in jail almost a whole year. The whole year, just sort of—So I couldn't even remember at this point what my thoughts were.

ES: In general, the federal government?

DH: Once again, this, the whole Congressional challenge represented a tremendous split in the staff. That is, the Mississippi staff and the staff in other places, because once again this wasn't communicated and there wasn't adequate dialogue between the entire staff in terms of what they were doing, what the significance of it was. Not only to the staff, but once again, we didn't—that is people in other areas—because we didn't have the information from our staff so we couldn't communicate it to local people. So local people in Alabama knew there was something important and knew there was something everybody was involved in and we should be rooting for, let's say, but in terms of details and in terms of being able to interpret the significance of it, either our interpreting it to somebody else or somebody interpreting to us, it just never happened as far as I'm concerned.

ES: In '64 and '65 winter and spring, there was a big controversy within SNCC over structure. Do you remember that?

DH: I was in Africa.

ES: You were in Africa?

DH: Thank God.

ES: And then you left shortly after that.

DH: When did we go? We went in August of '64 and we came back in December.

ES: John Lewis and you were away all that time?

DH: Well, twelve of us went to Guinea. We were in Guinea a month and then everybody else came back the first of October and John and I stayed.

ES: Did SNCC pay for that?

DH: Partially. Harry Belafonte raised some of the money and the Guinea government paid for part of it.

ES: How come you went? How was that tied up with what else you were doing?

DH: SNCC had had some contact prior to that with a delegation of African officials traveling around the U.S., and we had met them and so forth in Atlanta. Harry Belafonte was doing a show or gathering material for his own performances in Guinea, had met President Sekou Toure a couple times or something like that. They were talking about the civil rights movements. President Toure said it would be a good thing if we had some representatives from the civil rights movement here to talk to La Jeunesse, the youth movement in Guinea. So out of these discussions Harry suggested that some people from SNCC go over and meet, talk, learn and rest. So I think all the project directors went, as well as Forman and John.

ES: You don't remember any of the controversy after you got back in December?

DH: No, because I didn't attend any of those meetings.

ES: Did other people from the Southwest Georgia area attend them?

DH: I'm sure they did. What it was all about I really couldn't tell you. The question of who made decisions and how always was difficult for SNCC. Who makes decisions; how they're made; this kind of thing. I think staff members were feeling that although it was supposed to be an organization with no formal heads or figurehead, this wasn't in fact happening, and that the staff should be represented more. Prior to the time we left, I guess, we had formed a council or an executive committee or something like that and there were two people from Southwest Georgia on that. Three or four, five from Mississippi. Two from Arkansas. Two from Alabama. And transacted business in this way. Essentially it didn't do the job that was necessary. Well, the significant decisions probably were made on the local project level anyway, and never made when —

ES: You never felt that decisions were being imposed on you from Atlanta?

DH: No, I didn't feel that way. I don't think, to tell you the truth, that too many people felt that way. There was a general overriding feeling that some people generally got their way or the idea that they propounded generally got approved by one means or another. But I don't think it was actually imposed as such. There was some feeling, however, in the local project in Southwest Georgia that ideas were imposed and I never found this out until...

ES: By the local leadership?

DH: No, by the local staff. That ideas were being imposed—and this was in regard to C. B. King running for Congress in Southwest Georgia. I was project director at the time and I met with C. B. and local community people and we talked about it. I guess maybe fifteen of us from Albany decided that we were going to run C. B., and I thought it was a good idea and more or less said, "SNCC in Southwest Georgia will back him and support him a hundred percent." I'm sure I've forgotten how I presented it to the staff, but apparently—and this came out long after the campaign and the election was over—that a lot of people didn't go along with this. Not a lot, but some people in the staff didn't go along with this and they had some real disagreements in terms of wanting to work on the campaign and opinions as to whether we should be working on the campaign.

ES: They felt that they would have chosen another candidate?

DH: Well, I don't think it was in terms of another candidate. I just don't think they wanted to work on —

ES: What was their reason?

DH: Their reason probably was C. B. personally. Their own personal impression, attitudes toward and about C. B. I don't think, in fact I'm quite sure they could have come up with another candidate in place of C. B. I think what it amounted to was supporting C. B. to the extent that we did which was —

ES: They weren't opposed to the idea of running a candidate?

DH: No. No. No, they were opposed to C. B. as the candidate. They were opposed probably, or my impression is, to the amount of time that we gave to his campaign which may have been seventy-five, eighty percent of our time during that period. This never came out in terms of the work we did. It came out in terms of a discussion months after the campaign.

ES: Why did you leave SNCC? Was it for personal reasons?

DH: Well, I left I guess because I was tired, and I had evolved to the point where I felt it was a waste of time to be running candidates at that time in Albany and Americus, possibly in other counties. But we were running local people for city councilmen, sheriff or whatever, and they were getting crucified. I just didn't have the energy to put up with it anymore. I thought it was a waste of time. There was a local election in Albany and somebody was running for city council and maybe people got anxious about it and they went out and had posters and whatever, and I just sort of sat around and just couldn't get interested. The day of the election I just couldn't take anybody down. So it was time for me to go.

ES: When was this? When you went into jail?

DH: Yes. In the summer of '63 five of us were arrested in Americus. We were in jail for about a hundred days, ninety days. When we came out of jail basically because of our own mistakes we hadn't developed the kind of organization that we should have, or we didn't provide the back-up that we should have and the people in Atlanta fooled around. This is a time when we clearly didn't get the support we needed. Here was probably *the* significant issue to work with in Southwest Georgia, perhaps in the country at that time, and nobody touched it.

ES: What was? What was the issue?

DH: The fact that you had five people in jail under a death penalty for a hundred days and nothing was ever developed around it. You had a tremendous community organization in Americus, but nobody from the other projects or Atlanta came in to provide any assistance, direction or significant support.

ES: Why didn't they?

DH: For 150 reasons, none of which are important. This was Mississippi Freedom summer. It was March on Washington. So it was any thousand number of things. Most important, it was an organization that had grown insensitive to—it was an organization whose central administration could not administer a hundred or forty or twenty different places at the same time adequately.

ES: Already by that summer of '63 they were that over-extended?

DH: There were too many people in the field versus too few people in Atlanta operating too inefficiently to adequately deal with everything we were doing. Americus is a shitty, terrible little town out in the middle of the country. Three, four, five thousand people. It's more than that, of course, but certainly they were in need of some support, if just moral support. As I said, just prior to going in jail was probably the most important or one of the most important parts of my involvement in Southwest Georgia because we didn't have money, we didn't have anything, but we developed this, literally, a machine in Americus. What we didn't do is provide notes or some sort of documented material on what had gone on on a daily basis, who key people were, this kind of thing, so somebody coming in could sit down for two or three hours and be able to move with some efficiency. For instance, this first form that we filled out I told you about that was being filled out in '61, this wasn't done in Americus because we went into Americus in February '63. Okay, there was a prime need for it right then. There was a prime need for almost a log on what had happened from February to August, whenever we got arrested. It was very interesting.

The leaders of the movement fell into three segments. One was a very, very old deacon of the church. That's how he was known, as a matter of fact, as Deacon Evans. He lives way out in the country, not in the city of Americus. Now, he was president of the Sumter County movement. He was too old to go to jail, too old to really significantly involve and influence people and was more, not even the titular head because he didn't have the respect of the people in Americus. There was always some difficulty in bringing the people from the country together with the people in what was called the city. The reason for this was that the first people who were active in Sumter County were the rural people and this guy in particular, Deacon Evans. The mass meetings were formerly held out in the rural areas because no churches, nothing in Americus itself would give us a place to meet. But eventually, as the movement gained momentum, we moved into Americus, cutting off a certain number of people in the rural areas. Deacon Evans, who had been the head of it in the rural, came into the city but was not very well known, not respected certainly, and this caused somewhat of a problem.

Another faction was the students. Obviously the activists, the people who did things, took the chances, took the risks, the people we were most closely involved with. All high school students, junior high school students, elementary students, for that matter.

The third faction was once again a professional or middle class such as you had in Albany, but was represented by one family which has been running a funeral home in Americus for fifty years. They acquired a great deal of wealth and they provided the financial backing for the movement. So you had these three forces sort of pulling against each other and when we were arrested in August we had just the embryo of a solid coalition of these three factors. We hadn't built it up to the point where it could survive alone, but at the same time we hadn't provided or given ourselves the insurance of including, let's say, a worker from Albany or a worker from some other area who could just sort of step right in there and take over. This was our mistake, primarily my mistake. A hundred days later it was just lost to a great degree. The county people after that were just almost totally out of the movement. The community participation was lost to the extent that it had been and you had the students and the Barnums really.

ES: This funeral family?

DH: Yes.

ES: Who was arrested with you?

DH: John Perdew.

ES: Oh, and Ralph Allen?

DH: Yes.

ES: After that it never really picked up.

DH: Well, it picked up but certainly not . . . It picked up again the summer of '65. SCLC came and then they had a tremendous demonstration. I think that was the first time in the history of the movement that a white had been shot and killed.

ES: [Jonathan] Daniels?

DH: No, no, no. I don't even know the white guy's name but a white guy was shot and killed, local Americus guy.

ES: Yes, that was in Alabama.

DH: No, no, this was Americus.

ES: Right, but the Daniels thing was in Alabama.

DH: Yes, yes, had been shot and killed by local Negroes.

ES: Oh.

DH: And they had massive demonstrations but nothing ever happened. By that time I was in New York. I was also in the hospital.

ES: This white guy who was shot by local Negroes, was this a political thing?

DH: There was a demonstration going on and he shot into a car or something like that and there were whites riding through the Negro community shooting and so forth. He shot and the Negro shot back. He got killed and the two guys got convicted of murder. C. B. defended them but they still got convicted.

ES: Were they executed?

DH: No, life. Substantial sentences, whatever.

* * * *

ES: Were there many whites in the Albany movement?

DH: Yes. This was a significant difference in how the two original SNCC projects developed—not factions, groups. The first group that went to McComb and the other going to Southwest Georgia. Sherrod always and still firmly believes in integration as perhaps the important goal of the movement.

He brought whites to work in the Deep South and in integrated teams. He was the first one to do this in SNCC. This was the summer of '62. The project was always significantly integrated, meaning perhaps fifty/fifty. Sherrod left maybe the middle of '63 and until he came back down there this year, there were few whites. I only counted one or two whites on the staff while I was there.

ES: So since mid-'63 the number of whites just kind of went down?

DH: Where it has increased in every other project. The Mississippi Summer Projects, Arkansas. Well, it increased and then it, of course, maybe '64, beginning of '65 they started cutting back again until whatever it is now.

ES: What effect did this have, when Sherrod left and the whites left, also?

DH: Well, they didn't leave with Sherrod. They sort of —

ES: Drifted out after him.

DH: They drifted out and we just didn't take any others in. I think the effect was no great effect in terms of our own work. We did the work. It's around that time, too, we began increasing the number of new counties we were going into. It made it immeasurably easier. I don't think it seriously hampered the operation. We may have lost some publicity in the long run. It may have lost us some of the technical and skilled kind of things that happened in Mississippi that didn't happen elsewhere, i.e., development of credit unions, cooperatives, although this was done in Southwest Georgia. There was a domestic workers' union in Americus long before there was in any other place in SNCC. At one time they were talking about setting up a radio station in Mississippi and then they had all these radios in the cars. You know, these kinds of things where they got a student from MIT down to actually set up the radios, or they got a white student from some place else to set up the *Southern Courier*, maybe, from Harvard. You know, these kinds of technical things with these kids, and they recruited kids for these exact purposes. Now, this was never the way it was gone about in Southwest Georgia. We just said, "We want white students to come down and work on voter registration in a black community, work on demonstrations in Cuthbert or whatever." It wasn't for the specific kind of task that ultimately they worked out in Mississippi, which I also think was a significant mistake on our part.

ES: What was?

DH: Not getting specialists in a sense, people down to do specific kinds of things, to set up. Maybe some guy at Harvard is particularly skilled in setting up a union or doing research on this. John Perdew, for instance, who's white, his forte is research and while he was in Southwest Georgia, although he didn't come down to do that specifically, helped out the project a great deal by doing research that he just did personally.

ES: Why did the project in Southwest Georgia stop recruiting whites after Sherrod left?

DH: I became project director after Sherrod left. I differed with him in my view that integration was the ultimate goal. Well, at that point probably I didn't disagree with him on that. I disagreed with him that we should have integrated teams working wherever we worked simply to show that integration could work. I just didn't think it was necessary. It was eminently more dangerous for everybody concerned. It became increasingly difficult to house white students in that local community. People would be much more inclined to house a black student than a white student. It decreased the pressure on them in a local community, whereas they could say that if somebody heard, if X is working at a factory and his boss heard that somebody was living with him that was a SNCC worker and he was black, he could say, "No, no. That's my cousin from Baltimore," or something like that. Whereas, he obviously couldn't say that if it was a white student.

ES: Did you conceive SNCC's ultimate goal as integration at this point?

DH: When I first went down I didn't. Coming from the North, my initial view was probably being able to sit at a lunch counter, a white lunch counter, sit in the front of the bus or whatever. I don't think I came down with a view or even developed a view initially of what SNCC's ultimate goal was. As I stayed, I viewed SNCC's goal, not so much as a lot of people, essentially to put ourselves out of business by registering everybody and forming all these local pockets of power, local community organizations, but one as developing a highly skilled cadre of community and political organizers that could go into almost any area and be skilled enough and be flexible enough to provide some support to either a local community group in terms of ideas, in terms of resources, in terms of basic organizational skills, or to develop this kind of organization and assist it until it could operate on its own.

ES: And the purpose of the community group would be —

DH: To do whatever it wanted to do. See, once again you start getting into the philosophy of the thing. Are you coming in to tell people what they should be thinking or what they should be doing, or are you coming in and assisting them to do whatever they want to do? It seems to me although you can have an overall national or, as it were, general overriding philosophy,

you can leave the actual decision-making and the selection of targets or whatever you in fact are going to do in the local area up to the local people.
ES: Then these people wanted to do voter registration and that was why you went into a voter registration project? Is that a fair statement?
DH: Well, I couldn't say that in terms of Albany because I wasn't there when they first went in. In terms of Americus and Sumter County, once again, the people wanted to become involved in the movement doing essentially whatever the people in Albany or wherever else a movement was going on, doing what they were doing.
ES: The people in Americus just wanted to be part of the movement that was going on in other places?
DH: Right, and they knew voter registration was going on so they wanted to register to vote. I don't think for the most part they articulated that they wanted voter registration as such to get involved—well, the adults did, as a matter of fact—to get involved in elections and the electing of officers who would represent them. The kids, obviously they wanted to get into direct action, demonstrations and the logical step, an almost necessary step to direct action, is some field work, some experience, some idea of what they're doing and why and what kind of influence they're going to make and alternatives. So sort of deal with both ends. Initially we went in there to work on voter registration, but developed ultimately into direct action demonstrating around public accommodations. But it took us six months to build up to the point where we felt that the kids were ready to get into direct action with the kind of responsibility that was going to be necessary in that area. Once again, an extremely hard-core area. Well, I think a great amount of our success was the fact that we had kids, high school, junior high school and some elementary kids. We had a thirteen-year-old girl stay in jail for as long as we did, for a hundred days, and we had kids staying in jail for periods of a month, two months, and some up to three, and some in jail for a month; out for two days; in jail for another month. This kind of thing. Of course, you can't prepare anybody actually for this kind of thing, but you can —
ES: So a great amount of your success was, you started to say.
DH: Was the ability that the community wasn't split even more than it ultimately was by the fact—Albany or Americus had a great portion of its student community in jail, I would say, longer than most of the other areas in the country, longer than, let's say, Birmingham. Most of the kids in Birmingham were in jail a week, two weeks, three weeks at most. The average probably in Americus ranged around a month, a month-and-a-half.

Now, for parents, all those families involved this meant some tremendous sacrifice, especially if they had two, three. Some people had two, three kids in jail at the same time. That was a success and what sustained effort—I was in Americus this fall, in November, and although there wasn't any great organizing going on, there was a local election and there was a Negro up running for city council and there were people out on Sunday morning distributing leaflets. There were people talking in every church about the fact that election day was two days away and their car pools had been arranged, and this kind of thing. Something is happening. There are people working and there's just no kind of outside support now at all.

ES: In general what do you think SNCC has achieved?

DH: That is broad, isn't it? What has it achieved? Oh, God, it's achieved so many things it's impossible. It's given countless communities vehicles, methods, resources of expression of content and discontent. It's given alternative courses of action. It's provided organizers, either outside or developed internal organizers, within those communities. It's certainly brought heretofore nonpolitical segments of the population to be much more politically aware, much more politically active than they had been. It's forced national opinion and national concern—that's not right. Not national concern, but it's forced national opinion with other groups and other activities to pass some meaningful and some not very meaningful legislation. It's probably provided the basis and the forerunner of what is now called the New Left. It's forced a lot of moderates and liberals, white liberals to face issues that they've been dodging before. To a certain extent an international dialogue has been better established with other student groups, with other organizations. Certainly SNCC has had a significant influence on the whole peace movement.

ES: In what way?

DH: Well, by providing people, ideas. By the whole concept of the beloved community, although the beloved community probably is more of a Martin King type of concept. I think once again your activists have come out of SNCC, activists who may have been volunteers in SNCC for a summer or two and have turned up some place in the peace movement. Certainly SNCC influenced significant numbers of young, black and white—well, generally the pervasive kind of influence that Malcolm had on people right across the board in terms of their thinking about what this country is, what their responsibility is to it, what its responsibility is to them, perhaps as a group, as a race, as a segment of society as well as individuals. I'm sure I haven't touched on everything.

ES: What are you doing now?

DH: Well, I work for an educational . . . I was about to add, from the number of guys that were in SNCC from the beginning—not from the beginning but let's say fairly early in the game, '61, '62, early parts of '63—if they've left the formal movement, if they've left an activist role in the movement, certainly if they're in professional or semi-professional kinds of positions now, some of the people have a fair amount of influence in certain kinds of things that they're doing now. Poverty programs, foundations, community development work, education. Also, I think that a national dialogue has been established among students to a greater extent than existed, say, pre-'60. The ability of people in SNCC to travel around the country to speak and to organize on college campuses, to speak at college campuses was very important. Certainly one of the distinctions of this country and that of most other countries is that in just about every other country in the world the whole student population is a strong political voice and segment of the political institutions of that country and in this country it's not. But to a much greater degree than it was, say, in '58.

ES: Yes, I agree.

DH: I'm working with an educational firm in Boston.

ES: I've heard it suggested that that's a sign of strength in the American political system. That the students aren't particularly strong shows that it's stable. Students are strong in places where there is massive support among young unstable elements of the population, especially where students might bring about a coup d'etat, that sort of thing.

DH: Well, it may represent —

ES: It means that we have old established leadership.

DH: Right. Well, it means that the leadership or the institutions in this country are more firmly established, are more firmly entrenched than in most other countries.

ES: Do you think that SNCC in the course of its history has developed a new type of leadership, a new kind of person who's now a leader, new norms for leaders, perhaps?

DH: That is, is a Stokely Carmichael significantly different from a Charles McDew?

ES: Yes, and in what way if so?

DH: No.

ES: He's been in since the beginning, anyway, Stokely Carmichael.

DH: Well, vocal. No, I wouldn't say so. I think that the newer leaders, national leaders that is, are more vocal than were previous leaders. Vocal on things that others may have thought and may have been in-house kinds of ideas and concepts that have now just come out into the open.

ES: Why have they come out into the open?

DH: There was always a fairly strong [black] nationalist element in SNCC. It was sublimated. It was under the covers as such, but it was always there. There was a strong, vocal integrationist segment that isn't there now. The nonviolent and the anti-nonviolent element was certainly always there. This was just never articulated at all. I mean most people in SNCC I think admitted freely that they were nonviolent tactically at that moment for that particular occasion, but by and large I don't think the vast majority of the people in '61 were any more nonviolent than the people now.

ES: You're talking about everybody, not just leaders?

DH: Yes, right. Yes. Let's say proportionately fifty, sixty, seventy percent of the forty people in '62 or '61 were anti-nonviolent and maybe it's up to eighty-five or ninety now. I haven't the slightest idea. I would tend to think it's pretty high, though.

ES: Is there a different type of member now in other respects?

DH: My contact since '65 has been only with —

ES: Say between '61 and '65 then.

DH: Oh, yes, certainly. I think by and large the people that came in pre-'63 were people who came in to devote a year minimum to their active, Southern involvement, let's say. Whereas, subsequent to that you had people coming in for two months or you had people coming into project—hop, so to speak, take a tour of the South. Work in one area for a month, work some place else for a month and then disappear.

ES: That's an interesting point. Pre-'63 means pre beginning of '63?

DH: Yes, right.

ES: Were they more likely to be Northerners in this later period?

DH: Oh, yes. Right.

ES: That would account for their —

DH: I'm sure that the proportion of Northern students who went to Southwest Georgia in the summer of 1962 went up and then increased throughout SNCC by '63. Northern students, white students increased.

ES: How about the educational level of students?

DH: Once again, in '63 we were recruiting college students primarily. Prior to that we were recruiting perhaps drop-outs or young people out of work in local communities where we were working. We were recruiting even nonstudents. Mrs. Hamer, people in Albany who were forty, fifty years old, or elementary school students. There's a set of girls in Albany who I guess their participation started maybe around the eighth grade or something like that and they worked all the way up. Some of them are in college now. Well, I guess they weren't in eighth grade, but they were young and every year they sort of stuck to it.

ES: This change in the nature of the membership, what generalization would you make for that? What effect has it had?

DH: Well, once again, it's the same sort of debilitating affect on the entire organization in that you didn't know people. People didn't know you. There wasn't this camaraderie among people. There was much more reluctance in terms of calling up Joe from Harvard in Alabama and telling him to come over and assist in something in Albany than there would be in calling Hollis Watkins from McComb, Mississippi to come over and assist. Hollis being a real movement person, a local guy, a high school drop-out who returned to school ultimately. There probably would be no respect for Joe Harvard's ability to come in —

ES: Must you pick on Harvard?

DH: Or, Mike MIT, to come over and in fact step into a situation, assess it quickly and be able to either step up in the middle of a mass meeting and move people or say what needs to be said, or suggest something important or get out and lead or assist or whatever in a demonstration. Whereas, as you bring Joe Harvard or Mike MIT over you're going to have to sit him down and go through a whole lot of training program with him and then hope that he may be able to talk to the community. As I said, as more and more white students came in I think there was a growing, not quite nationalism, but anti-white feeling among black workers, and as more came in it sort of increased and they said, "The hell with it. I'll do it myself or it won't get done." This kind of thing. I think also, as college students came in, their concerns were not as single-minded, let's say, as a Southern black student or nonstudent or as a Southerner or perhaps even a Northern Negro, although generally Northern Negroes or blacks were classified pretty close to a white in terms of competence, ability and judgment and so forth.

ES: How about in terms of problems of organizing?

DH: Well, yes. Competence. Well, in terms of dealing with the community and that is, the community's view of him?

ES: Yes, right.

DH: Well, that was almost individual but it generally amounted to his competence because the community was going to view him as he projected himself or herself. But I would say generally the Northern students brought in many more concerns and weren't as narrow and focused in their view of civil rights as the Southern students.

ES: Would you say they were more radical?

DH: More what?

ES: More radical?

DH: No. I wouldn't classify it in terms of radical or moderate or conservative. I would classify them in terms of not only a concern for civil rights, but also peace and also civil liberties and also campus freedoms or intellectual freedom. You know, a broader spectrum of concern rather than whatever way we viewed civil rights, which was fairly narrow.

ES: Do you want to add anything, Don, to my questions?

DH: No.

ES: Is there some area that you still wanted to go in that you think I haven't covered, like the . . . ?

DH: Not terribly. I would say also that the organization's dependency and respect for, and consideration of the ideas of people like Zinn and Ella Baker and other adults, professional advisors as such, decreased significantly over the years. I think, once again, simply because of the size. Ella Baker is a one in ten thousand, one in a hundred thousand kind of person and just a tremendous person in terms of a resource and in terms of bouncing ideas off to assess direction and credibility and so forth. You just don't get to know a person like this and she's not around twenty-four hours a day and as more and more people came in, something like, "Who the hell is this old lady here?" which was one of the saddest kinds of things that I thought happened. Zinn, also. People at SRC, Southern Regional Council in Atlanta, in various other places. In the early days we acted without a complete idea of the consequences or of how we're going to extricate ourselves. Then later on we began, as we tended to get money and tended as an affluent organization, when we had something to lose, started considering: "Well, can we afford to do X, Y and Z?" When we were in a position of having nothing we'd just go out and do it.

ES: The fact that it had money was sort of a moderating sort of thing?

DH: Very much so. Many, many people, both inside and outside of SNCC have said that SNCC, its best organization, its best effort, its most successful periods were when it was flat broke or heavily in debt and, of course, later on, travel, credit cards, all this kind of stuff just got out of hand.

ES: It's broke again, now. Maybe that's a good sign.

DH: I don't know. I think also SNCC never really utilized, sat down and fully utilized everybody's talent as much as it could have. I don't know whether it's doing that now. I would tend to think not. Basically, I think, the organization in '62, everybody was an idea; everybody had ideas; everybody had responsibility; everybody felt they were a significant and important part of the total network. I can remember—well, we had meetings like this all along, but I remember—one of the things that was amazing all the way through was the striving to be honest with ourselves and honest with the situation we were dealing with. You just can't do it as well with 300 people as you can with sixteen or twenty. People tend not to open up with 300 people in the room because you're talking to 280 people that you don't know. I guess that's about it.

ES: Okay. Thank you.

Charles Jones

Q: I think the questions we were talking about before were sort of beating around the bush a little bit. The central question is about SNCC's goals. What do you think are SNCC's goal or goals now?

Jones: I think, as I understand it, I think . . . the goal is to concentrate the resources now available in getting to the black community, the non-middle class, non-affiliated, non-mobile black community a sense of identity, a sense of worth, a sense of self-love which I think is essential for any group of people or any individual before he can proceed to make any kind of constructive life for himself and his family.

Q: Did SNCC have another long-range goal?

Jones: Well, let me say quite candidly that having been out of the decision-making processes of SNCC for the past three years I can't speak with any kind of authority. I would rather not deal so much with where SNCC is now because it would be my own reactions, my own reflections as I view it primarily from discussions with Stokely and people in the movement rather than the press. I think there is a basic difference in what Stokely is saying and what SNCC is saying and what the press reports, the difference being that Stokely was talking in a very logical, very analytical way of the problems of the black community and the white press is responding to their own problems and editorializing and interpreting what Stokely is saying on the basis of what kind of reactions they have to them. So essentially the whole Black Power battle, or lack of battle, the whole Black Power reaction has been primarily the reaction of the white community to the concept and the threat inherent and hasn't been so much the reaction of Negroes or Stokely.

Q: So there isn't a big Black Power dialogue going on in SNCC now?

Jones: Well, I'm sure there is but what I'm saying is the quality of it and the direction of it is somewhat different than what the *New York Times* or the *Washington Post* or other papers that are primarily white opinion-makers, not just the written press but the radio and TV quarter. These are essentially repeating interpretations by these sources, these institutions, of what they hear Stokely saying.

Q: Has SNCC's goal changed over time?

Jones: I don't think their goal has changed. I think the form of presenting the goal has changed.

Q: Could you expound on that?

Jones: Yeah, sure. The things we were thinking about when we first got together in Raleigh were primarily the interests of the black community. Because of our own, maybe lack of political sophistication, or because of the sophistication we had, we chose to present that form as an extension of the tradition of the civil rights movement but we never called it civil rights, that being the coalition of white, middle-class, labor, Jewish interests toward developing a concept of democracy and the cause of brotherhood which was essentially conceived by and developed by white middle-class people.

Q: Does that imply that SNCC all along was really concerned about non-middle-class Negroes, but was making it look another way?

Jones: No, it implies that SNCC has been saying pretty much the same thing it always has been saying but the way it's been understood has been different lately. The concern of SNCC as I understand it has been for the mass of the Negroes. The mass of the Negroes are not middle class so as that interest manifests itself consistently throughout this whole dialogue of the last four or five years, the understanding of it has changed, although the scope and the concern of SNCC has been pretty consistent.

Q: Within SNCC did people in the very early days, 1961, think in terms of the masses of Negroes?

Jones: Of course. That's why we went into Mississippi and Georgia and worked on organizing the total community, bringing in and developing leadership from all segments but primarily the poor segment because that's always the position that SNCC has been concerned about, the mass of the black people in itself definitively is a statement that SNCC is primarily concerned about poor people, because most Negroes are poor. That percentage which are mobile and middle class, of course, are effected by their concern but we always manifested that interest in all of the organization we ever did, to my knowledge.

Q: How about SNCC's methods? Do you think there have been changes over time and could you discuss that?

Jones: Well, when you say SNCC I assume you are talking about the effort of the organized group after the spring of 1960, which does not necessarily encompass the sit-ins as such in terms of the first wave of them, but resulted after the first conference in Raleigh in April and then the development of a staff in the summer of '61. Now in response to your question about methods, after we organized the staff the methods were pretty consistent. That is, we would go into a community and attempt to organize and did organize the complete community, that is Negro community and where possible white support.

Q: So you don't think there have been any big changes in SNCC's methods since, say, the summer of 1961?

Jones: Only in degree. That is, the resources that we developed to enable that approach to be more effective through the central office, the research department, the fund-raising in the North, etc., is separate from the actual community organization, were simply added dimensions to support the basic approach of attempting to involve the total black community.

Q: How about SNCC's policy about nonviolence? Was that sort of a changing method? Could you discuss how that occurred? When were the big turning points for that?

Jones: I'm not sure I understand what you mean.

Q: In other words, before SNCC had a consistent policy of nonviolence and now it has a somewhat less consistent policy of nonviolence and the whites at least seem to interpret this as some kind of a major shift in methods.

Jones: Well, I think that's the problem of the whites. I don't think SNCC has any problem with nonviolence or has ever had any problem with nonviolence. What we said initially about, and that was a large and long dialogue within SNCC from the first time we got together, about nonviolence as a way of life or nonviolence as a tactic and there were those who pursued it as a way of life and those who pursued it as a tactic. But in terms of action there was always a commitment to nonviolence. We never went beyond the action phases of discussion of nonviolence. We never said, for instance, that once you were not engaged in an organized demonstration that you should not protect yourself. In the last two or three years this has come out more that it has been said and several people have taken the position that people should protect themselves.

Q: You said self-defense was always accepted except during organized demonstrations?

Jones: Well, I'm saying that we never discussed it in any public context except those who were purists in the sense of nonviolence as a way of life.

But there was never any discussion about what happened outside of a demonstration.

Q: So people were essentially left to follow what they thought was the best idea?

Jones: Of course. I might point out that I think the recent discussion about self-defense, to me represented a healthy next step in the process of growth of a concept of nonviolence.

Q: Why do you say that?

Jones: Well, I say that because I believe that the expression of one's integrity in the context of a choice between preserving his own life or eliminating someone who would, in the absense of any aggressive action, any defensive detaining action, destroy him is healthy. I never went so far in my own pilgrimage into nonviolence as to feel that to allow a nut to kill you was healthy. As a matter of fact, that seems to me to be an expression of something less than mental health. Because if you think you are important as a person, then to preserve that when there's a clear choice, a very clear choice, an unescapable choice of yourself being destroyed or someone else, I would have at that point no problem in preserving myself, absolutely not. I think I'm much more important than a psychotic Klansman. They are, as far as I'm concerned, a lot of psychotic middle-class bigots. Assuming that the choice is clear and it's unescapable that it's going to be your life or that person's life.

Q: Let's get on to some more specific things about the history of SNCC.

Jones: Yeah.

Q: After the Highlander Folk School conference you were put in charge of the voter registration section. Could you describe the events leading up to that conference?

Jones: I'd been in touch with Tim Jenkins for some time back as far as '56, '57 in NSA and during the initial stages of the sit-ins and demonstrations, and through that whole spring and summer Tim and I had been talking and into the next year. One of the things we wanted to do was to bring together some of the guys that emerged as strong leaders as a result of the sit-in. So Tim, in the summer of '61, it was around June or early July, arranged a conference or a discussion here in Washington with Belafonte and recruited several people into Washington for that purpose. Charles Sherrod, Diane Nash or now Diane Bevel, Lonnie King, Chuck McDew.

Q: Who was that after Diane Nash?

Jones: Lonnie King and Chuck McDew. And as a result of three days of discussion we decided that voter registration was the most important issue to be dealt with.

Q: Diane Nash was there?

Jones: Yes.

Q: She agreed?

Jones: No. We discussed with Harry at that point the necessity of having some money to proceed to determine how many guys were ready to take full time at working at this. And Tim wrote up a proposal that involved about $3,000 and Harry promised to get some money.

Q: This was sometime in the spring of '61?

Jones: No. This was the beginning of the summer, late June. Then we went back to where we had been. I was out at the University of Illinois. I was there for some kind of seminar. And in the meantime Tim had set up a conference, a seminar funded by the Field Foundation in Nashville of again the key leadership that emerged from the sit-in in Nashville and directed by Harlan Randolph. I guess there were about twenty some of us there, including all the names of the people I've given you.

Q: What was the purpose of this conference?

Jones: To evaluate the existing problems, to determine what were the issues, to determine how to communicate those issues and how to organize around those issues.

Q: Do you know James Laue?

Jones: James Laue? I'm sure I do but . . .

Q: Yeah. He also wrote a Ph.D. thesis on SNCC and he seems to think the purpose of that conference was to train something like almost a core of professional revolutionaries. Was there anything of that in it, a core of professional leaders rather than the somewhat amateurish leadership that had gone on before?

Jones: Yeah. I suppose that's his words. I've given you my estimation of it.

Q: That was in August or July?

Jones: No. I don't recall exactly whether the conference you ask about was just prior to or during, I think it was June. Diane had a lot of problems understanding how voter registration was direct action in a tradition of *satyagraha* and she had some logic which went something like this: "voter registration involves politics; politics is dirty; therefore voter registration is dirty and immoral. Nonviolence is truth and good; therefore to attempt to mix voter registration and nonviolence is immoral."

Q: She seems to have gotten over that.

Jones: Yeah, well see, what happened then was that Diane proceeded to organize a group of people who believed in pure nonviolence. This group had essentially come out of the "nonviolence as a way of life" and she didn't understand voter registration to be that, so she wanted the whole thrust of SNCC's staff to be *satyagraha* she called it. And we wanted, we meaning myself, Charles Sherrod, Chuck McDew, Stokely, Dion [Diamond]. . .

Q: Oh, Charles Sherrod was in your group?

Jones: Yeah.

Q: Did you mention Stokely?

Jones: Yeah. Dion, Tim Jenkins. As a result, primarily, of that three-day analytical discussion in Washington, in which we went through the whole problem and decided on voter registration and were insisting that voter registration be the main thrust of SNCC.

Q: You haven't mentioned Bobby Kennedy's Justice Department officials. Were they involved too? I think Zinn does mention them.

Jones: Yeah well, that's another aspect of this thing going on concurrently with, well, following the discussion with Harry and developing concurrently with the seminar in Nashville. Tim, Chuck, Sherrod and myself after the Belafonte session continued to work together. Tim and I had incidentally been . . .

Q: Was Sherrod there too in Belafonte's office?

Jones: Yes. I'm trying to get this timing straight. It was either prior to the Belafonte thing or it must have been right afterward. Tim and I went to a conference down in Virginia being sponsored by the Phelps Stokes Fund. It's a retreat and there were present representatives from the Justice Department, several foundations, several Negro college presidents. And Tim and I proceeded to develop the program of a group of students working full time going into the South. And this involved necessarily then what role the Justice Department would play pursuant to the Civil Rights Act of '60.

Q: SNCC before this didn't have a staff, a full time staff?

Jones: They had one guy who was working after or between the . . .

Q: Ed King?

Jones: Ed King. Between the Raleigh conference and that meeting up in Tennessee. And the discussion concerning the role of the Justice Department was essentially going into the South for the first time in this context would require the protection of the persons by the federal government. So our discussion with Justice was in relation to procedures of implementing the protections made possible by the voter registration Civil Rights Act of '60, principally the section which protected voters, potential voters, those registering and those assisting them to register from any harassment, threats, intimidation, violence, etc. We continued those discussions. We also from that meeting set up a meeting of foundations and other people. I have some hesitancy at this time of going into some of the details because a lot of this is confidential.

Q: These were what—Taconic Foundation, the Field Foundation, the Phelps Stokes Foundation—where there any others?

Jones: New World. And as I recall we were discussing the Rockefeller Foundation. And again the issue here was . . .

Q: The reason I ask about the involvement of the Justice people was that I had the vague impression that one of the reasons that Diane Nash and her group were so opposed to the voter registration idea was that they were suspicious of the involvement of the federal government.

Jones: Yeah, but that follows the logic that I outlined to you earlier.

Q: She was opposed to the federal government?

Jones: She was opposed to anything that had to do with politics because politics was immoral and nonviolence was moral and that was her logic, quite succinctly and explicitly.

Q: Who else agreed with her?

Jones: Well, Diane proceeded then during the course of the summer after the Belafonte meeting here to contact people in support of her position and those people were, as I remember them now, Bevel, the Right Reverend James Bevel, Marion Barry, Brooks—John Brooks I think it was, Jim Forman.

Q: Forman?

Jones: Forman.

Q: Wait a second. She contacted him because she thought he was with her position?

Jones: Matter of fact he was.

Q: Someone else told me this but I just thought she picked him because she was bringing somebody from outside who could be executive secretary.

Jones: Diane was never objective. She contacted Jim because Jim wanted to come down and she had been talking to Jim in Chicago and he was coming down as a part of her staff, and I will get into more specifically how this worked in a minute. Again, all this is so you can develop the chronology of that summer because all of those things were essentially in how the staff operation got under way. The meetings with the foundations and other people were to develop the idea of voter registration, Justice [Department] in terms of the Civil Rights Act, with the foundations in terms of a research program known as the Voter Education Project. There were several meetings in '60 with Tim, Chuck, Sherrod.

Q: That's connected with the founding of COFO?

Jones: Yeah, but not with the founding of COFO as such. COFO followed from the founding of VEP. I'll explain how that happened. Now we then all converged on Nashville for the seminar. All these things had gone on prior to that.

Q: Diane started contacting people before?

Jones: We had gotten Tim. Well, Tim and I had been working in NSA since '56. In '60, the summer of '60, we were working together and got Tim elected National Affairs Vice Chairman of NSA. I was kind of acting as campaign manager, coordinator or campaign manager. And one day in Philadelphia Dion Diamond came into Tim's office and we talked to him about the program. He wanted to come in. Now other things going on prior to that were the Freedom Rides.

Q: What was Dion Diamond's view?

Jones: Yeah. I'm just saying that's how the contact with Dion came in. Dion came down and became part of the voter registration thing. Let me digress for a second and . . .

Q: To the Freedom Rides?

Jones: Yeah, we'll go back even further than that. After the summer conference of '60 we developed an executive committee of SNCC. Chuck was made chairman and there were representatives from each state.

Q: Chuck McDew?

Jones: Chuck McDew. After the conference in '60 in Atlanta, Chuck was made chairman. And on the executive committee were several people, principally, but not exclusively, Diane, Sherrod, of course Chuck, Smith, Ruby Doris, myself and other people, I don't recall everybody. Of course, Ella was advisor and incidentally has always been a very strong, very powerful person in SNCC, essentially because we all respected her very much and loved her very much.

Q: I was very impressed with her when I met her.

Jones: Now, during the fall that year we met in executive committee once a month or something like that. And in the January meeting of '61 a group of guys in Rock Hill, South Carolina along with Tom Gaither, who was working with CORE, had been arrested. They were from Friendship College, had been arrested for sitting-in at a lunch counter and they chose to take the thirty days rather than pay bond which was a current issue in SNCC at that point, jail versus bail, and was Diane's thing.

Q: She favored jail.

Jones: She favored jail. So in that discussion it became very clear that we had a very clear decision to make about jail versus bail. And I remember Sherrod saying, "okay, it's very clear to me what we've got to do." And I said, "yeah, I'm ready to go to Rock Hill." And Sherrod said, "well, I'm ready." So we both looked over at Diane and she fumbled around and finally said, "well, I guess I'm ready too." And then Ruby Doris wanted to go.

Q: You were in Atlanta then?

Jones: Yeah. So we decided to go to Rock Hill and join the people in jail. So Sherrod, Charles Sherrod, myself, Diane and Ruby Doris went to Rock Hill and we got arrested. We went to trial the next day and were found guilty of trespassing and we were sentenced to thirty days and we went to York County chain gang, York County prison camp. The girls went too but they were separated and we were working with John and the other guys and we were there for thirty days. Now that's important in that it explained some of the background of the relationship between us and Diane and the executive committee function of SNCC.

Q: You all spent thirty days in jail?

Jones: Yeah. On the chain gang in Rock Hill. The personal relationships and the way the organization was functioning at that point we were trying to coordinate the efforts of students all over the South. Now we came out and I went back to school and everybody went back to school.

Q: Could you spell out what you meant about the history of your relationship with Diane, why you told that story.

Jones: Yeah, because it's important to understand the interrelationships between these people going back to at least the summer of '60 which will also shed some light on the decision that was made in '61, the summer of '61 in Nashville about the direction of the program.

Jones: Now after the chain gang experience which is in itself another experience I don't want to get into now, we went back to school.

Q: You went to school in Atlanta?

Jones: No. I was in school at Johnson C. Smith University in Charlotte, North Carolina. In the school of divinity. My local board tried to get me into the service at that time, claiming I wasn't in school and I was on the chain gang. And the president of the college and the board of directors . .

Q: They put you in jail, then they tried to draft you because you were in jail?

Jones: Yeah. And the president of the college and the board of directors took on the local board. The school took on the local selective service board and said that I was in school, that I was accepted back full time, that they reserved the right to determine who was a student in good standing and requested that the local board tend to its business. Well of course I can go on with that, but anyway in late spring, I guess it was in May, CORE in New York was talking about the Freedom Rides. And a group came to Charlotte, that was Jim Peck, James Farmer, John Moody is another name, another guy.

Q: These are all CORE people?

Jones: Yeah. Definitely. John Moody had been active with the group here that Stokely had been working with, and developed in Washington, somewhere. Moody was with Stokely . . . Anyway, they came through Charlotte and so we met them at the bus station. We had a planning discussion that night and some of them stayed at the house and caught the bus the next day. I was very much concerned about the group because I knew what they were getting into and some of them knew what they were getting into and some of them didn't. Anyway we followed them on down and then they ran into Birmingham, Alabama and then boom, all hell broke loose. I was going into finals. Oh, I had to write about twenty papers that semester because I had to make up some stuff because I had been out for thirty days and we had to make it all up, we had to comply with the requirements of divinity school at Johnson C. Smith University. Diane called me one night after the people had gotten beaten up in Birmingham and said, "what do you think about following up the Freedom Rides?" And she called me as SNCC executive committee, and I said "fine, we have to, there's no question about it." We had not been as successful in the Rock Hill thing in bringing together all of the students in the South. There had not been any one thing that had brought students out of their local sit-in movement activity into a joint action kind of program other than the executive committee of SNCC, and that one of the things that we were trying to do with the Rock Hill situation was provide that focal point for organized, cooperative action. And it was successful in that a couple of busloads came in from Nashville, but not totally. So this then provided the handle for bringing together as many students as possible throughout the South. So I said, "of course we have to follow it up." And then I called Chuck McDew and I called Sherrod and she called several other people. And I finished my exams at 12:00 one day and I was on the bus at 1:00 the same day going with another guy, I'll think of his name in a minute, from the school of divinity who was from Birmingham, going to Atlanta, going to join the Freedom Rides in Montgomery. Diane and another group had gone in just prior to that and joined the group in Birmingham, or around Birmingham, and they were in Montgomery. Clyde, Clyde Carter was the guy that went down with me from Smith. Clyde and I got to Atlanta, we went out to the airport for some reason, I don't recall why. Oh, we were going to fly in so we could join the first group from Montgomery into Mississippi. We ran into, at the airport, John David Maguire, Bill [William Sloane] Coffin. Bill was the chaplain at Yale. John Maguire was from Wesleyan. George Bundy.

Q: Not *the* George Bundy?

Jones: No. There's another George Bundy, a law student at Yale. These were white professors, ministers, teachers, Negro law students. So we decided rather than fly down, we would start the second wave from Atlanta. So we spent the night in Atlanta and the next morning proceeded by Greyhound, or was it Trailways, from Atlanta on the bus. We got to Montgomery and the crowd was very large and hostile. We got there about 1:00. The first group had left going to Mississippi at about 7:00 or 8:00. And we spent the night, there were numerous discussions and Bill Coffin was working with the Peace Corps at that point. And they were friends of George Bundy and I got to know their confidants, some of their confidants. They were on the phone with Bobby Kennedy . . .

Q: What do you think was the significance for the Freedom Rides?

Jones: Well, I was explaining that. Anyway we decided to go down. The next day we went down. All of us got arrested at the bus station in Montgomery and that included Ralph Abernathy, Fred Shuttlesworth, Wyatt Walker, myself, Clyde Carter, George Bundy and John Maguire and Bill Coffin, the whole group with the exception of Martin. We stayed in four or five days. Anyway, that case was appealed. Anyway it was finally resolved by the Supreme Court, which is another thing. We all met at the Supreme Court for the hearing of the case and sat in the judge's chambers, not the bench but in the chambers that were reserved for the judges and guests. But we had acted and, of course, the Freedom Rides continued to send waves in and that, of course, was Stokely and quite a few people. Dion had gone in on that and Sherrod had been on that first wave and they got to Jackson and organized a lot of people. All right. That had essentially accomplished the bringing together of students from all over the South, and North too, but primarily the South in a project. It was coordinated and it was Southernwide rather than local cities. It also brought together these same people that we've been talking about since we started. Okay, now we all met back at Nashville, Tennessee. Incidentally, Reggie Robinson had gone down to McComb—well, that's another thing I'll talk about in a minute. We're all now back in Nashville and then the Highlander meeting was coming up. Now, one other important thing. Chuck, Tim, Sherrod, Chuck McDew, Tim Jenkins and Charles Sherrod and myself, Dion and Stokely had been talking during, I think, the first week, this conference was after the first week of summer, about the whole thing. No one had been in touch with Harry since Washington. Well, they'd been in touch but no one had followed through since Washington. No one wanted to take the responsibility. So I then proceeded to call Harry in Lake Tahoe and say, "where is the bread that you were supposed to get?" And he said, "let me call Martin and you call Martin and call Martin up in Martha's Vineyard."

Q: He was going to get the money from King?

Jones: Martin was involved. So I got to Martin. Martin said call Wyatt Walker, call Wyatt. It seems that Harry had gotten some money from somewhere to SCLC for voter registration for pretty much the same thing we've been talking about. Same $3,000. And he told Martin to give up that money. Well anyway, we got back to Martin and Martin called Wyatt and Harry called Wyatt. So Wyatt sent me in Nashville a check for $1,000 which I then deposited in a bank in Nashville and necessarily then became the focal point for everything that took place from that point until we turned the money over to the group much later. So I had the money and we then began to solidify very quickly. And then it was a matter of where the money was going to go. Who was going to have it, whether it was going to be the voter registration staff or the nonviolent *satyagraha*.

Q: Well, the money was raised for the voter registration, wasn't it?

Jones: Not this particular effort as such.

Q: What happened to the other $2,000?

Jones: Well, we got it at a different point. I guess for my own ego purposes it's important to point out that nobody wanted to take the responsibility of calling Harry or take the responsibility of handling the money, so I did. So we then all gathered at Highlander Folk School. I had been delegated within the group the responsibility of carrying the voter registration at the conference. I developed a program for effective . . .

Q: How come this was done through King?

Jones: Martin?

Q: Yeah.

Jones: Well, it wasn't done through King, it was done through some money that Harry raised.

Q: No. How come the money that Belafonte raised was given . . . ?

Jones: No, this was much prior to our first discussion with Harry that the money went down there.

Q: I see. Right after the Freedom Rides. Then you had been getting money from Belafonte?

Jones: No. We didn't get any money from Harry at all. There was no money involved up to that time of the call to Harry in Lake Tahoe. Except Harry, well somebody had paid for the flight.

Q: Before the Washington meeting Belafonte had already raised this $3,000 for you.

Jones: Not for us, no. For voter registration. And it had gone then to SCLC.

Q: And then after that you had the Washington conference and he agreed to raise more money.

Jones: He agreed to raise some money.

Q: Some unspecified sum.

Jones: See, we were not working with SCLC. It was two different functions at that point.

Q: I was just wondering why it did happen that way.

Jones: Because the money wasn't being used, first of all, by SCLC. I mean it was just sitting there. They didn't have a program.

Q: It seems odd for one organization to give money to another.

Jones: Well. I won't go into it but you have to understand the nature of Harry's relationship with Martin and SCLC. It was money that Harry had raised and it was earmarked for voter registration and Harry said that the money should go to SNCC and told Martin to tell Wyatt that the money should go, well, to us.

Q: Well, then later on you said it was a question at SNCC, a matter of debate where the money would go.

Jones: Well, yeah, what I mean is, it was earmarked to us for the use of determining whether or not, as a matter of fact, we could establish a staff, a group of guys. About two pages back you'll see that right after the conference in Washington, when we presented Harry with the necessity of having money, the money was to be used to do research and contact the guys to see whether sufficient people were ready.

Q: That was the Washington meeting.

Jones: That's right.

Q: But this money was before the Washington meeting.

Jones: Yeah, but it doesn't make any difference about where the money came from. The fact was that Harry had made the commitment and it was then that I called him in Tahoe that we were asking where the money was and he proceeded to get the money. It's not important where the money came from.

Q: It seems funny to me that he raised the money for purposes of developing a SNCC staff.

Jones: No, he didn't.

Q: He raised it for voter registration?

Jones: You see, this is prior to. When he got the money, money probably gotten back in early spring and there was no such thing at that point as a SNCC staff working full time. And the money had gotten transmitted to Atlanta, and was in the bank in Atlanta. Now subsequent to that, completely unrelated to that as such, we got together with Harry and the whole thing we've been talking about developed. So when I called Harry . . .

Q: Didn't SCLC think that Belafonte was kind of an Indian giver?

Jones: I'm sure that's true, but that wasn't our problem.

Q: Okay. He had given it to them to be used for voter registration.

Jones: They had raised it.

Q: They raised it?

Jones: They had gone to him. He got this money. It was earmarked for voter registration. Well of course there were some problems in Atlanta and that's why we went to Harry and to Martin. But that's something else.

Q: What happened was when he raised the money he thought it was for voter registration and then he changed his mind and decided it would be to develop a SNCC staff?

Jones: But they aren't inconsistent. They were the same thing, because when we agreed in Washington we were agreeing that we would be working on voter registration. That was the only purpose that we left Washington with an agreement with Harry, ourselves and Harry. So the money went for voter registration.

Q: The only question is why there was a debate in SNCC afterwards on where the money would go.

Jones: Then you understand Diane Nash's role in the whole thing. Diane wouldn't go along with the consensus that the rest of us had reached. She wanted the money to be used for nonviolence, *satyagraha*, which brings us right down to the succinct issues at Highlander Folk School. And everybody was there except Forman. Everybody was there including Ed King who was with Diane because we, well, a lot of reasons, no need to go into them. And we had a very intensive debate that everybody participated in. I presented the voter registration program and Diane presented the nonviolence *satyagraha* program and we got down to a vote on what the emphasis of SNCC would be. And Ella was very key on this too. She was trying to keep us all together and she did, and again, it was a fact of our respect for her though we would have gone against Ella if Ella had taken the position that the money should go for direct action.

Q: Okay, you were in the Highlander Folk School and Ella Baker was holding the group together.

Jones: Well, see, we'd been trying and trying and trying and trying with Diane to get her to come in and she kept insisting not to, so we had the votes to carry the thing but there was concern on all of our parts that we have everybody with us, though we had gotten to the point where that was absolutely not necessary. We were going to go.

Q: Diane did threaten at that point to break away from SNCC? Was there a serious danger of that, of SNCC splitting?

Jones: I thought there would have been. But then there was a matter of who would have been with her and the resources and her definition of why she was out there, going back to the premise I told you earlier about voter registration being politics and politics being immoral, therefore voter registration being immoral.

Q: Did she eventually change her mind? What did happen?

Jones: So we went into the whole thing, discussed quite a while, got quite involved. So we hammered away at a compromise and Ella was there.

Q: She's very modest but I got the impression when talking to her that she had . . .

Jones: And the compromise was that we have two programs in SNCC, voter registration and I would be head of that and direct action and Diane would be head of that. I still had the money. So we went back to Nashville and finished the seminar, which was excellent, incidentally, was exactly for the purposes for which it was designed.

Q: You had speakers?

Jones: Yeah, we had all kinds.

Q: Who spoke there?

Jones: I don't remember. Now Bob Moses had as a result of several things, primarily his working in Mississippi to get people to the 1960 conference, run into Steptoe and several people down there, and he had gone down the beginning of the summer, around the end of the summer of '61.

Q: Which '60 conference did he work to get people for?

Jones: SNCC. The only big conference in 1960, the summer of '60. He went back and went down to McComb, Mississippi and was working there the summer of '61. He'd been there through all of this stuff. And meantime several people had gone down with him. Reggie Robinson was one, a guy named Travis Britt was another. I called Bob and told him we had some money. And he was then part of the voter registration program. And we started sending him some money which was the best thing since popcorn. We pulled Bob out of there. Well, we did several things. One, we left Nashville. We all congregated in New York City at the Atlantic Hilton or the Atlantic Sheraton and discussed detailed plans of going into Mississippi. The plan was that we would go to McComb and have a staff meeting, have a meeting in which we would develop the whole specifics of the administration of the program. We'd already begun to talk about it.

Q: Why did you decide on Mississippi?

Jones: Well, because Bob was there and he didn't want to pull out and several other people who were active at that point were in McComb and we wanted to get with him and also we wanted to go out and have a first meeting. So for all of the psychological and physical obvious reasons we wanted to start it right in the hub.

Q: Would you say that choosing to go to Mississippi, go into the very worst area, is connected with SNCC's concern with self-love and dignity for the Negro?

Jones: Yes. See, it was a symbol, Mississippi was a symbol. We had to break that psychological symbol, both in our own minds and the minds of the people in the rest of the South and the country. So Diane was at the meeting in New York and we decided to go away for two weeks, all of us to get ready for the possibility of death, also the possibility of revolution and changes in the South. And we did. We each got a little money, I gave everybody some money and everybody went to different places. Most people went home . . . I went home and we were to meet back in New York in two weeks and then proceed to Mississippi. Diane wanted some money to get her people together and she wanted more, she wanted a heck of a lot of money, but anyway . . .

Q: Did Diane go to Mississippi?

Jones: Yeah, well I gave her some money. She went and did her stuff and got her people together and she came back. We all met in New York. Tim Jenkins, Chuck McDew, Charles Sherrod, Diane and myself. And I had an old car, a Pontiac '55. And we proceeded to drive from New York to Mississippi. Stopped in my home, stopped in Sherrod's home. Diane was very sick at one point. We got her to a doctor.

Q: Did Diane go on in the car?

Jones: No, Diane split somewhere. So anyway, we stopped in Atlanta and that was the first time for me in the car.

Q: First time for what?

Jones: That we had gone to Mississippi. Chuck Sherrod had been to Mississippi, but not the rest of us. I never in my life will forget going into Mississippi. We had stopped just on this side of the state line to get some gas and Sherrod had gone to the bathroom and gone to the white bathroom and the man pulled out a gun.

Q: In Mississippi?

Jones: No, this was in Alabama. We had stopped for gas and he almost shot Sherrod. We had that experience and then we went across the state line. We had been singing and stuff. The minute we passed that state line everybody in the car was crying. And then I think McDew started singing. We all started singing. We carefully picked our way to . . .

Q: What were you singing? Do you remember?

Jones: *We Shall Overcome*, I think, was the thing we started off singing. Everybody was scared as hell. That's what happened and we realized how profound that concept of Mississippi was to everybody. We drove on down to McComb, went through Jackson and got there about 10:00 at night. We were riding up the dirt road and Reggie Robinson says, "oh yeah." The next day we started to meet, Diane's people had come in by that time, by the next morning and we're all around together and we started all developing the program. We agreed on forty dollars a week. And then somebody said that there were . . .

Q: How many of you were there then?

Jones: Oh hell, there were about fifteen of us.

Q: That was all of SNCC?

Jones: Yeah. Somebody said there were some kids in jail. Marion Barry had come down in August. This was September 4th. Marion had come down early in August and gotten these kids involved in a sit-in at the Trailways bus station, Woolworths, and they all got arrested and they were in jail and they were in there about three weeks.

Q: In Jackson?

Jones: No, in McComb. I went to see them and they had been there and there was Hollis, Curtis Hayes, Brenda Travis, Hollis Watkins, one other guy. And those kids were just full of confidence, singing. That was the first time they had any kind of experience like this and we came back and decided we had to get them out before we could do anything and so we raised money. So we all split and went in different directions to raise $5,000. Diane's people, our people, Sherrod, McDew and myself and we went and Chuck McDew and myself raised $5,000. We all gathered back a month later.

Q: Where did you get it from?

Jones: I don't remember. Norman found some.

Q: Norman?

Jones: Anyway, we got back and I got the kids out.

Q: That was for them?

Jones: What?

Q: What was the $5,000 for?

Jones: For bail for those kids. Anyway, we got the kids out and we didn't have to use that check. I don't know how we did it but anyway we then continued the meeting and got the kids out. They wouldn't let one of the girls back in. Brenda Travis.

Q: Back in where?

Jones: School.

Q: That's right. She went to a reform school.

Jones: So we had a mass meeting and that was one of the great mass meetings of the movement. The tension was high, I'll never forget that.

Q: How did you get people to come?

Jones: We just got them out there. And that place was packed and we came marching in singing all of us there.

Q: Was SNCC working anywhere else at this point or was the whole staff in McComb?

Jones: Bevel preached, Reggie was leading it, and Sherrod was singing and preaching. And the tension just built and built.

Q: They just preached about politics?

Jones: Yeah, they were talking about the situation there. And the thing was so great that none of us went to bed that whole night. It was after the meeting and people were just ready. The kids were going to come out of school the next day and we stayed up all night. Nobody could sleep, wanted to sleep, just stayed up communing, because that had been the thing that brought us spiritually together. Very emotional.

Q: Exactly when was this mass meeting?

Jones: It was about October 5th or 6th. The next day we all gathered up at the office. Bob Zellner came down that morning, yes he did. And he looked out the window and here came a huge crowd of kids, about 136 in the school. He came into the office upstairs and talked about what it was going to involve. Bob was very concerned about the fact that this was going to be direct action and we were going to have to stick with those kids and follow through.

Q: What school were they from?

Jones: McComb something. The high school. And we agreed that we would stick with them. And it was also agreed that I would stay out.

Q: These kids wanted to do direct action?

Jones: They wanted to go to the courthouse and insist that Brenda Travis be allowed back in school. I was to stay out and organize pressure and public attention around the issue.

Q: Zellner was concerned about the safety?

Jones: No, that was Bob Moses.

Q: Bob Moses?

Jones: Bob Moses was concerned that we stick with those kids.

Q: He wanted you to stick with the kids?

Jones: Yeah, no question. And he was saying in a very serious vein that he didn't really, he wasn't at first very committed but once he saw it developing he was seeing how serious this thing was.

Q: Was there any feeling that this would distract from voter registration?

Jones: Not terribly. Bob expressed it more than anyone else, but once it developed we were in it all together. So they all walked down to the courthouse and everybody got arrested. Chuck can tell you about it. Are you going to see Chuck?

Q: Chuck McDew?

Jones: Yeah. He can tell you about what happened down there.

Q: Everybody, the whole SNCC staff?

Jones: The whole SNCC staff, all the kids, everybody but Reggie was arrested.

Q: Skipping back a little, the mass meeting, was that mainly about voter registration?

Jones: Voter registration, what had happened and the movement.

Q: I was wondering about how the split worked out. I mean the problems of those two courts.

Jones: Oh, well, see one of Diane's people had gotten the kids in jail and all of us went out to get them out. So that in effect, that bridged, began to bridge the gap. Marion Barry got them in jail and had split. And we were supposed to go around the country raising some money. I mean we were all extending ourselves.

Q: And then what happened?

Jones: All right. Everybody got arrested except Reggie.

Q: How did he escape?

Jones: That's another story . . .

Q: I'm just kidding.

Jones: He's been involved in quite a few things. I was the only one out at that point, back of the little grocery store. And the cops had a warrant out for me and they would come in and I would put on . . .

Q: And you also were arrested?

Jones: No, I wasn't. See, I was the one that was to stay out and make the contact with the world. And this is a very profound thing to understand. Those guys went in there knowing full well that they were going to get arrested and the potential consequences of that arrest. In McComb, Mississippi we had absolutely nothing at that point in terms of office. There was no kind of office operation, nothing of what we know now in terms of any kind of contact with the press or anything. And those guys went. We all moved on the faith in each other that we would do what we had to do to save their lives and to get them out and to get the movement going. And they went in, went down there with the knowledge that they were likely to get arrested and that I would be the only cat out there between them and death. And, of course I was aware of that too. So we started the phone calls. The cops would be coming in. I'd put on this white jacket and be back there chopping meat. I must have messed up $5 worth of pork chops. I didn't know what I was doing but the guy's be asking for Charles Jones. "No, sir." I'd be just back there.

Q: Did you say "No, sir"?

Jones: Oh, of course. And I'd go back to the phone.

Q: Why were you chopping meat?

Jones: Well, I was a butcher. I had to be there because if I had been arrested then it would be all over. No one else was out. So I had to go into this disguise. They didn't know what I looked like, they just had a warrant for Charles Jones. As a matter of fact that warrant is still outstanding. So then I started calling. I called Jim Forman. I called the SNCC office in Atlanta and Jim had just walked in the office. Had just arrived from Chicago, just walked in the office. I told him to see me and he said, "okay baby." I never met him in my life and from that point he worked. Then we started calling. I called Harry, I called the Justice Department. Anyway, we were in touch with a group in Chicago at that point, the press. See that was the only link. That was the first contact with the world with SNCC in that kind of situation. These kids, you know, everybody in jail, and we were getting all kinds of publicity.

Q: Did the Justice Department do anything?

Jones: Well, we got this word that the Klan came down and told some Negroes that they were going to take Bob Moses out of jail. They were taking everybody over to Magnolia, which is the county jail, about eight miles from there. We got the word they were going to take Bob out and kill him. [Herbert] Lee had already been shot by this guy, a state representative [E. H. Hurst], and he was first on the list and Bob moved up to number one on the list of the Klan to be killed. So I called the Justice Department and told them all this and they told me to talk to the local FBI guy and told him where to come to find me and he came up and I told him what the scene was and he said, "oh, I don't think so, I know them people. I've been living with them. I don't think they'd do anything like that." And then I called back [Washington] and I told them to get somebody down here because their guy was from the South and he was saying "oh, I don't think they'd do that." So, John Doar [a Justice Department Civil Rights Division lawyer] . . . I'll never forget this as long as I live. I was sitting back there. People were still in jail and, lord knows, were relying on the Justice Department, to protect people. I called Burke Marshall and told him "get on the FBI, man" and Burke said, "it's a matter of jurisdiction." And I sat right there not knowing when the cops were going to come in. And all of a sudden John Doar walked in and he said, "I'm John Doar." I said, you know, "very good" and I was relaxed and I had all the might of the federal government. I told him the whole scene and he said, "well, I'm sorry but there ain't nothing that I can do."

Q: Did he come down from Washington just to tell you there was nothing he could do?

Jones: I don't know why he came but he said, "I'm just as scared of them as you are, man, there's nothing I can do." I looked at him and here was all the force, honor, the military technology, power, of the greatest country, the most powerful country in the history of the world, represented in the form of John Doar, and he says to me, "I'm just scared as you are, man, ain't nothing I can do." And that pretty much completely shook me out of any illusions that I might have had about the federal government.

There was a Dr. Anderson where I was staying and he had a gun . . . And I was very pleased that he would have just as soon shot anybody that came up to the door.

Q: He was just a local Negro?

Jones: Yeah, a local Negro doctor. So we decided to get Chuck out. I couldn't be seen. If I was ever picked up again it was all over. So Anderson got together some money and went and got Chuck out. Chuck came in. I'll never forget that evening. He came over and we embraced. Chuck probably never would say this, but tears came to his eyes and tears came to mine. The money order was in his name and mine. It was either/or, that's what it was. Charles Jones or Chuck McDew. So he went down to the bank and cashed it and went and got everybody out.

Q: Where did that come from?

Jones: This was that $5,000 money order we had gotten to get those kids out. Chuck can tell you about that. And he went into the bank with that $5,000 money order. Anyway, we got everybody out and we were having a meeting at Anderson's house and we were talking about how we're going to follow up and stick with the people. And Diane, of all people, and Bevel were saying, "uh, uh, we're leaving." We decided that we had to get organized so we decided everybody would go to Atlanta but Chuck. Chuck made that decision. He was going to stay. Everybody pulled into Atlanta to organize.

Q: Didn't Bob Moses stay?

Jones: No. Nobody but Chuck. That was another beautiful scene. And we pulled into Atlanta to get organized. We decided that Sherrod had developed a thing about Southwest Georgia and I was staying around for a while but then I wanted to go to Atlanta. I went to Atlanta. I mean I went to Albany and joined the Albany Movement. At that point the function of the staff became a group thing and I passed, somewhat reluctantly, I was still young and insecure, but I kind of began to pass all the authority I had as a result of the money and the money.

Q: Did you say it was in your name?

Jones: Yeah.

Q: How come?

Jones: Well, I had to take out the responsibility.

Q: Could you follow up? Before we go into talking about Albany, do you want to follow up on what happened in Mississippi with the McComb project?

Jones: Well Chuck stayed there during the time we pulled back, during the time we pulled back to Atlanta to organize.

Q: Did he get anything done?

Jones: Well, once we left everybody was saying, "ooops, SNCC done snuck." And Chuck put up a little sign on the door saying, "SNCC ain't snuck, SNCC done stuck."

Q: How long did he stay there?

Jones: He stayed there a month and a half, something like that. So at the Atlanta meeting Bob went back, Dion went down, Chuck stayed and they, all the kids, got kicked out of school.

Q: All the high school students?

Jones: The ones that had been demonstrating and gotten arrested. So Chuck and . . .

Q: Mississippi has no compulsory education law?

Jones: Well, yeah, but for a criminal activity like that you don't deserve an education. You know, like going down to the courthouse and saying we would like to have our fellow students back in. Of course they kicked all of them out. And Chuck and Dion and Bob started Nonviolent High School for those kids up in the office. Nonviolent High. Chuck was teaching.

Q: That's its official name?

Jones: That's right. Nonviolent High School. Dion was teaching Physics. Bob was teaching English Literature. They all combined.

Q: Did they teach anything besides standard subjects?

Jones: They all combined on Negro history. That's where we got into the stuff about textbooks in Mississippi. I remember they had a section in there talking about the "war of Northern aggression."

Q: That's the civil war?

Jones: Yeah, the "war of Northern aggression" and how the "best friends to the semi-savage," this was 1961.

Q: Was this textbook used in Negro high schools?

Jones: Oh, yes, the "best friend" to the semi-savage African was not the Northern so-called liberals, abolitionists, but the kindhearted loving Southern patriots. Then we finally got all those kids into school in Atlanta, I mean in Jackson.

Q: The regular public schools?

Jones: No, it was a private high school. Dion was left there and Chuck, for a while Bob, Dion was there by himself a lot, at least he was pulling there by himself for a while. He's, incidentally, white. That's the response to your question.

Q: Right. Yeah, that's what I missed. So after Atlanta it sort of slowed down.

Jones: Yeah, Dion was supposed to have been there but more and more came up from CORE. They came up and were calling them Freedom Rides through McComb and they got arrested and a lot of publicity and looked around and Dion wasn't there. But we stayed there and Bob stayed there.

Q: You worked in Albany. Could you tell me how that got started and what happened?

Jones: Yeah, Charles Sherrod had done a research paper proposal on Southwest Georgia. The end of the summer of '61 in that first organization meeting right after McComb in Atlanta we considered program proposals and considered Sherrod's proposal and decided to support that proposal.

Q: What else was considered?

Jones: A project called MOM, Move on Mississippi, presented by Diane Nash, in which she proposed to organize the state of Mississippi for a grand mass march on the state capital.

Q: March on Mississippi, or move on . . .

Jones: Move on Mississippi.

Q: That was rejected?

Jones: No. The Committee would support that and the Albany project, continue to support McComb. Sherrod and Cordell Reagon proceeded to Albany. I worked in there for a while and went back for a trial in

Montgomery on the Freedom Rides, did some fundraising in New York and then about three weeks later went to Albany.

Q: How was the Albany experience different than the one in McComb?

Jones: We had done much more community contact. We had developed the approach around a mass community involvement, total community involvement. Voter registration and direct action, which action was separate from voter registration. That is to say, that an attempt to register to vote in most parts of the South at that point was very much a direct action. In light of the intimidation, shooting presently being conducted both in that section of Georgia and Mississippi and throughout the South.

Q: Was this mass, or community involvement different from McComb?

Jones: Yes. Different in that we organized the Albany movement prior to action or simultaneously with action, but most of it was prior to the action. We established an umbrella structure that involved all of the local groups, NAACP, citizens groups, and then proceeded to set up an office which was in the community and paid for by the community, made possible by our personal contact and involvement of people. We went to the bus station. There were three or four people who went to the bus station which was located adjacent to a Negro community—Harlem, they called it—and this was . . .

Q: They called it Harlem?

Jones: In Albany. And this was as the students from Albany State were going home for Thanksgiving. A couple of people got arrested when they went into the white section. Keep in mind that this was after the Interstate Commerce ruling and after the Freedom Rides. One of the persons was a girl—Bertha Gober—who decided to stay in jail rather than be bailed out. And she stayed in over Thanksgiving Day and the day after and we took that occasion to develop the issue by extensive coverage, most of which we did including pictures that we took of her in jail behind bars by means of a camera we took in unbeknownst to them, to Chief Pritchett, and her statements of why she was staying in, which were printed in a Negro weekly of Southwest Georgia. The *Albany Herald*, owned and operated by a Massachusetts resident who had come to Albany and out-Southerned the Southerners, who would not carry either full factual accounts or wouldn't carry any account at all.

Q: Did it in fact print this whole incident?

Jones: In an article buried in the back pages. We proceeded from that to institute these meetings at which time we talked about the whole problem of voter registration and discrimination in Albany. Now that's prior to the trial of Bertha. At the trial itself, during the trial we had been in touch with several students at Albany State College who then organized on campus. We had had an organization there and the president had told us not to come around talking about these black issues. As a result of that organization, at the trial there were 200 students who walked from Albany State College, who walked to the courthouse. At that scene police proceeded to attempt to disperse the crowd and I took the offensive and told people to proceed to walk around single file not blocking the sidewalk. And the action involved not only students but picked up many other people in the process of emotion. It also projected me as a "particularly light-skinned, blue eyed Negro" spokesman in the *Albany Herald*. Negro.

Q: They wrote out Negro?

Jones: Yes, I'm quoting the description. That action precipitated a very large mass meeting. At which point the Albany movement relationship as we had previously developed it began to emerge.

Q: Local leadership, you mean?

Jones: Our roles were defined primarily as a catalyst in developing leadership.

Q: Was SNCC successful in developing local leadership? That is, did the movement carry on after SNCC left?

Jones: Yeah. That was obviously around November when the national celebration of the turkey commences. Now around the first of December the Freedom Rides, Jim Forman, Tom and . . .

Q: Tom?

Jones: Hayden, Tom Hayden

Q: Oh, Tom Hayden.

Jones: Tom Martin, a lieutenant. Was that his name?

Q: A white guy?

Jones: A white guy who went down to McComb, came down to McComb that first time, a very important kid on the staff, was up at Brandeis the last couple of years. I'll think of his name. On the train they used the "white waiting room," whereupon several of us did and whereupon we proceeded to walk to our cars. We were all, several of us, were arrested for disorderly conduct and taken to jail in a Cadillac. Most all of the Freedom Riders were arrested, and myself, Sherrod and . . . proceeded to organize. Several of us came out, all of us came out the night of the mass meeting and proceeded down the hall and we had all been . . . and the next day a large number, in the hundreds, went down to the jail to protest, most of whom, a large number, were arrested and it was during that whole week some 1,200 people were arrested. We were up to Nashville, Albany, Georgia during that week. Several key members of the executive committee of Albany negotiated with the city. They got certain notice that they would release all of the people in jail, would not press charges, would open up the interstate bus station and train stations. So on that agreement we all came out. Martin came in in the meantime.

Q: Did the facilities remain integrated?

Jones: Hell, no. Not only did they not prosecute, they did attempt to prosecute the cases. They also continued to arrest people at the bus station and train stations.

Q: So they went back on their word completely?

Jones: Yeah, that was in the finest tradition of Southern gentlemen integrity.

Q: In general, in the Albany movement what do you think was accomplished?

Jones: The development of a mass approach, a complete mass city approach to the problems, everybody coming out.

Q: Was progress made toward the solution of any of the problems?

Jones: We had to subsequently go into a bus boycott, voter registration campaign, a federal suit, picketing, other jail arrests for lunch counters. The federal government was very shaky in most of its feelings with that whole situation. Howard Zinn pretty accurately describes the role of the federal government in that thing.

Q: What happened with the Move on Mississippi?

Jones: Nothing.

Q: Never?

Jones: No. Diane went down and after the Albany movement we came back and had an executive committee meeting. All of us were very anxious to know, we had gone to Albany and thrown in all our other resources and gotten Albany going and we all came back anxious to find out what Diane had been doing in Mississippi on the MOM project and asked Diane how many people she had ready to go and she said, oh, about twelve.

Q: You mentioned before the founding of COFO. Switching over to that could you explain how that developed out of VEP?

Jones: Well, Bob Moses stayed in Mississippi, began to make contacts throughout the state, got some funds from the voter education project for some research in the problem of voter registration in Mississippi generally. And got it funded through an organization he had developed which was a coalition of community organizations in Mississippi which I guess is what COFO is. He had drawn together all of his efforts in Mississippi into that organization.

Q: Into COFO?

Jones: Yes. And this was funded through the Voter Education Project.

Q: What do you think was the significance of COFO over all?

Jones: The organization on a statewide level is just another dimension to the organization on a citywide level that we had in Albany. Local organizations dealing with . . .

Q: Was there collaboration with groups like the NAACP?

Jones: They were all members of COFO. Well, I would rather not go into that because of my limited knowledge of the in-fighting that was associated with COFO except to point out that there was at all times, there were problems with NAACP. We ran into them directly in Albany. As a matter of fact there was a point in the organization of the Albany movement where the regional director informed the Albany leadership, many of whom had been old NAACP workers that either they direct all their activities to NAACP or NAACP would pull out completely. And our approach to that was to take a position that everybody should be a member of the NAACP. We should all be working toward getting everybody in Albany to be a member of NAACP. And as a matter of fact that was all they were doing in Albany anyway, that was the extent of their program so we shouldn't have any problem.

Q: That is, having everybody as a member was the extent of their program?

Jones: So we pretty effectively coopted them.

Q: This is a program in Mississippi?

Jones: Albany.

Q: In Albany. Wait, I'm confused.

Jones: No, I stated earlier that we had problems all the time within NAACP and we had handled it in Albany to some great extent the way it was handled in Mississippi, where they took that kind of position.

Q: What was going on in SNCC in 1962? Could you tell me about the various events that led up to the decline of the summer of . . . That seems like a period people don't talk about much.

Jones: Cut that [tape recorder] off a sec . . .

Q: In '63 people started working on FDP and stuff. '61 was Albany. In '62 Greenwood was . . . things were going on there.

Jones: Cut that off a second and I'll think. The organization in Albany, the follow-up, went through the winter of '62 and spring. We initiated the bus boycott, we went back, Charles Sherrod and myself went back one day to the bus station and were arrested as we were proceeding to get the bus, arrested for loitering. We were in touch with the Justice Department who promised faithfully to prosecute the case. We got back into mass demonstrations in the spring and early summer. As Martin, who had come in during the Christmas thing, came back in, in relation to a trial pursuant to an arrest that involved him during the time he was there in the December or early January part of it. He came back and they decided to prosecute the case in contradiction to their agreement during the negotiations in December. We started another phase of mass demonstrations and mass arrests.

Q: This was in early '62?

Jones: This was in the spring and early summer of '62. It was at this point that the city of Albany got an injunction, a temporary restraining order against any further demonstrations, using a very curious argument based on the Fourteenth Amendment which went . . . [tape cut off] Martin had come down for the trial and the fact of the trial itself was a repudiation by the city of its promises in the December negotiations. This then triggered other mass demonstrations at the city hall. The city then got a temporary restraining order from the district court using the very strange

Q: Restraining what? Demonstrations?

Jones: Yeah. Using a very strange legal concept of the Fourteenth Amendment, an argument which was essentially this: that demonstrations require the presence of policemen; policemen who are present during demonstrations could not handle other complaints of other citizens in the community; therefore, the demonstrations were denying other citizens, white citizens, equal protection of the law. So we should be restrained from engaging in any activities, First Amendment protected or otherwise because it tended to deny equal protection to white citizens. A temporary restraining order was granted. We appealed it and it was lifted. Then we went into the restraining order itself.

Q: Was this all in federal court?

Jones: Yes. Heard by one J. Robert Elliott, a Kennedy appointee, payoff to Southwest Georgia segregationists and I'm going to deny any authorship of the statement because I may have an occasion to be in Judge Elliott's court. He was in the finest tradition of the Southwest Georgia segregationist tradition.

201

Q: Well, I'm sure he'd take that as a compliment.

Jones: Well, I'm not sure.

Q: But I won't quote you.

Jones: We then counterclaimed and raised several issues about the suit. The Justice Department entered the suit *amicus curiae*, primarily on the theory of clean hands, which means that a man cannot come into an equity court if his own hands are not clean. The theory here related to the fact that the city had perpetuated segregation and it cannot then come into court and ask that persons who are engaged in conduct to eliminate those practices which are constitutionally invalid—"the city cannot be heard to complain of the activities of those attempting to eliminate unconstitutional practices." The judge took his time in dealing with all those things, but anyway, the case was finally resolved. But that grew out of the late spring '62 reactivation of Albany, Georgia?

Q: Did you work with Greenwood?

Jones: No. Mississippi.

Q: Do you want to talk more about Albany?

Jones: No. I left Albany and the active, front-line movement of SNCC in September of '62 and went to Mexico, at which place I recuperated physically and psychologically. And have been associated with SNCC in various forms subsequent to that, but in terms of active, full-time work, I have not been involved in that.

Q: What would you say were SNCC's greatest successes in that period?

Jones: Well, I think that the fact that the movement developed and was actively coordinated by young Negro students was the most important thing that happened in that the leadership, the direction, the content of the programs were being decided by Negroes. The other thing is I think we dramatized . . .

Q: What sort of thing do you think SNCC—well, that's been happening in SCLC too, with the Negroes?

Jones: In fact that very independence is the most important thing we gave to the whole movement.

Q: How do you distinguish SNCC from SCLC, the movement?

Jones: One, the ability to organize from the grass roots and from nothing to a viable movement. At this point SCLC would inevitably come in.

Q: Why couldn't SCLC do that or did it try?

Jones: Well, I'm not sure they didn't, but it was at least the fact that we were young, idealistic, though very practical, very committed people.

Committed to working for nothing if necessary, committed to an idea of living with, organizing with, sharing with the lives of the people on a full time basis is the basic difference. Plus we tended not to play the institutional games. When people had money and said, well, we'll give you this if you get rid of Chuck McDew or Charles Sherrod.

Q: Did anyone actually . . .

Jones: Yes, of course. We'd say, well, take this and ram it.

Q: Careful, this is on tape.

Jones: And this was pretty consistent for the first couple of years. I'm not sure what happened after that.

Q: You felt that SNCC had taken the initiative in asking for funds for voter registration?

Jones: Well, it wasn't SNCC at that point but the people that were involved prior to, during or after, as an accurate description of what happened will reflect.

Q: How would you evaluate the Voter Education Project?

Jones: It provided the resources to get the job done, principally money.

Q: You have no complaints about SNCC?

Jones: Well, yeah, you asked me about the successes.

Q: Okay. Have you any complaints against it? Want to talk about that?

Jones: No, I think it objectively did an effective job of bringing together all of the organizations. At the time I was involved in SNCC, I was more concerned about how it related its resources to us, assuming the premise that we were doing the most important (and the most) work.

Q: Okay. Now what do you think was SNCC's biggest problem? Areas which you thought weren't so successful?

Jones: For some reason I have a block.

Q: What did people talk about when they talked about SNCC? What were the kinds of things that were discussed, what were the issues?

Jones: I think I'll let you establish your own criteria on the basis of what information you get. . . . A lot to criticize . . . See the reason I'm not responding to this is you have to assume some premises that are agreed on from which you can then decide what are effective and not effective. As a matter of fact there were no premises at that point. We were developing them as we went along. On the basis of premises we developed at that point we were successful. As a hindsight analysis of someone else's premises of what we were doing at that time, I'm sure many people will come up with all kinds of things. It is not necessary for me to do that. It is not desirable for me to do that. I don't think it's for me important. So I tend not to be terribly concerned about failures in the sense of who or what criteria of what is a success or failure. In terms of my own concepts of our objectives, I thought we were very effective. The problems were those that naturally flow from young leadership acquiring all of a sudden a tremendous amount of power and attempting to deal with that in an altruistic, human-oriented context.

Q: How big was SNCC at the time you left it?

Jones: I guess there were fifty people.

Q: Was there already beginning to be any sort of problem of, you know, who makes decisions?

Jones: No. There were points at which persons attempted to assert, because of their belief in the correctness of their idea and approach, themselves, but the worth of an idea and program was in direct relation to the amount of self one was able to put into it and effectiveness that one could develop from placing oneself into it. And there was a hell of a lot of trust and a hell of a lot of love and a hell of a lot of confidence at this point in each other. People were encouraged and supported in doing what they could do best. And this was based on the fact that they were in the movement and everybody was important. Everybody had a right to say, and say as fully as possible, what he wanted to say. And his right to say it was respected and the content of what he said was respected, and inevitably had an effect on the ultimate decision, whether people completely disagreed or not.

Q: You said something before about a change in SNCC's mood around the time you were working in Albany.

Jones: Not SNCC.

Q: Not SNCC? Something about love and trust?

Jones: No.

Q: Okay.

Jones: No. This was primarily the result of Martin's involvement in Albany and the different type of approach Martin and company brought to relationships to people. I always tended to recognize and give support to local leadership. Martin tended to recognize and give support to Martin at the expense of local leadership. So that once he left, the impetus principally associated with him receded and the day-to-day responsibilities of what he had created tended to fall back on the local leadership itself, which created some problems in Albany in terms of the attitude of the people, of the leadership there toward kind of distrusting.

Q: The reason I ask about the problem areas is that SNCC in a later period used different tactics on developing political power, such as the FDP, and I figured one way of finding out why was to ask about the problem areas. Let's see. Is there anything else you want to add or do you think you've given me a pretty full picture of what went on?

Jones: I would just suggest that SNCC probably is and was one of the most important human social group developments in our recent history.

Q: I think so too, that's why I'm writing this.

Jones: Because of the basic commitment to people, human problems, human values and the commitment of the total self to achieving a recognition of those and the total fabric of American society.

Q: Do you want to say anything more about what happened to SNCC since you left it yourself?

Jones: There's no question but that my experience with SNCC has presented me with a much larger dimension of my own self, has developed within me a much greater sensitivity to people and myself and given me a very profound sense of strength, integrity, love and determination. Had I not been in it I would have been a much less effective human being, both to myself and other people.

Q: Do you think SNCC had this effect on other people too?

Jones: There's no question in my mind that it had.

John Lewis

John Lewis

Q. You were talking about Albany, what it did. I've written something I can't read here. It was a defeat for both SNCC and SCLC in a sense. Oh, I know what you had just said. You just said that in a way they tackled too much.

A. Yes. In the city of Albany I think there was an attempt on the part of both SNCC and SCLC . . . For one reason they had the whole community involved. They went out in a sense to make Albany an open city; to remove the barriers of segregation and racial discrimination in all aspects of the city of Albany, rather than attacking particular and specific places, selecting particular spots in the city, or particular streets and corners, where, even with the selective buying campaign—or economic boycott or withdrawal—or even if they would hold a demonstration. And I think the cleverness of a police chief like [Laurie] Pritchett . . .

Q. How was he clever?

A. Well, he did things very cool. He knew that if there was violence or retaliation on the part of policemen—if they would rough up demonstrators, if they would beat up people, that this would tend to increase the participation of the Negro community and would give a greater sympathy to the movement in Albany, from people not only in Albany, not only from white people but from people throughout the country and throughout the State of Georgia. And Pritchett had this whole thing that he would meet non-violence with non-violence, and it's a very interesting point.

Q. Especially for a policeman.

A. That's right.

Q. Do you want to add anything about Albany?

A. No.

Q. The next thing you mentioned was the challenge at the convention. Now, what did SNCC expect to happen, actually, at the convention?

A. I think that SNCC, as an organization, expected that the Mississippi delegation would at least be recognized; recognized and seated as the official delegation, representing the Democratic party of the State of Mississippi; because the SNCC people had worked very hard leading up to the Democratic convention. They worked during the spring. They lobbied and talked and pressured members of the platform committee, pressured state delegations, all over the country, got some of the freshmen committee people with the delegation from Michigan, from Minnesota, from Wisconsin, from Oregon, and certain members from New York and Pennsylvania and Massachusetts and other areas.

Q. What happened at the convention? What prevented that from happening?

A. Well, the issue was never really brought to the floor. The platform committee went through many changes and delayed the decision and the White House put a lot of pressure on people saying that there must be a compromise, that it must not be brought to the floor. If it had been brought to the floor, the Mississippi people were convinced, and their supporters—people like [Representatives] Edith Green and [William] Fitts Ryan and other people—felt that if that issue had been brought to the floor the Mississippi people would have been seated. But the President . . .

Q. You mean the FDP people?

A. The FDP people would have been seated. But President Johnson and other people put pressure on the so-called liberal establishment, on people in the Civil Rights movement like Roy Wilkins and James Farmer and Martin Luther King and Bayard Rustin and Joe Rauh.

Q. Why did Johnson do that?

A. I don't know why, but I think because of his relationship with Senator Eastland and his relationship with Senator Stennis. And he kept saying that if this thing is brought to the floor . . . He was telling members of the platform committee that he won't get a good man for the vice-presidency, that they had to make a choice between keeping this thing off the floor and getting Humphrey.

Q. The platform committee or the credentials committee?

A. It was the credentials committee. Right. If they wanted Humphrey as the nominee for the vice-presidency, then they had to keep this thing off the floor. And a lot of the members of the credentials committee told some of the SNCC people who were lobbying there that they had gotten calls from the White House, from different staff people, saying that if you do such and such a thing, your husband won't get this job or get this appointment—that type of thing. There was a lot of pressure on both sides. And then I think the challenge of Congress was another landmark in both CORE and SNCC, and then we just could not be satisfied, and SNCC played an important . . .

Q. How come SNCC went on to do that after what happened at the convention?

A. Because I think they felt that there were possibilities in that and they had to try these different methods. I mean, there were some people in SNCC at the time that you had to take through different changes and different steps, knowing that they would not work, but they must experience that.

Q. What effect did these two challenges have—the convention and the congressional challenge?

A. On SNCC?

Q. Yes.

A. I think some people no doubt gave up. SNCC gave up, lost faith.

Q. In?

A. In the possibility of bringing about change through the so-called democratic process.

Q. Did you give up then?

A. No. I don't think I've given up now. I don't think so. I've said on many occasions that in spite of what happened and all of that I don't consider myself bitter. I might be angry and I get angry about a few things, but I made up my mind as an individual, a long time ago , , , I don't know how you make up your mind to say this, but I said that I will not become bitter; I will not become so frustrated and let hate and bitterness engulf me, control me. Because I recognized the fact, when I got involved in the movement in 1960, that the struggle was going to be a long, hard, tedious struggle and you're going to have to pace yourself, and I didn't expect that in two years or three years of sitting-in and demonstrating and getting people to register to vote, that there are going to be radical changes all at once. I didn't expect that. I am disappointed though that things did not move as fast as they should have.

Q. Yeah. Anything about the challenges you want to add? . . The last thing you mentioned was the summer project.

A. The Summer Project.

Q. How was the decision to undertake the Summer Project made?

A. Well, it was made by SNCC but primarily by the whole of SNCC, and primarily under the influence of Bob Moses. For some time, in the fall of '63 (and my copy of those things, it's home in Alabama), there was a great debate in SNCC, and Moses led the debate; that SNCC should move its office out of Atlanta and move to Mississippi. Everything should go. Some of us opposed it strongly, and fought against it like I don't know what.

Q. What were Bob's reasons for wanting it moved?

A. He said that if we want to work in Mississippi, and this was where we were going to put in a great deal of effort . . . this is where the staff should be; the national staff should be there.

Q. Was this temporarily, for the summer?

A. No, this was on a permanent basis; we should move the press, everything, there, and that's where Jim and I should spend most of our time . . . and that we should stay in Mississippi rather than staying in Atlanta. Then people started debating if Mississippi was a safe place to go; it was bad for communication and bad for transportation and you couldn't keep your records there and your organization could be bombed and everything could be destroyed and blanked out. And Moses insisted that we do it, and in the end he started laying groundwork in his own mind about the Summer Project . . . .

Q. Why was he so eager to have the office moved? It seems like those arguments are reasonable ones, about it being unsafe.

A. Well, because he felt that by being in Mississippi the Mississippi project would receive greater attention from SNCC because it was there. Mississippi would become the home of SNCC.

Q. Why did he want the Mississippi project to have so much attention?

A. Because he felt that it would need that attention in order for the project to be effective and to be carried out you needed the communications setup; you needed a guy like Julian Bond to handle press and Dottie Zellner. You needed people like that there; you needed the WATS line in Mississippi. You needed the press that we had at that time. You needed a darkroom, and all of this equipment. You needed to be in Mississippi, he felt.

Q. Yeah. Was there something of a power struggle there? Did he want more power?

A. No, I don't think so. That never came across to me. I don't think so. I think Bob saw Mississippi as, in a sense, his territory at that particular time, and he was in charge of it. But he had a lot of problems with Mississippi Negroes who happened to be on SNCC's staff, who at that particular time didn't want any white people to come into the state. And SNCC finally decided that it would want to support the Mississippi summer project and...

Q. Why did these local leaders not want any more white people?

A. Well, I guess they had had some experience with a few people in '60—thirty, I think—and they . . . In a sense, they just didn't want anybody to come down. Because they felt that people were sort of taking over from them who would be typing, you know. And you can see that; you can understand that. Some little Negro girl who dropped out of high school who had been typing maybe forty-five words or twenty-five words or thirty words a minute, and here's some white girl down from . . .

Q. Smith College.

A. Smith College, from some good college, who can type maybe seventy-five or more. I don't know. And, you know, instead of taking two or three days to get out a newsletter, a paper, these kids were turning things out in a few minutes or half a day or so. And I think kids felt like they were being moved; they would be displaced and what they considered theirs would no longer be theirs. I think they had that fear.

Q. Weren't they sort of right?

A. Oh, yes. That was right. And that's what happened. There's no question about it. And I think that may be one of the bad points about it.

Q. Did Bob really persuade these people that the Summer Project was okay, or . . . ?

A. Oh, yes, he did.

Q. He went over their opposition?

A. I think he persuaded some of them, and then for some it went over their opposition. Some worked with it in spite of their opposition, and some just tended to withdraw from that whole area; just worked in their own little world. But I think the good things that came out of the Mississippi Summer Project of '64 overshadowed the bad things . . . I recall during the spring of '64 some of us traveled all across this country (I've spent a lot of time in the Midwest and the Far West) recruiting people for the Mississippi Summer Project. Speaking or telling people to come, and all that type of thing. Well, we brought the country into Mississippi. There's no question about it. It was a marvelous idea. You had all these young people who also happened to be white, because young white people were able to come. They didn't have to spend the summer working hard to get back to their college, but a lot of Negroes had to spend the summer working in order to return to school in September. You had these young people getting involved in the type of thing that Kennedy was saying about the Peace Corps, but this was local, at home, the domestic scene. And a lot of the people, I think, a lot of the young whites, and a lot of the young Northern Negroes were educated in

213

the process on what was going on. They taught people a different thing. And I think it gave the Negro people in Mississippi . . .

Q. What did it teach them?

A. It taught some people how to read and how to write. They taught courses in Negro history. They taught people about their political structure in Mississippi. Even what the qualifications were for being able to register and vote, things like that . . . See, I think, perhaps more than anything it's a gauge of Negro people in Mississippi. A deeper feeling that you're not alone. Because people are concerned about what's going on. It gave them a sense of strength, and a sense of a source of happiness, a sense of confidence that you're not alone and you're not struggling alone. There are people throughout this country who are with you. And it was saying to the Negroes of Mississippi, "All white people are not alike."

Q. After the summer was over, did this lead the people of Mississippi on to do new and more exciting things?

A. And to doing things on their own. And I think Fannie Lou Hamer was the best representative of it . . . I don't know if you've seen this book or not—*Strangers at the Gate*, by Tracy Sugerman. She wrote this . . . There were people who wanted change, but they hadn't dared to try to come out and do something, to try to change the way things were. But after the 1964 project, when all of the young people came down for the summer, an exciting and remarkable summer, Negro people in the Delta began moving; people who had never before tried, though they had always been anxious to do something, began moving.

Q. The whole Freedom High movement that we were talking about before?

A. Came after.

Q. Was developed after?

A. Came after the Summer Project. Right. And she talked about how she felt it was the Kingdom of God and all of that that took place in Mississippi, and I think she's a good representative. If you can you really should try to talk to Fannie Lou.

Q. Were the events of the summer, and the kinds of developments that occurred in the summer related to the Freedom High thing, which occurred right after?

A. I think so.

Q. How?

A. I think a lot of people, after they went to the Democratic convention in Atlantic City . . . they didn't get that many people to register in Mississippi during the summer of '64.

Q. Not many?

A. No, not many people registered. Many people, many, many people tried, but very few people were successful in being registered. I think a lot of people were tired and weary. I really think so. I don't know too much about it because I left the country right after the Democratic convention; I went away for two and a half months to Africa. But I think there was a sense of monumental fatigue, after the '64 Summer Project, and after the Atlantic City convention. And people felt that they had to try something else; they had to try something different. They had to do something different. A lot of people just didn't do anything. That's when SNCC went through that whole period of saying there shouldn't be an organization. I was away the first time, the first week in November. You may recall in November . . . .

Q. There shouldn't be an organization?

A. There shouldn't be a structure. There shouldn't be a chairman. Somebody proposed that in October and November 1964. The latter part of October 1964. There shouldn't be an executive committee and there shouldn't be an executive secretary. You should have a revolving type committee. Moses supported some of this stuff. And some other people. Let people just be free to do anything. There shouldn't be a bookkeeper. We'd just have a revolving committee, and the people who wanted to do this could get together and discuss this and that, and a lot of people felt SNCC should become one of these "soul" type sessions, where people just get together and talk out problems, and that type of thing. And that was really the essence, I guess, of Freedom High.

Q. We've sort of already discussed that. Do you remember the Holly Springs meeting?

A. The Central Committee meeting at Holly Springs?

Q. Yeah.

A. Yeah. I remember that meeting. I think it was at the end of '65.

Q. What happened there? The spring of '65. Was it people from Atlanta went out to Mississippi?

A. Yes.

Q. Were you there?

A. It was a Central Committee meeting. When the Central Committee met at Hollis's [Watkins] house, I did go there.

215

Q. Yeah?

A. I think that was when there were attempts to read the lists of names of people that were on the payroll.

Q. Yes, that's right.

A. And what people were doing. They sent letters to different people, saying you had to say what you'd been doing over a certain period of time, or you'd be dropped from the staff.

Q. Before the Holly Springs meeting?

A. No, that was after Holly Springs. But the decision was made at Holly Springs to do that kind of thing.

Q. Uh huh . . .

A. I don't recall very well what took place, but I knew that was one of the...

Q. Who were some of the people who were sent letters asking for accountings?

A. I would say a large . . . over half of the staff. I just don't know their names. I can't think of one particular person right now.

Q. Was anybody actually dropped?

A. I don't think so. Not at that particular time. I don't think anyone was really dropped from the staff. I really don't recall.

Q. Hmmnn. Over half the staff of Mississippi were sent that letter. That was in connection with trying to make sure the people were really doing something?

A. Yes. Maybe someone made a speech once at a staff meeting and stated to people that "you must shape up or ship out." Maybe I saw that at the Holly Springs meeting, a few people became bitter about that "you must shape up or ship out" or something like that. What they were really saying . . .

Q. Who was doing these things? Saying "shape up or ship out"?

A. I took the position that people had to start working, and I think a lot of people supported that. Ruby Doris [Smith] Robinson, for example, supported it. On the other hand, I remember [Ralph] Featherstone at that meeting, and I think Ivanhoe [Donaldson] was there. Cleveland Sellers was there. And I think Cleve supported that position also, but he got in a lot of trouble trying to implement it, I think. That "shaping up and shipping out" idea. But I don't know what happened. I think a lot of people straightened up; people sort of shipped out. People sort of shipped out on their own, before they were shipped out.

Q. I see. So, did a lot of the Freedom High group, after that, leave SNCC entirely?

216

A. Oh, yes. I would say the majority. Like, in New York alone, I don't see that many people, but that's the whole ex-SNCC right here. Right in New York. Probably there are more people living in the city of New York who were on SNCC's staff than are on SNCC's staff now.

Q. Yeah . . .

A. Have you talked to Howard Zinn at all?

Q. Yes, I have. I have to talk to him some more too. Was this at all connected with disappointment in the way whites worked out in working among Negroes?

A. I don't think so. See, I think in SNCC it didn't appear, because SNCC people go through what they may call their "black nationalist" thing, and then get out of it. Because I know one person who went through it, she was all caught up in it, very early, but no one else was on this "black nationalist" kick. And now she tells the people in the Atlanta Project, she just wants to come out of it . . . and she's one who'd been fighting for continuity. But I don't know what happened to her . . . that was Ruby Doris back in the early days. She went through this whole period of . . . and she became . . . her closest friend, I guess, happened to be white. But then later . . .

Q. What happened? Then she became friendly with the whites?

A. Yes, she became very close and very friendly with whites, you see, and she tried to convert others, who . . . In the summer of '66, right after the national meeting, who were really going all the way, like keeping the Atlanta Project, she was telling me, she said, "I went through the same thing, and there's nothing to it," you know.

Q. Because she was trying to dissuade them from being such black nationalists?

A. Yeah.

Q. Yes, that's interesting. Now . . . At the Holly Springs meeting, were these people whose names were read off on the payroll, were they all actually there? Did they get a chance to defend themselves?

A. Oh, no. There was no one at the meeting: The Central Committee, maybe one or two other people . . .

Q. And say Bob Moses spoke for all these people? Because, how did they find out what they were doing? How did they decide who to send letters to?

A. Well, just reports . . . I don't know, was Moses at that meeting? I don't know if Moses was there, it seemed like he was there. No, but there were a lot of people, not just Negroes but a lot of white people who worked with SNCC, not just the Summer Project people, but white people who had been working who were also caught up in this Freedom High bag. And I must say, a large segment of them are here in New York now. Talk to Casey. Casey was one of the real subtle leaders of this whole Freedom High thing that "people must be free to do, free to think." Casey Hayden, Mary King, Emmie Schrader were these types. And they would go from one thing to...

Q. You said Jane Stembridge?

A. No, I didn't say Jane Stembridge because she was sort of out of everything by that time, I guess. Another young lady named Emmie Schrader, a good friend of Casey. But they had been involved in some project down in Mississippi. Then they got involved in becoming photographers and then filmmakers, and they'd be going from one thing to another thing, and the Central Committee just got sort of fed up with the whole thing.

Q. So the Central Committee . . . I still don't quite understand what they were doing at the Holly Springs thing. These people weren't there to defend themselves?

A. No. They had reports on the different areas, and you had a project director who was a member of the Central Committee, and he sort of had to give an account of what was going on in his project.

Q. Ah ha. Each project director . . .

A. Right. So, if ten people work in his office in Southwest Georgia and the project director happened to be Roy Shields, then they would say, "What are these ten people doing?"

Q. Oh. I thought it was just the Mississippi staff that was asked to report.

A. At the Holly Springs meeting?

Q. Yes.

A. Oh. Probably the Mississippi staff were the only staff that was dealt with at the Holly Springs meeting, but eventually, at different meetings, all the SNCC staff, including all the people in my office, had to deal with that kind of . . .

Q. I see. The Holly Springs meeting was just for Mississippi?

A. I think so. I really don't . . .

Q. But actually, later on, they had other meetings where everybody . . . ?

A. Right. I think maybe the Holly Springs meeting was only Mississippi. But eventually the whole staff was dealt with the same way.

Q. I see. Did you favor that?

A. Well, I favored trying to find out what people were doing. I did favor that.

Q. Okay . . . Now, at the May 1966 meeting, when Stokely was elected chairman, what happened there? How was it that you weren't re-elected?

A. Well, what happened there . . . The meeting had lasted for a week, and late Friday night, I guess, around 11:00 or something, it was time to elect officers for the new year, for next year, and the house was open, and two or three people were nominated, I guess. Stokely and myself and somebody else, I think. But I think one of them was a joke, and they withdrew it, or . . .

Q. Had your election been opposed before? I mean, in previous years? Had you ever . . .

A. No. Once in '65 about six people were nominated, including myself, and I remember that very well. There were about twenty some people on the staff then, and I think there were about six people nominated, and most of the people only received votes from the person who nominated them. I think the person who received the next highest votes received something like ten.

Q. Who was that?

A. I think it was Lafayette Surney, I'm not sure. But several people were nominated, I remember, in '65. And I received 200 and some odd votes. It was no problem. In Nashville I was nominated and I think maybe [Willie] Ricks or Stanley [Wise] or somebody else was nominated. Anyway, the person received one vote or something like that, and there was a standing vote, with the candidates in the house, and when it came down for the vote I was elected chairman.

Q. Where was this?

A. In Nashville. I was re-elected chairman in Nashville.

Q. But what year?

A. Sixty-six. In May of '66, when Stokely was elected . . . It's very . . .

Q. Chairman of SNCC? You were re-elected . . . You were re-elected chairman of SNCC in Nashville?

A. In Nashville. I don't know . . . It's a very bitter thing in history but things like this happen. I was elected chairman of SNCC in '66, re-elected, and by a wide majority—I don't know what it was; it must have been something like sixty-six to nineteen I think, with quite a few people abstaining.

Q. Was Stokely running against you?

A. Yeah. Quite a few people abstained. Because there had been a serious debate, a discussion, but it got much more serious and much dirtier later. Then, the thing came up with the White House Conference and they needed somebody to be elected . . . See, Forman opposed my election, and he lost

. . . Have you talked to anybody else about the Nashville meeting and election or anything?

Q. No.

A. You haven't talked to anybody about that yet?

Q. I'm getting just your story.

A. My story. So you have to talk to other people.

Q. I will.

A. You should go back and read *The New York Times* on it also, and maybe somebody else . . .

Q. Well, how long after this Nashville meeting were you de-elected?

A. De-elected. Well, just a few hours. It was around 11:30, and then I guess around 5:30 that morning . . . . What happened . . . Some people got up and said . . . I had been attending these White House planning sessions. Earlier during '66 Johnson had appointed me, along with some other people, civil rights people, to the Planning Commission, Planning Council, for the White House Conference. And I'd been attending those sessions. And the White House Council was made one of the things that "we don't want a chairman to attend the White House Conference or White House meetings" or something. That was one thing.

Q. They didn't like it that you were involved in it.

A. Right. And another thing, people were opposed to my relationship with SCLC, in particular. Martin Luther King—we have been somewhat friends over the years, I guess. I got to know him back in '58. Well, you know, the strange thing, "we need somebody who will tell Johnson to go and do this," and somebody . . . I won't use the phrase or the word because it's not pleasant non-violent words. Those were some of the things. And the whole thing of "whiteness" and non-violence or violence issue. And "We need someone who will spend more time in the South and stop speaking on white college campuses," and that type of thing.

Q. Well, Stokely hadn't done that.

A. That's right. But that was a strong point: that they needed people to stay in the black communities, speak to the black people, live with the black people and stop spending all this time speaking to white people on white college campuses. That was one of the strong things.

Q. Did you in fact spend a lot of time?

A. I think I spent something like 60-40% of my time . . . I would say that maybe the first year as chairman of SNCC . . . Maybe in '64 I spent over half my time on the white college campuses. But in other years—'63 and

'65—I think I spent most of my time in the South. I spent most of my time on the white college campuses in '64 because in the spring of '64 in particular, and after, we recruited people for the Summer Project.

Q. Yeah. Okay. Now, how was it that there was a second election? That seems illegal to me.

A. Well, a guy came in and challenged the elections. He challenged on the same principle that we had challenged in Mississippi; that the elections weren't constitutional, that we violated our own laws and rules and SNCC doesn't have any rules or laws or anything. And this guy's not even on the staff or anything. But people used that, okay? So . . .

Q. Who was this guy?

A. A guy named Worth Long.

Q. Oh, yeah.

A. Have you talked to him?

Q. Not yet.

A. I'd be interested in what he . . . So, there was another election there, and all the people who'd been elected . . . See, at one point, Cleve had been elected executive secretary, had been elected program secretary, and Stokely had been elected executive secretary . . . Or maybe he refused, and Ivanhoe was elected executive secretary, but Stokely refused the position of executive secretary after I was elected chairman, and then a lot of the people after I was elected chairman left the room. The great majority of the people left and went home, went to (we had this meeting outside of Nashville) the place where they were staying, to their cabins, and went to sleep. And they didn't know anything about it until the next morning, or the next day. Because some of them had left and gone back to Arkansas and some back to Georgia, and they didn't know what was happening.

Q. That sounds pretty illegal.

A. And that's what took place. And that's never been told.

Q. That's why the vote went the other way? Because these people had already gone home?

A. People were asleep or people had gone home. For the most part that's why it went the other way. Again, I think a lot of people had been influenced . . . It was a very trying moment for a lot of people. Some people cried and went through all types of changes about what happened. But they got very sick over it. Personally, I was very cool and very calm through the whole thing. I was, you know, a little disturbed about seeing SNCC come to that point.

Q. Were you really illegally . . . ?

A. Well, not altogether because I was illegally de-elected, but to see an organization get so carried away. An organization that had played in honest measure a very important and significant role on the American scene. Then fall down to such tripe . . . "We need somebody to say to Johnson to kiss my . . ." You know. That type of thing. And "John Lewis won't say that to Lyndon Johnson." You know. "We need someone to tell Martin Luther King to go to hell," you know? It got to things just like that. A lot of the people were very sorry about it. Members of the staff sent me letters and things. But, that's beside the point. I guess I have to write that in my memoirs some day. That's why it would be very interesting to read your dissertation. It was a very trying moment, for a lot of people.

Q. Did SNCC very shortly after that change its policy?

A. At that meeting the whole question of "whiteness" was debated. "Black consciousness" and "black power" were not used, the phrases were not used, but . . . We had to stop talking to the white press, we only talked to the black press, and later they started talking about white people, they had to get off the staff. And you know, since then, I really have lost contact, so I cannot say much more. I resigned, submitted my resignation on July 11th.

Q. Had this been sort of a gradual development?

A. Oh, yes . . .

Q. Thinking more in terms of blacks?

A. Because I just noticed in this article that this guy was writing—Paul Good in the *New South* in March of . . .

Q. Is that also true that you are one of the few who accepts nonviolence as a way of life?

A. I guess he meant the people in SNCC.

Q. In SNCC.

A. Yeah. But another thing, this guy Paul Good, I'm not just using this, but it may be helpful in getting the transition of a particular thing. Did you see a copy of the *New South* anyplace?

Q. No.

A. But early in the game I said something like this: "I've been thinking about leaving the movement . . ."

Q. When was this?

A. This was while I was in Rome in April 1966. "I have been thinking about leaving the movement . . . It would be very hard for me to leave with all the years put in, all the time and energy. There seems very little change.

Back in 1961 I felt we were achieving something, but then my expectations were limited. Our expectations increased and I get the feeling that the rate of progress isn't increasing with the efforts we put into it. Maybe we're not using the right methods. I don't know."

Q. Do you still think that? That maybe you were not using the right methods?

A. No. I think we were using the right methods, but I don't think we used . . . We haven't used all the possible methods and techniques . . .

Q. More marches, do you think, would be good?

A. I think we have to use more marches but they must take a different form, a different pattern. That type of thing. I think the non-violent movement itself has got to become radical now, to meet the demands and the needs of the people, to evolve different forms of protest.

Q. Did you say the movement has to become more radical?

A. Yes. Become radical enough to meet the needs of the people.

Q. Like in the economic sphere?

A. I said this in Rome in April, 1966. The national meeting took place May, 1966. "I may very possibly be replaced in the future. We are having a meeting in May, and if most of the people in SNCC decide to end the nonviolence, then that's the way it will be. I wouldn't want to see it happen. I can't even promise I will be nonviolent in every circumstance. If someone was beating my mother . . . I don't know. But what else can you try to live by?"

Q. Okay. What do you think has been SNCC's greatest success?

A. Its greatest success? As I said earlier, I think SNCC has demonstrated more than perhaps any other organization that has been on the American scene in the past five or ten years, what a few people can do. What they can set in motion. I think with the sit-ins in 1960 and the Freedom Rides in '61, but particularly the sit-ins, SNCC started a fire. A different type of fire burning in this country that influenced so many institutions, so many other organizations in America. I think it had a tremendous impact on the federal establishment, on organized religion, upon the academic community . . .

Q. Earlier you said, when you were quoting yourself in Rome there, you said the rate of progress of the movement is slowing down. How do you account for that?

A. I think the lack of commitment, the lack of courage, the timidity of the federal government, in a sense, to be responsive to the demonstrations, to the protests of the people. I think SNCC, along with other organizations, along

223

with a large segment of the American people, has presented opportunities for the government to be responsive and to meet . . .

Q. Why do you think they weren't responsive?

A. I think for political reasons. In a situation like the Mississippi challenge, for example, the government was prepared to act on the basis of a great consensus in Mississippi and on the basis of political expediency, rather than on what was morally right. And see, at one time (and Moses used to put a great deal of emphasis on this stuff) . . . There was a certain amount of ethics—I guess you may call it ethics—or a certain amount of morality that engulfed the whole civil rights movement. Not just SNCC but the whole movement had an obligation or a mandate to inject some of this ethic, or inject some of this morality, into the body politic. And I think SNCC has lost that now, because SNCC at the present time is using some of their very methods. They're using some of their very language; they're using some of the things that we were fighting against.

Q. Black Power?

A. Yes. See, I think that an organization like SNCC had an opportunity to say that we do not necessarily want to become a part of that which we're fighting against. We do not want to copy that which we're fighting against, but we want to make it something better and something different, and right now it's picking up the same methods, using the same vicious and evil system that we have been trying to destroy.

Q. Well, what do you mean by . . . Such as what?

A. Well . . .

Q. What methods is SNCC using that are so bad?

A. That are so bad, and so violent? See, I'm a believer in this whole idea that you cannot separate means and ends, and that if you're striving for what we liked to talk about in SNCC in the past and what some of the people in the national movement liked to talk about—the beloved community. A community at peace with itself. What some people would call an open or a redeemed society. If this is our goal, if this is our end, then our means and our methods must be somehow caught up in our goals and our ends.

Q. Would you say that using political methods, trying to get political office, trying to take over a community, like Lowndes County, is incompatible with seeking the redeemed community.

A. No, I'm not saying it's incompatible. Not at all. Because I think the so-called good people, the so-called people who believe in nonviolence, who believe in a beloved community and an open society, in an interracial society, must get involved in the political arena. I think this is a must. To take an effort, to take a morality and to make it something different, make it something better. On the other hand, I don't think we should put all of our emphasis and all of our stress on bringing changes through the so-called elective process, through the political arena, through the whole legislative process. We must also deal within that whole area of reconciliation—man-to-man, that type of thing, races to races.

Q. Yes. Do you know what happened to the people in SNCC who supported you, after Stokeley took over? Did a lot of them leave?

A. Well, I don't think all of the people left. I don't think so. I think a lot of people are still there. I think people fitted into other things. But, on the other hand, I think there have been massive turnovers since the national meeting. Different people . . . Not just white people. There were a lot of white people there who were asked to leave or something. But different people left. I think some people stayed as long as they could afterward and then they left. I think Marion for one stayed as long as he could. People say he was fired or he resigned from the new Washington office. I don't think he could have officially submitted a resignation, I don't know. But I know he's going to resign from the SNCC staff. That's what Julian Bond told me. Julian's one of my closest friends.

Q. He made a public statement saying it wasn't.

A. It wasn't because of that. Right. You should talk to him. People make public statements, they have one reason for making a public statement, and another reason for . . . I don't know, but I couldn't say. I'm not going to question his . . .

Q. What has been SNCC's greatest difficulty? The greatest obstacle to its success?

A. Unwillingness to come to grips with this. That is putting it too simply.

Q. Southerners?

A. I say it's unwillingness to come of age, in a sense.

Q. What do you mean?

A. It's an unwillingness to live in the real world.

Q. Could you give me an example of how that's hurt SNCC?

A. See, I think the greatest need right now is for SNCC, as an organization (I don't know whether it can do it or not), to really organize young Negro people, young white people in the South. I think the greatest contribution that SNCC can make, with its limited resources, limited staff, limited funds and all of that, is to concentrate primarily in the Deep South—the whole

South rather—and on organizing the young Negroes and the young whites in the South into a powerful political force for change. Not just getting people registered, but training people, teaching people how to conduct a campaign. And getting people elected and not just runing people for the fun of running people. Go out and get people registered and get people elected, and that can be done and SNCC can do it. And I think that's what SNCC can do and stop spreading itself so thin, going all over the country. Talking about black power here, black power was just like Freedom Now—a slogan, and rhetoric. It was just like the slogan "one man, one vote," but I think "one man, one vote" was a possibility, a little more than "Black Power." "I have a dream." All these things that we've been chanting, and "Freedom Now," and "one man, one vote." It's rhetoric, it's slogans. You do not have the ABCs, you do not have the one, two, threes of how you do it. What are you going to do? Something is missing.

Q. Would you want to add anything about SNCC?

A. No. (interruption) . . Let me give you a little history . . . See, I went on the Freedom Ride. I was one of three students who went on the original Freedom Ride for CORE. I left school without taking my final exam, my senior exam, at . . .

Q. You mean three SNCC students?

A. No, there were three students, three SNCC-type students, I guess, one from Morehouse College, one from the Atlanta student movement, and one from the non-violent action group in Washington. I went on the Freedom Ride in mid-May of '61, and I was beaten, on the Ride, in Rock Hill, South Carolina. Then I got off the ride because in the meantime I had made an application with the American Friends Service Committee to go on the VISA program—Voluntary International Services Agency. To go to India for two years on an assignment. So, I left the Freedom Ride to go for this interview, to Philly. And in the meantime I was supposed to rejoin the Ride in Birmingham, or Montgomery, and they had the violence at first going into Anniston, Alabama and they had violence in Birmingham, and CORE dropped the Freedom Ride. And I came back to Nashville and got involved with the Nashville students, suggesting that we should pick up the Ride, or continue the Ride. And we talked to a lot of people, CORE people, they said, "Don't do it," they were flying on to New Orleans. And people in SCLC, including Dr. King and the local people in Nashville, said "you all cannot go, it's just like committing suicide." So we decided to go. Ten of us were selected to go on the Ride and to continue the Ride from Nashville, and I was one of the guys.

Q. Who was with you?

A. There were ten people . . . Ten Nashville students . . . There was Paul Brooks, Katharine Burke, a young guy named William Harbour.

Q. What other SNCC people were with you?

A. I don't know any names that stand out right now. Most of the people after '62 or '63, they really didn't get involved in SNCC as a southwide group. They stayed with the Nashville Student Movement, and after that they graduated from college and got involved in other things. So none of the names I can think of at this particular time of that original ten really stand out. I can't think of a single one. And I was chosen to be the spokesman for that particular group and went on to Birmingham and we were put into protective custody and all that. And later, we went on to Montgomery, where I was beaten again, and left out on the street unconscious and I think all of that has something to do with it; people didn't forget that. And then I went back to Nashville in September of '61 and I was elected chairman. See, Diane [Nash] had been chairman of the Nashville Student Movement in the past, and then I was elected chairman of the Nashville Student Movement, and when it was . . .

Q. When was that?

A. That was '61. September of '61. I was chairman of the Nashville Student Movement during the school years September '61-'62 and '62-'63, and when there was no other protest movement going on, there was something going on in Nashville. Massive demonstrations, 3,000-4,000 students involved in theaters, hotels and motels and that type of thing. And the Nashville Student Movement, being a part of SNCC, was a movement to be reckoned with, because it became a powerful movement in terms of getting things accomplished. So that's why two of the chairmen of SNCC have been from Nashville; from the Nashville Student Movement.

Q. You mean Marion Barry?

A. That's right. And some of the best people (and I'm not just saying that), but some of the best people that made up SNCC, people like Diane [Nash] and [James] Bevel and Marion [Barry] and [Bernard] Lafayette, all came from Nashville. Jim Lawson was their teacher.

Q. Okay. I sort of want to skip ahead to something else, and that is the whole Selma-Montgomery march, where Martin Luther King was involved.

What happened there? Was it some sort of thing where Martin Luther King made everybody stop and pray and turn back?

A. I didn't go on Tuesday because I was released from the hospital on Tuesday, so I wasn't there. I came out and I was there just before the people left, but I didn't participate in that particular effort. On a Sunday we marched, or attempted to march, were beaten and then Monday I guess we just sort of regrouped. What day did he turn back? On Monday or Tuesday? On Tuesday . . . Let's see—7th, 8th, 9th—I guess it was on Tuesday that he turned back, maybe.

Q. Did SNCC know he was going to turn back?

A. No. SNCC didn't know. I don't think people were aware . . .

Q. What did SNCC think about it?

A. I think some of the people in SNCC were bitter and angry about it, but I say this, and I say this for the record: I think SNCC forfeited its right to criticize the march from Selma to Montgomery, in a sense to say anything about it. If I can give you a little history here. I don't know if anyone else has talked to you about the march, but this is pure, honest history of what happened. The day before the march, the Saturday before the march, we had an executive committee meeting in Atlanta, in the basement of a local restaurant on Hunter Street. And the SNCC people, almost every person, opposed the march from Selma to Montgomery. They said that people shouldn't march. They said it was another trick of Dr. Martin Luther King to get people hurt and everything. We shouldn't march, we shouldn't support it, we shouldn't have anything to do with it. And it was the official decision.

Q. Did you agree?

A. No, I didn't agree. And another cat didn't agree, and that was Bob Mants. See, I took the position that the march was one of the most available weapons, was the most powerful weapon that we had to dramatize the desire of the Negro people in the Black Belt of Alabama and throughout the South to vote, and that we should march. It was a means of protest, and that we should march. Some people said if we should march, the only reason we should march is to protect the people, because people gonna get hurt and people gonna get killed, that type of thing. But when the vote came down, people voted against SNCC officially participating in the march. And I don't know what the vote was but I know two people who favored the march, and that was Robert Mants and myself. I said I was going on anyway . . . I guess this was when the whole consensus thing broke down . . . So I said

I would go as an individual; that I was a citizen of Alabama and I had a right, I thought, to participate in this particular demonstration, and that I was going to march. So, I left that Saturday night, driving with some SNCC people who were going down to observe, I guess. Some individuals who favored the march who were not members of the executive committee, went to Selma, and we marched. After all the violence and everything in Selma, after that first attempt to march, SNCC people got involved. The people who had voted against the march got involved, as far as saying that they wanted things to go in a particular way, in a particular direction. Some of the people, as individuals, were willing to cooperate and try to . . . Selma, during that whole period leading up to the march, had been a cooperative venture, since January 18th, between SCLC and SNCC. And since that time, I spent almost all of my time, almost every single day in Selma. Maybe I went to Atlanta on the weekends. From January 18th, all the whole month of February, except for about four days when I was on a speaking thing . . .

Q. Was there a certain rivalry between SNCC and SCLC in Selma?

A. I don't think there was necessarily a rivalry. I think some people disagreed on certain techniques and certain tactics and things like that.

Q. For example?

A. There was a debate over people signing a roster in order to get a number . . . A little thing, a little insignificant detail. But I don't think there was any real debate and division over major points of the whole Selma movement. Some people say that Martin Luther King betrayed them, betrayed the people; that he sold out the day he . . .

Q. Why do they say that?

A. On the bridge; that he made a deal with the federal government and that type of thing. See, and I think one of the basic principles of the philosophy of non-violence is that you always give your opponent a way out. You don't try to crush someone, but you try to leave room for them to get out. If they want to save face, let them save face. I think that was Kennedy's thing with the Cuban crisis. He never threatened to destroy Cuba, or destroy the Soviet Union if Khrushchev didn't move the missiles out of there. I know there's a lot of debate about that. But he sort of left a way, an honorable way, for those guys to come out. And I think what Dr. King did was said in a sense, "while we may lose in this particular demonstration today, we may lose the battle, but we will win the war. That we may lose on this Tuesday, but two weeks from today, we gonna be on our way to Montgomery." And it was not . . . To me that was not a big . . .

Q. Well, I don't understand. If he hadn't stopped there, then . . .

A. If he hadn't stopped there, there were real possibilities of another serious, probably more bloody, clash between the demonstrators and the state troopers of Alabama.

Q. The whole thing was about whether SNCC would have police protection on the march, or something like that?

A. I don't think so . . .

Q. If there had been another bloody clash, SNCC might not have been able to go on to Montgomery? I mean, the march might not have been able to go on to Montgomery?

A. If there had been another clash on that particular day . . . Eventually the people would have made it to Montgomery, but there would have been so many innocent people hurt and beaten and probably some people killed, when it could have been avoided . . .

Q. That bridge incident . . . What was the name of the bridge?

A. The Edmund Pettus Bridge, over the Alabama River.

Q. Were you . . . There was some sort of incident where you were leading people over the bridge? I mean, you were stopped and beaten by the police?

A. Right. That was Sunday. That was the first attempt to march. There was the Sunday March 7 march. Hosea Williams, who represented SCLC, and I were marching, supposedly as an individual. But it was really SNCC . . .

Q. But that had nothing to do with King turning back?

A. Oh, no. King was not there that Sunday. He stayed in Atlanta preaching at his church. There were different rumors about why he stayed away. Some people say the FBI or somebody in the Justice Department said that he could be assassinated and he shouldn't march, and he would be fired on when he got on the bridge. And so we decided to march, and then I was beaten and gassed, with other people.

Q. Oh, did SNCC people suspect that King turned back not because he feared a bloody clash, but because he feared being assassinated?

A. On that Tuesday?

Q. Yes.

A. I don't know about that Tuesday. I think people in SNCC generally just felt that probably he gave in to the pressures of the federal government. But they felt on that Sunday that he didn't march because of the possibility of being assassinated.

Q. Oh. Just that one day?

A. Yeah.

Q. What was the significance of that whole march?

A. The Selma march?

Q. Yeah. In general, and also in terms of SNCC's relationship with SCLC.

A. The Selma march, I think, must be considered a landmark in the civil rights struggle. Because it was the first time that we were able to involve more than just one city, more than one county, but several counties in the black belt of Alabama, into one massive movement. And at the same time we were able to bring the nation to the South and show, point out, what Negroes have to go through in being denied the right to vote. And the Selma crisis created such a concern, such a restlessness on the part of a segment of the American people. I remember on the Tuesday following the Sunday Betty Garman . . . have you talked to Betty Garman?

Q. Yes, I have talked to her.

A. Well, she was the Northern coordinator, and one night she called the Selma office when I was there and she gave me a list of cities for the demonstration . . . SNCC was a powerful force during that period . . . There were demonstrations in more than eighty-two major cities in the United States and in Canada, and I would say over ninety percent of those demonstrations were in cities SNCC had something to do with, including the one in Canada at the American consulate. But you had hundreds and thousands of people in the streets. In Michigan, the governor—Governor Romney—and the Mayor of Detroit were marching down the street together; and people all over the country, because of what happened in Selma.

Q. This was in . . . what? Spring of . . .

A. Sixty-five. March of '65. I think the Selma march was the beginning of a further deterioration of the relationship between SNCC and SCLC. Just in little problems, personality conflicts and things like that. We had some people on our staff who were very critical. They couldn't fit into the SCLC bag. SCLC put a great deal of emphasis on strength, a great deal of emphasis on the leader type thing.

Q. Did this make a momentum, this Selma march. Was it more successful than the march on Washington in this respect?

A. I think so. Because the Selma march, something concrete came out of it. The march on Selma created such a national crisis that the President of the United States had to go on nationwide television and deliver a major address, which I think was a marvelous speech. He said something about the "moans and the groans of the people," and when you get a government official saying something like that, that "the cries of the people have summoned us all here," that brought even a President, even the highest legislative body, decision-making body in the country; one of the most respected, I guess, legislative bodies in the world: the Senate, the members of the House together, I think that is saying something to the South. Because I think if Johnson had not made that speech on March 15th, if there had not been any type of justice from the federal government, if he had not sent troops to Alabama, I think the summer of '65, or the spring of '65 could have been serious. There could have been disorder in every major city in this country. Because they talk about a credibility gap now concerning the war in Vietnam. But, I think SNCC had had the feeling for a long time that there was a credibility gap in the whole civil rights area. The government was saying one thing and not doing what it was saying it was doing; making promises and not keeping those promises.

Q. Do you think this somewhat changed the minds of some people?

A. I think the Selma thing . . . Maybe not "changed" the minds of some people; it was not a detour, but a postponement of certain actions.

Q. I would say a growing disillusionment.

A. Right. But now, you know, I think what could have happened if Johnson had not made that speech, and some other thing, like supporting and protecting the marchers from Selma to Montgomery, what could have happened at that time is happening now. I think it's sort of like Selma with the Meredith march, and we're seeing much of it now and I think you'll see more of it this summer. And if I may make a point about the James Meredith march . . . I think SNCC's involvement in that march . . .

Q. Yes . . . ? What happened on the Meredith march?

A. See, what made the Meredith march different from the Selma march . . . The James Meredith march didn't have any substance. See, demonstrations grow out of a movement. There was no movement in Mississippi . . . I think, in order for any particular demonstration to be powerful and meaningful it should have some basis, some basic purpose. Or there shouldn't be a demonstration.

Q. Did SNCC participate in that?

A. In a sense they did, in a sense they didn't. And that's sort of wrong in itself, I guess, but it's true.

Q. In what sense did it?

A. The sense it did . . . The chairman of SNCC at that time made a decision—along with two or three other people, on his own—to participate in the Meredith march without the central committee or the coordinating committee. And at the Nashville meeting, just a few weeks before, they had been accusing other people who had been in elected office of making decisions without consulting other people.

Q. That was Stokely . . .

A. Yeah. And I think the Meredith march . . . There was no movement. I think few demonstrations, few marches, few protest meetings—anything—will surpass what happened in Selma. See, the Selma demonstration didn't take place in a vacuum; something led up to it. When we went there in September of '63, and then when SCLC came down, this was a type of joint effort, starting in January, that increased the momentum, you see. The Selma march was a climax of something, but the Meredith march was a reaction to a particular incident; that James Meredith had been shot, and people tried to create something out of that, which I think sort of fell through. I don't know whether I said it openly in public, but I don't know whether greater harm came out of the Meredith march, or good.

Q. What do you think were some of the other important developments in SNCC between '63 and '66? What were the big things in that period?

A. I think the development of the Mississippi Freedom Democratic Party. SNCC gave birth to that organization. The development of the Albany movement, in Albany, Georgia, the first time that a whole community outside of Montgomery, Alabama got involved in the SCLC and SNCC. But you've got a whole movement, a whole city, a whole Negro community going to jail en masse. I think SNCC had to create that, with the challenge of the Democratic convention and the party, the Freedom Democratic Party, and, after Atlantic City, the Summer Project has to be considered as a landmark, I think, in the history and development of SNCC.

Q. Well, let's talk about these different things in more detail. You mentioned the FDP first. How did that come about? What led up to its being founded?

A. I don't know if I'm the right person to . . . If you can talk to Frank Smith or somebody like that, because they were more closely in the Mississippi development. And people like Moses, and [Lawrence] Guyot. Have you talked to Guyot yet?

Q. Not yet, no.

A. People like . . . (unintelligible)

Q. He's in Mississippi too?

A. Yes, he's in Mississippi. They know the details of what really happened. I was not that closely involved on a day-to-day basis with the development or creation of the Mississippi Freedom Democratic party. I was not altogether in that "wing" to give everything to Mississippi.

Q. Why was the party founded, do you know?

A. Yes. The party was founded because the Negro people in Mississippi—more than 450,000 of voting age and only about 25,000 registered to vote—had been denied a right, denied *the* right to participate in the regular Democratic party. And they felt that . . .

Q. Why didn't they just found another party, instead of founding another "Democratic" party?

A. They felt that maybe by using the methods of the Democratic party, using the methods of being accepted, of getting into the establishment and participating, they would be recognized as a big, official political party. And I think at this point, after the Atlantic City thing, people became so bitter and so stern and frustrated about what took place, that they used all the methods, used all the tricks of the game and played the game, and then they were turned down. I think they felt this was the only way the people would have a voice in the decision-making process within the political arena in Mississippi. I think people really felt and some of us were really convinced that the Mississippi Freedom Democratic Party will be seated and will be recognized, and all of that. But . . .

Q. Yeah . . . Was this very effective in starting local leadership?

A. Oh, yes. By all means. Throughout the state, people participated in mock elections, you may recall.

Q. Could you go back? Let's go back to December of '63.

A. December of '63, right. When Aaron Henry and . . . Ed King were running for governor of the state, and I spent a great deal of time in the state during that particular period, down in the delta area. All across the state people had been organizing to different local, political organizations—precincts and county districts. People who had never voted before, who needed to get used to the whole method of trying to vote. Who had never registered. You had these different ballots and things—beauty shop, barber shop, grocery store, churches, homes and everything else—and in that election, if I recall, more than 80,000 . . . 82,000 I believe . . . I think it was 82,000, maybe more . . . Negro people voted in that mock election. In '63. And I think from that period, if you recall, a lot of whites too were involved in that, particularly from Yale and Stanford, I believe. Maybe somebody you should call and talk to who was involved in that is Al Lowenstein; have you talked to him?

Q. I'm going to.

A. Right. He's a good guy. I saw him not too long ago. I go down to his restaurant to eat a great deal. And I think he could give you some real insight on that. . . . And all those contacts that were made from that election were given to the different workers in the different districts, the different counties and the different communities. And those records served as a mailing list to get people to come to other organizations. So that whole mock election thing took on a prominent organization, that led into the real creation, engaged in MFDP as a real organization, I think. It was the beginning of the MFDP, in terms of having a mass base, a mass following in Mississippi.

Q. Okay. Now, the next thing you mentioned was the Albany movement. Actually in '61 and . . .

A. Sixty-one and '62.

Q. Would you evaluate that as a success? The Albany movement?

A. No, I think the Albany movement . . . It was successful in only one way. The fact that you got the Negro community aroused; you got people aroused. You got people in motion.

Q. But no really concrete . . .

A. No victories, or concrete gains. And a lot of people have said it was Dr. King's serious defeat. I don't know. If it was a defeat for SCLC, it was a defeat for SNCC also, for there were two organizations working there. But nothing really significant or meaningful in terms of change or victory came out of Albany. Chief Pritchett, the police official there, played it very cool.

****(Interruption)

When Kennedy died, I think something died within the movement itself. And I think something died within a lot of the young people. See, in spite of people being critical of Kennedy, and all of that, I think that, on the other hand, there was a great deal of hope and a great deal of possibilities with Kennedy; of being a friend to the movement and being a friend to young people in particular. Because people could tend to identify with him, he spoke their language.

Q. What were some of the other big turning points in those first few years of SNCC's history. Between say '61 and '63?

A. I think the central point, and it's the most important development in SNCC between '61 and '63, when people decided that they could no longer live in the college-community world, and because somebody had just brought the problems within the urban centers to their colleges and their universities; somehow they had to go out into what people in SNCC (because of the religious influence) called the "byways and the highways" of the South and take the gospel—Freedom—to the little people. Somehow you had to move beyond town and gown, and move out, for people to know anything about a town or anything about gowns.

Q. Yeah. Now, once they decided to do that, were there any big changes in the way they worked in these highways and byways?

A. Oh, yes, by all means. In the small towns, people were primarily based on college campuses or university campuses, whereas . . . I think in a sense SNCC's pattern in late '61 and all of '62 was a great deal like the early Christian church. You sort of went out there without anything. You really didn't know where you were going to stay. How much food would you have to eat? I mean, you really didn't know whether you were going to return or not. There was a great deal of faith. You just sort of were going out on your own; you became a missionary, in a sense. But not a missionary. You became one to go with the people, where the people are. If they're in the cotton field picking cotton, you would go there. And maybe help pick some cotton. If they were picking squash, you would help pick squash. Whatever the people were doing. You're there with them, stay in their homes, share their food and do everything they would do. But in the process, you're trying to build up their confidence, and starting to win their confidence, I guess. And at the same time, trying to get down to . . .

Q. Were SNCC people angry in those days?

A. You could say they was angry, but at the same time not angry. It was a good type of anger. It was a positive type of anger. It was against something, but it was also for something. It was against the whole system and structure of segregation and racial discrimination. It was also against the old guard Negro leadership. It was against . . .

Q. What about them?

A. Well, the old guard Negro leadership was that type of leadership that would tell people "you do this and you do that"; particularly an organization that happened to be based in New York, or be based in Atlanta, it was sort of looked on like they were looking down through a telescope, instead of going down and being with the people. They conducted membership drives and membership meetings and big fund-raisers and rallies and things like that, but at the same time they were not suffering the type of indignities and injustices that the local people were suffering. And I think SNCC resented this. This was what, I think, brought SNCC into being, a sense of resentment against old guard Negro leadership and against the pace of change.

Q. Too slow.

A. Yes, the thing was too slow, and they wanted things to move faster, much faster. They resented people who said we got to work it out through the courts. They were saying that we've found a method, we've found a way. That we can do it ourselves, and it was saying to other people, "You don't have to wait until Roy Wilkins comes to Jackson. You don't have to wait until Martin Luther King comes here, but you can do it yourself. Just organize yourself into a powerful force and do it, and . . . "

****(Telephone interruption)

Q. You were talking about how SNCC had the idea people could do things for themselves, and not wait for the courts or for big famous leaders.

A. Right. And from that very period . . . had created this, I think, marvelous idea, which is a very noble concept, that you went into a community not to become leaders yourself; that you do not go in there to establish SNCC and make SNCC the organization that everybody should lie down and worship.

Q. Did that work out? Did SNCC really develop indigenous leadership?

A. I think so. When you look at the state of Mississippi, and look at all of the people who have emerged over the past few years. And it would be good, you know, to talk to some of those people, like Fannie Lou Hamer, for example. I think Fannie Lou Hamer was a product of SNCC. They took her out of the . . .

Q. Was there a problem of the SNCC people trying too much to be leaders in working with people?

A. Trying to be . . . too much . . . ?

Q. In other words, telling them what they wanted too much?

A. I think that became a problem much later on, telling people what they wanted, rather than let people sort of decide. You make certain information available to the people and let the people make their decision. But I think there was always a conflict within SNCC, over this whole thing of some people deciding for people, in a sense, what they want. And at the same time, other people saying to people, "you decide for yourself." See, I don't know if people discussed this or not, but Gene Roberts did a story on people in SNCC, the so-called "Freedom High." Have you heard that phrase?

Q. I've heard it, yes.

A. Well, much later, after the summer of '64 but even before then, a great many people went through a period called the Freedom High period. This was when people did whatever they wanted to do, according to the spirit. You just go out and do anything, you're not responsible to anybody. There was serious discussion in SNCC once, some year and a half or two years ago—about firing people. People would say, "You can't fire us. No one can be fired from SNCC. SNCC is not an organization, it's not a union, it's not a club, it's a movement." And people would try to bring discipline. But I understand now, from somebody last night, that SNCC is getting back to this thing of trying to bring about some sense of discipline, a sense of organization.

Q. You think that's a good thing? How does that stack up with what you said earlier, about consensus? Group leadership?

A. Well, I think an organization like SNCC needs or must have some form of discipline, some form of leadership. On the other hand, you must be willing to reconcile the best qualities within the consensus, this whole other thing of consensus of group leadership, with the best qualities in this whole discipline approach. I think it would be the death of SNCC if it became so highly organized and became disciplined like the military. I think it would die of its own, you know, organizational structure, if that would take place.

Q. Well, why do you say that? Was there a lot of initiative coming up from SNCC workers in the field?

A. Oh, yes. I think . . .

Q. How about initiative coming up from the people who were working among the local people?

A. A lot of initiative from the local people. But a lot of initiative came from workers in the field. People were free. They didn't have to make reports and things like that. Particularly during '62, '63 and '64. But we'd get all these reports from the field about what people were doing. People were very creative. But, when SNCC came to . . . "we're gonna concentrate on Mississippi this summer; everything is gonna be for Mississippi and we're not gonna do anything in Arkansas," then the Arkansas people felt sort of left out, and the people in Southwest Georgia and the people in the Black Belt of Alabama.

Q. Was that part of the Freedom High problem?

A. I think so.

Q. Could you expand, and say exactly how?

A. Well, I think there was a danger . . . After the Summer Project in particular (and we were for the Summer Project), all the people started talking about Mississippi, Mississippi this, Mississippi that, and there were no resources, no new staff for Southwest Georgia or Arkansas or Alabama. Most of the funds had been routed to Mississippi. So the Southwest Georgia people felt like they were being treated like step-children, and I think Alabama people and Arkansas people felt the same way.

Q. Now, what position did they tend to take in the whole Freedom High controversy? Did they want more discipline?

A. They wanted more discipline. They all did. Because they felt that Mississippi was, like, they had so many people down there—so many staff people there—they were not doing anything, and in a sense that was true. They just had a lot of deadwood on the SNCC staff in Mississippi. I think people had some legitimate gripes, and that a lot of people became Freedom High.

Q. Was this connected with the problem of whites in SNCC too?

A. I think that had something to do with it. I think the whites in SNCC had something to do with it. I think a lot of people felt, after the Summer Project of '64, we just had a lot of people, white and Negro, I guess a lot of people were white, because most of the Negroes happened to be from Mississippi, and you couldn't tell the Negroes from Mississippi to leave home, and they were there, but their relationship with SNCC was sort of nebulous. Sometimes they were on the staff, sometimes they were off the staff. On the other hand, I think some of the local Negroes on the Mississippi staff wanted white people in a sense to leave the state; it was almost like "we've been here for so many months and we want to stay here and the local people want us to stay," and we went through that whole thing.

Q. Wait now. They wanted the white people to leave. So did they favor a tighter structure, too?

A. Who? The Negroes? I don't think so. See, I think Moses, more than any other person, played a great role in this Freedom High thing. There was a segment of the Northern whites and the Northern Negroes, and I may be a little biased here but I don't think so. Because I'm a Southerner, see, but

I think Moses had a tremendous impact upon a group of Northern Negroes, and a group of Northern whites. And not just in Mississippi, where they sort of made him their own little thing. He became the all-perfect and all-holy and all-wise leader, and I think that's one of the reasons he changed his name and all that stuff. Because of that. Moses had this whole thing that people should just be free. That people should be paid to just do anything. Somebody wanted to write a play, there's nothing wrong with writing a play or writing poetry. There's nothing wrong with that. It's good and necessary, if people want to do that. And then you got involved in this whole thing of defining work. What is work? It was a hassle . . . At that point, after '64, SNCC was going through serious, very serious internal problems. There was really a real split, and it was divided into many, many factions. It was not just personalities, but it was a whole thing of disciplined consensus, the participation of the staff in the decision-making process. That's when we abandoned the so-called "coordinating committee," and elected people from different areas of the South, and the whole staff became the coordinating committee. The whole staff became the chief decision-making body of the organization. The small committee that called itself the executive committee later, changed to the central committee.

Q. Were you still chairman then?

A. Yeah.

Q. Were the people who favored a tighter structure also the ones who tended to be more critical of whites' role in the movement?

A. I don't think so. I think there were some of them in both camps.

Q. Who were these Northern Negroes who were with Moses?

A. I think people like Courtland, Courtland Cox. Have you heard his name?

Q. Yes, I'm sure . . . What about him?

A. I think Courtland would be in the Moses camp. I think Stokely would have been in the Moses camp. Well, I will say Stokely, Courtland, Ivanhoe Donaldson, Charlie Cobb. I have this whole theory and I think if you had some real investigation it would bear me out, just from talking to other people . . . You know Rochelle Horowitz at all? She was sort of an outsider; she was never really that much involved in SNCC. But a few days from now, Rochelle and Tom Kahn and I think Ivanhoe are going to get together, I guess it's on February 1st, and sort of have an interview/discussion . . . what SNCC was like . . . so many years ago.

Q. Oh, will that be published in *Dissent*?

A. I think it probably will be published. So we're going to get together on the 1st or the 2nd. Next Wednesday, I guess.

Q. Here in New York.

A. Here in New York. Yes.

Q. Will that be open to the public?

A. Oh, no. It just gonna be at somebody's apartment so they can just ask those questions, and probably just three, four, or five people. So you might watch out for that issue of *Dissent*.

Q. How come you chose those people instead of choosing people who were more important to SNCC?

A. Well, I think for this reason. Perhaps Tom Kahn more than . . . Who happens to be white . . . You know Tom Kahn?

Q. Yes . . .

****(interruption)

Q. Courtland?

A. Courtland . . . Courtland Cox, Ivanhoe Donaldson, Stokely, Bob Moses they went through this period of . . . Bohemian . . . Village . . . And all their friends happened to be white, and they sort of grew up and lived, for the most part, in a white world, attended some of the best schools and some of the best universities and all of that. And after the sit-ins—when the sit-ins started in 1960 they were in a serious dilemma.

Q. They what?

A. They were put in a dilemma of seeing young black students in the South being beaten, harassed and put in jail for trying to get a cup of coffee or a hamburger at a lunch counter, and somehow they wanted to identify with that. And so they had to in a sense throw off their past and disown their past, and they became very bitter and very angry, and they all came South, and that's where most of them are today . . . and I think this has something to do with the participation of some of the people that led them to this issue, particularly, the Northern Negro. I remember at the national meeting one young Southern black guy said, "most of us from the South do not need a white to tell us that we are black; we don't have to wear signs saying we're black. We don't need it. We do not need to wear afros to say we are black, we know we are black." And I think that is saying a great deal.

241

Because I still maintain there is a great difference in the young Negro people who get involved in the movement—those from the South and those from the North.

Q. Is there a certain guilt on their part?

A. I think it's guilt, and I think the frame of reference is different.

Q. It's interesting that this group—Stokely, Ivanhoe and so on who were later involved in SNCC at the time when whites were more and more excluded from the organization . . . How do you think that adds up?

A. Well, I think that's part of the pattern. See, I think it's a very interesting theory. I think maybe somebody should do some research on it and really trace it.

Q. A psychologist.

A. That's right! It would be good for a psychologist to . . . You know Bob Coles?

Q. I haven't met him yet . . .

A. You've got to talk about . . . He's on the board of the Field Foundation also. He's a good friend of mine. I know him very well. He's very close to SNCC.

Q. I'm planning to . . .

A. Well, you should talk to Bob Coles because I think he knows a great deal about a lot of these people. But I think this follows, that at a particular period in the very early stage, when they were very young, they went through this period where they wanted to disown their own background, disown being Negro. At the same time . . . I think this happened in other situations and other cases that had nothing to do with race; that people moved from one extreme to a position of moderation on one thing, and then they'd move from that to another position . . .

Q. Another extreme?

A. Another extreme. And I think that's what has happened to a select number of people in SNCC. I don't know that much about some of their backgrounds, but I know just from talking to people, talking to Bob [Moses]. I doubt seriously if he would speak to me today. I don't know. Maybe he would. But I understand he refuses to speak to any white person and he selects the Negroes he likes to talk to.

Q. Why do you think he won't talk to them?

A. To the white people? He said they live in a different world, and there's no way for him to communicate, to understand. He cannot understand, he cannot talk to them.

242

Q. And yet he was a leader of the whites, when he was in the South.

A. That's right. He was one of the guys who fought for whites to come into Mississippi when everybody else was against it. But today, three and a half years later, he's saying that he cannot talk to whites; he cannot deal with them. And the best schools and colleges. He was at Harvard and studied philosophy . . . a good student . . . I guess he taught at Horace Mann. A math teacher. . . Hunter College . . . Interracial background. Studied the philosophy of science.

Q. It is kind of ironic that the people at SNCC with the most interracial background are now the black nationalists.

A. That's right. And I think there's truth in that. I really haven't seen anything in writing about it, but it would be great for somebody to do a study of that.

Q. I'll probably include that in . . . some of that on the chapter on that.

A. That would be very interesting. You really should talk to a lot of people about that, particularly Sherrod. I understand he is going to be up this way in a few weeks . . .

Q. Most people haven't told me that. I sometimes ask the question whether in the Freedom High movement there was any split on issues between Northerners and Southerners, and they usually say no.

A. No, people tend to sort of evade that. Even one white kid I was talking to the other night, who had been very active in SNCC in Jackson, Tennessee came by here—had worked for SSOC [Southern Student Organizing Committee] and Hamlett. You should talk to some of the Southern white students who were involved.

Q. I've talked to Jane Stembridge.

A. Jane Stembridge. Sue Thrasher, who is at the Institute for Policy Studies in D.C. Ed Hamlett, a young white cat from Jackson, Tennessee. Sam Shirah from Alabama. As a matter of fact, he's from Toronto. Well, he was born in Toronto . . . Bob Zellner . . . You've talked to Bob. Because, I do think that young white Southerners and the young black Southerners—and maybe I'm becoming biased and prejudiced, but I think I'm trying to be as objective as possible—there's a greater sense of knowing each other, a greater sense of understanding the language, the culture—whatever you want to call it.

Q. More than, say, white and black Northerners?

A. Oh, yes. I think so.

Q. I think you're right. Jane . . . I was just talking to Jane yesterday, and she said something like that . . .

**** (turned machine off) . . . (inaudible question)

A. Well, I was not out of SNCC during that period. See, they had the coordinating committee, and I was a member of the coordinating committee during that whole period from '60 . . . I guess the first time I was elected to the coordinating committee it was the fall of '61. So I attended all the meetings and things like that. And I took a very active part in it, between going from Nashville to Atlanta and during the summer I was very involved in some of the projects and things. Chuck McDew resigned as chairman, he said because of health, and he didn't come to the meeting. But in the meantime he sent me a telegram. I have just looked at some stuff on the desk, there's a telegram that he sent to me saying that we were having an emergency meeting of the coordinating committee; this was really not the coordinating committee. In theory it was the coordinating committee, but we didn't have that many representatives on different college campuses at that time. So I came to that meeting and the house was open for the election of the chairman, and I had . . . In all seriousness—I'll be very frank and very honest: I had no idea that I would be elected chairman of SNCC. I had no dream, no thoughts on anything. I'd been very active in the Nashville Movement, at that time. I had been chairman . . .

Q. Who sort of pushed your candidacy? Who was eager to see it happen?

A. Well, I understand that Forman . . . I later understood that Forman was interested in it, that I become chairman.

Q. How was that election procedure?

A. Well, the only thing that happened, I think Forman made the motion, or somebody made the motion, that . . . well, the house was open for the nomination of the chairman, and I was nominated, and this was not a meeting of the Conference. It was not an annual meeting, but it was in June. We usually have our annual meeting in April, and McDew had just been re-elected, I guess. And so I was really elected to serve out his time. And personally, I don't see anything evil about it.

Q. Was . . . Did the whole organization elect you, or were you elected by just the . . .

A. The coordinating committee. But it was not a conference of students from all over the South, who usually elect the chairman; who had been electing the chairman, but just the coordinating committee.

Q. And usually when they elected a chairman it was everybody?

A. Right. The representatives from all of the colleges and things like that. Then, that was in June of '63. April of '64 they had a new election, and I was re-elected chairman by the whole organization, the conference—the usual thing. And the same thing happened in '65.

Q. Was there anybody who opposed your candidacy?

A. In '60?

Q. At first. The first time.

A. Oh, no. There was no one.

Q. So, I guess it wasn't that . . . really important.

A. No, no one opposed. And the rumor was at that time—I understood later—that either Sherrod or myself would become chairman. I didn't know anything about it, I guess because I was in Nashville and it's not that close to Southwest Georgia. But . . .

Q. Why do you think you were chosen?

A. Well, I think because . . . I think two or three things. And I'm not saying this in an arrogant or boastful sense. I think I was elected chairman of SNCC and the reason I served the period I did was because more than any other person at that time (and it's a pretty arrogant presumption, I know, to say this), I had demonstrated a type of commitment, a serious commitment to the philosophy and to the discipline of nonviolence, perhaps more than any other person.

Jane Stembridge

ES: What were SNCC's goals when you were a member?

JS: I think the goals were for a long time changing, and actually, not too long before I left SNCC officially—I stayed on in Mississippi to work—but when I left SNCC in '64 the goals were just beginning to be formulated. Still, stated, I think, in fairly vague terms: organizing grass roots, people organizing Negroes in America, registering to vote, economic freedom, slogans, without a specific program on the whole. However, in local communities, in individual communities where SNCC workers had gone, programs had developed. People really knew what they were doing. Local people had taken over the leadership, and this was true in many areas all over Mississippi, and some in Georgia and Alabama. It seems to me SNCC as an organization, though, still did not have specific goals and still talked in fairly vague and general terms.

ES: Did goals get clearer and clearer over time starting from the beginning and it sort of continued?

JS: On the part of the field staff and the people who really were digging in and staying in local communities, goals became clearer and clearer, more and more specific, less and less broad. One of the problems with SNCC having goals as an organization was a conflict between people who did work in the field and who were in touch with specific every-day problems on a local level and people who of necessity had to run the office and do the administration of the office in Atlanta and elsewhere.

ES: They saw the purpose of the organization in very different terms?

JS: I think so and I think this is why it took so long and perhaps SNCC is now just beginning to state goals, SNCC as an organization, to really state goals.

ES: Could you expound more on this business of the field and the office and the different views of the organization?

JS: The office staff exists primarily to keep the staff in the field there. They had to raise funds, publicity to protect us, especially cases like the Mississippi Freedom Summer when so many hundreds of students came down there.

ES: But they saw SNCC's purposes as different than the field staff saw SNCC's purposes?

JS: I think so. I think when you're in the office, when you're doing this kind of work all day, you tend to want to maintain the organization as such. You're oriented toward the survival of SNCC as an organization, almost as an end in itself. Not really, but you can very easily get trapped in this and I think a number of people did, who—sometimes through no fault of their own—were confined to the Atlanta area, say, or the New York area. The field staff seemed much more in touch with what was essential, what we really wanted to do, which was to help local Southern Negroes develop leadership, state their problems, begin to try and do something about their problems, jobs, political involvement and so forth. The field staff saw itself as playing a very crucial but temporary role in this whole thing. Go into a community. As soon as local leadership begins to emerge, get out of the community so that that leadership will take hold and people will not continue to turn to you for guidance. You work yourself out of a job rather than trying to maintain yourself in a position or your organization. It doesn't matter if you go in and call yourself a SNCC worker or a CORE worker or just a person who's there. That wasn't the important thing. This is really the opposite of what you get from Atlanta. Not just there, from any of the offices where people really aren't in touch with local problems very much. You get a desire to maintain the organization, wear the uniform, wear the buttons.

ES: Did this translate itself into different views or areas of controversy inside SNCC?

JS: A great deal of controversy over this issue and it took a long time for us to understand what was happening. We got all tied up in personality conflicts within the organization, when I think really what was happening was simply two sets of people doing two very different jobs, both jobs being important and failing to say, "Look, we're doing two different jobs. Both jobs are important and therefore we're going to have this conflict if we don't constantly talk about the fact that we're doing these two different jobs." Failure to recognize that, getting into personality battles and so on.

ES: Did this take the form of a conflict over the structure of the organization?

JS: Yes.

ES: Could you talk about that?

JS: Well, it happened gradually. It came to a head in '64. The field staff—and again I generally say field staff because there were people working who differ from this point of view—but over all the field staff felt that there should be a very loose structure, that there was a bottleneck in the organization, that money, cars, whatever the field staff needed, was getting tied up in the organization. That in order to really do the job so that they could work in the field and be what we said we wanted to be, which was a group of organizers, again, working ourselves out of a job. Not an organization that needed to perpetuate itself. So people who had been holding the job of chairman and this and that and the other ought to move out, ought to let somebody else be trained for this kind of leadership. Why did they need to stay in these jobs? This seems to be the opposite of what we're really saying to people. So various proposals were made for alternate structures, a revolving structure, a revolving directorate which would travel to the field, have much more contact with the field so that this gap between the office and the field would narrow. Training young local Negroes for these jobs within the organization. The proposals were made. There was never an open confrontation of the issues. There was enough fear in enough people to prevent this from happening. People who had jobs wanted to hold onto those jobs for one reason or another, and people who had jobs were convinced—or so they said—that this was the best structure. They weren't always personally afraid to give up the job, but they were convinced that this was the only way to structure the organization, honestly. But the insecurity and the personal needs got in the way so that we never really faced the issues, and finally there had to be a coup and we would just take over and structure it the way —

ES: What was this coup?

JS: People who came up through the field and whose whole orientation was that of the organizer finally declared themselves directors in leadership of SNCC and that in the future they would make the policy.

ES: Who do you have in mind? What people?

JS: Well, I was in Mississippi when the change in structure came and I'm not sure who said what at all. I'd prefer to say simply that those people who had come up through hard work in the field and who really knew what the local people wanted got tired of . . . There's another point to be made on the change in leadership. It's not simply desire for a looser structure, different goals in terms of being more closely tied to what local people wanted. It was also a rise of militancy among the field people. They felt that SNCC was not being hard-nosed enough, was not really saying what it was after, which was helping the Negro in America to become free politically and economically and have some power. It was power that was going to bring this freedom. It was not prayer, they felt, and it was not continuing the way we had been continuing. It was not going slow, certainly. It was power. This is the line you get from SNCC now and when these people—and I say these people because I really don't know who all figured in the change in leadership—when they did take over then SNCC began, I think for the first time, to have unifying goals and to state them in that way: give the black man power; enable the black man to get power, or take power. Along with this, of course, was disillusionment of the white kids who were working with SNCC. They had felt for quite a while confused about their role in the movement and in SNCC specifically. They began to get hurt, angry and either to leave or to be asked to leave so that SNCC now has very few if any—I really can't say—white people on the staff.

ES: That sort of brings up my next question, which is: There was conflict between the loose structure people and the tighter structure people. There tended to be a division between the field and the office. Were there other divisions that were characteristic, like whites on one side and blacks on the other? People from Mississippi versus people from Southwest Georgia?

JS: No, it didn't break down according to states in any significant way. Mississippi people were probably more vocal on the issue of loose structure. That's only because more Mississippi people were there. We had done more work in Mississippi. I think the Southwest Georgia people and the Alabama people would have taken the same line. Mississippi seemed to make itself heard more. Most of the white people who were with SNCC at that time and who had been for quite a while were advocates of loose structure. It's not true that most . . .

ES: Does that imply that they were all the time more militant—which went along with loose structure?

JS: They said so. I think what's really true is that they were perhaps angry for all kinds of reasons, angry people. Beautiful people but very angry and I'm not sure angry about race. I've seen white Northern upper middle class kids at a rally in which someone is advocating black power and saying "Down with the white man," I've seen these white kids clapping. They can't mean it. They're white. They do mean it in the sense that they hate themselves. They wish they weren't white. They're trying to be black. There's been a lot of that. I think the white kids were definitely militant and very, very dissatisfied with the whole progress of the society. From the war in Vietnam to the conditions of the Negroes in this country. I don't think they were any more militant on race than the people in the Atlanta office. That's what I'm saying. I think that would be very unreal. But more revolutionary because they're interested in more issues. They're not just interested in race. More angry about more things, but less angry about race because they're not Negroes. They can't be as angry. They haven't been treated—I'm sure I'm as angry as Jim Forman. I'm not now. I'm sure that when I was in Mississippi I was as angry as Forman. Not about race.

ES: Did the white students come from radical backgrounds whereas the Negroes didn't?

JS: Not a lot of the white students came from radical backgrounds. Most of the white students came from middle class backgrounds. Most of the Negro students did not.

ES: How about the Negro college students?

JS: No. Most of the Negro college students, at least from the South, were first-generation college students. Their parents were still farming, sharecropping and barely able to keep those kids in college. This was true of Southern Negro kids, at least.

ES: I was going to ask: were SNCC Negroes predominantly Southern?

JS: That is . . .

ES: SNCC staff, not local Negroes.

JS: SNCC staff, right, but the thought that went into the organization, the decisions that were made, were made I would say mostly by Northern Negroes.

ES: Did that create a problem?

JS: I think so. I think there was a different kind of anger. I think there's much more anger in the Northern Negro. I'm by no means saying that Southern Negroes are happy. But I've gotten the feeling at times that Northern Negroes had to convince Southern Negroes that they were in fact angry, which is a very kind of way-out statement to make. But I've gotten that feeling very strongly at times. And that the role of the SNCC organizer was to convince Negroes that they were angry, first.

ES: Was there some resentment by Southern Negroes in SNCC of Northern Negroes taking over?

251

JS: There was resentment from uneducated and less educated people about more educated people taking over, more competent people. They always do that. That's the same old thing. What's new about this organization: "Let him do it. He can do it." They didn't say "North-South." It was a question of education, skills, how articulate a person was.

ES: Did the less educated ones tend to be loose structurally?

JS: I'm not sure that there was any correlation. There were a number of young Southern Negroes on the SNCC staff, say high school or a little college background, who tended to be in favor of tight structure, who wanted positions, titles, identity, never having had any. Who saw the organization as something that should last in and of itself. It was the first thing with which they identified, the first thing that gave them the feeling of importance. I don't think that all of the Southern Negro kids wanted a tight structure. Many of them had a much better idea of what was more important, what we really wanted to do.

ES: What did SNCC people look for in their leaders?

JS: I think the first thing was "What's this guy been through? Has he really been there? Does he really know what he's talking about?" His jail record; where he's worked; what he's been through; what gives him a right to speak, much more than where he went to school, what he studied, where he comes from.

ES: How about his intelligence?

JS: I don't think that was particularly relevant.

ES: That kind of builds in militancy.

JS: It was a hero cult kind of thing. Now, when you say "the SNCC staff looked for what kind of leader?" there were a lot of people in SNCC who wanted this kind of leader. There were other people who did look for a sensitive, intelligent teacher. The tremendous influence that Bob Parris [Bob Moses] had, who is very, very intelligent and very sensitive. He was a teacher to most people in SNCC.

ES: What sorts of SNCC people looked for the more sensitive and intelligent type?

JS: Most of the white kids looked for that kind of leader. Southerners. I would say all the white Southerners. I would say all the white Southern kids looked for that kind of leader and maybe it's simply because we white Southern kids couldn't take the militancy. We wanted somebody gentle. But I think there's much more to it than that.

ES: What about Negro Southerners?

JS: Well, some turned to Bob for their leadership. Others turned to people who seemed more militant, who talked louder, who seemed to talk with more anger in their voices, who perhaps were more angry than Bob. A kind of get-up-and-go kind of person. "This is what we're going to do. Let's go and do it now." Whereas, Bob would outline much more basic long-range crucial goals. They were harder for some of the young Southern Negroes to grasp, to really feel that if we do this we're doing anything. We want to get out and demonstrate. We want to get out and act right now. Not that Bob was opposed to that, but just that he saw things in the long range.

ES: You were with SNCC right from the beginning. You were at the Raleigh conference.

JS: Right.

ES: Well, what was SNCC's goal then? What goals were stated?

JS: Well, there was a statement of policy which was written by Jim Lawson. He was one of the people who helped. He and Miss Ella Baker helped get that conference off the ground. I can't quote that, but it was love and brotherhood, freedom, justice—abstract. It was much more what Dr. King has stated as the goals of the Negro movement. "I have a dream . . ." kind of thing. A dream of brotherhood.

ES: You were a SNCC office secretary.

JS: Right.

ES: Was that like executive secretary?

JS: Not really. I was not on the coordinating committee. I carried out the wishes of the coordinating committee. In other words, I didn't have a vote on policy. Of course, in those days we all sat in together and there was a very loose structure and we came up with policy the best way we could, but it's not the same as executive secretary. The job was small. There wasn't that much to do. Newsletter, typing, trying to get people in touch with each other. But I did not speak for SNCC like Forman as executive secretary did.

ES: You were in a sense involved in SNCC's day-to-day activity as office secretary?

JS: Right.

ES: How did the program begin to take shape? How did it work out?

JS: Well, we didn't have a program. There was a coordinating committee made up of a representative from each Southern state and Washington D.C.

ES: How were they chosen?

JS: They were chosen at the Raleigh conference. These people were usually in jail or just out of jail. First we would try and keep those people in touch with each other. This is when the sit-ins were breaking out everywhere. As soon as a sit-in would break out, the SNCC office would try to get in touch with somebody who had been involved and give them moral support, try to get them to write to us, send them a newsletter. Say "The people in Tallahassee are also doing this. These are the names of the people in Tallahassee," and also, the first three months, simply work toward a big conference which we held in the fall of '60. That was a decision at that Raleigh conference to set up a temporary coordinating committee; the main purpose of this committee is to hold a conference in October which will try to get all these people together. It wasn't until October that anything like the goals or the program really, or even a permanent committee took shape.

ES: SNCC did have a program starting in October?

JS: Well, a program in still a very loose sense, and for the following year the main thing SNCC would do is; one, try and keep Southern Negro kids, college kids who were demonstrating, in touch with each other, try to keep the thing going; and the other big job was to try to get the word to the North and West so that we could get some kind of financial help for these kids who were being kicked out of school or this and that, losing their jobs. Money for court cases; money for bail, all this, and to get people moving behind this thing because there was tremendous brutality throughout the country, because there was no coverage in the South to amount to anything. Maybe the *Atlanta Constitution*, but outside that very little press. To act as an information agency. People were writing us from Seattle and God knows where. "What's happening? What can we do?" These letters said, "Please let us know. Can we send this or that or the other?" Somebody had to watch those letters and try and get all these people who cared about the thing in touch with each other.

ES: When did SNCC move out from being involved just strictly with the sit-in movement?

JS: Well, really when Bob went into Mississippi, which was early, that summer of '60. He went to find kids who would come to this October conference. We had one or two names that we got from SCLC, Negro ministers and what not in Mississippi, but in Mississippi, Louisiana and Alabama we just didn't have any names of students and nothing had happened, really. No demonstrations outside of the attempt to integrate the University of Alabama. So Bob went to find these kids and talk to them. While he was there local people in southwest Mississippi, first of all, asked him to give them some help in trying to start a voter registration campaign.

So he came back feeling that we should do that, we should help people start a voter registration campaign, at least there. SNCC did decide to do this and out of this, of course, we got involved in politics, specifically in getting out the votes.

There was conflict in SNCC about whether or not we should go into voter registration. My understanding of the conflict is those people who did not want to go into voter registration wanted to continue direct action demonstrations aimed at desegregating buses, lunch counters, this sort of thing. They wanted to because they felt we were making a bigger impact that way. We would get lost if we went down in these little counties and tried to start the vote. They felt that the vote is meaningless in this country, there's nobody to vote for. All candidates are the same, essentially. I think also, at least with some people, for the first time they had found a way to vent their anger and their fear and their frustration, by marching, by sitting in, even by going to jail. This was important, and to turn away from this right at the height of it was terribly hard for some people to do or to even conceive of doing.

ES: Was this really the height of it, though? Wasn't it sort of down at that point?

JS: Well, it was not the height of it, but there was still considerable momentum. Those who wanted to go into voter registration felt that in order to continue direct action demonstrations it would require a great deal of energy to whoop it up again, as it were, to keep the thing going. I don't think that's the main reason we went into voter registration. Plus the people who wanted to go into voter registration were more politically oriented in the first place, wanted to get into politics, thought this was the way to do it. Also, we had been asked by local Negroes to do this, and after all, why did we exist except to do what these people asked us to do.

ES: Did you tend to favor voter registration?

JS: Yes, I did. Although, I have real questions—and these questions are much larger now than they were then—as to what the vote is worth. Also, I'm not political, but in the issue there, I was for voter registration, yes.

ES: Who were the people who weren't?

JS: I think most of the Southern Negroes wanted to continue the demonstrations and direct action. These were the kids who had never been allowed to eat in Woolworths and so on. This was something very real.

ES: What significance did the Freedom Rides have for SNCC?

JS: What do you mean what significance?

255

ES: How did it affect the organization? What course did it take?

JS: I don't think it affected SNCC as an organization except the idea of people coming from the North or coming from outside the South to do something in the South, which happened again and again in SNCC.

ES: Was that the first time that happened?

JS: Yes. The Selma march, the call goes out for people to come. This has been an important part of SNCC programs. Of course, a lot of publicity was focused on the South because of the Freedom Rides, but as an event or as a technique I don't think it had much influence on SNCC's later goals.

ES: How did SNCC's voter registration program work out in practice?

JS: Well, it didn't. I mean these people weren't allowed to register to vote, or just a handful of them. Trying to get people to register to vote—I mean the program failed.

ES: It went on for several years, though, didn't it?

JS: Right. It failed in the sense people did not get registered to vote. It did focus attention and eventually brought some pressure on the Southern states and some federal presence there so that now in some counties, even in Mississippi, Negroes can register to vote. But as far as putting masses of Negroes on the books, no, which is what it would take to change anything, anyway. We had mock elections and our own freedom registration books and our own candidates, a protest election because we couldn't get registered. The price that was paid in loss of jobs and violence and . . .

ES: Do you remember any specific programs where SNCC would go first?

JS: Well, first in Mississippi. Let me see. Trying to work in three countries, Pike, Amite County and Walthall County. The first request for help came from Amite County. Bob went down and some of the local Negro kids worked with him. The violence was so extreme in those counties that the local people and Bob, SNCC, finally decided that they would move out for a while and come back. So then we went to the Mississippi Delta and pooled together everybody who had been spread across these three southwest counties together and moved into Greenwood and Leflore County and worked out from there.

ES: Did that work out any better than McComb?

JS: Yes.

ES: How were they different?

JS: Well, it was different in that in Southwest Mississippi initially they had one person trying to work Walthall, another person in Amite and another person in Pike or just a few people. Whereas, when they moved into

Greenwood, they all worked out of Greenwood and they didn't try to work such a large area. And it's different. I mean they learned what they were up against, what kind of violence to expect.

ES: Did they change their tactics?

JS: They were more careful. That's the main change. I mean there's really just one way to do this, which is talk to people, and listen to people, and talk to people, and listen to people. At least at that stage of the game that's the only way to do it. It was done the same in both places, but it was done with more caution, more slowly, I guess, as a result, out of Greenwood.

ES: Basically the same kind of strategy. What about Albany? Was that different from the Mississippi project in any important way?

JS: I don't think so. I think wherever SNCC worked in the field in those days the pattern was pretty much the same. A person goes in and finds a place to live and begins to listen to people and talk to people and find local young people or older people who can talk with him and gradually talk instead of him and take over the thing.

ES: What led to SNCC actually going into the voting process and the electoral process, running candidates themselves?

JS: Well, running candidates of its own because there were no candidates to vote for. I mean none who were going to help the Negroes at all. In fact, the candidates were all racist, at least in Mississippi.

ES: Do you remember how that got started?

JS: Well, Mississippi started it first of all with a protest election, a mock election in which we ran Dr. Aaron Henry for Governor of Mississippi and Ed King for Lieutenant Governor. Then out of that the decision to really try and run your own candidates within the accepted or official, what have you, structure.

ES: How did the MFDP come about?

JS: It came out of the same feeling that there's no candidates for which we can vote, there's no party to which we can belong. What's the difference between the Democratic Party and Republican Party in Mississippi, or in the South, or in the country as far as that goes? Eventually the only way Mississippi Negroes can do anything is just to form their own party, the Mississippi Freedom Democratic Party, and then out of that gradually the feeling on the part of most of these people, the only way the whole country can change politically is if there's a third party.

ES: What do you think were the most important events or developments?

JS: Well, there were some events and there were some just kind of ideas that I think were crucial. Certainly one of the most important events was the trip to Mississippi and Alabama and Louisiana that Bob took. Out of that came the first discussion of going into voter registration, which is really to say going into becoming political. That's what that meant for SNCC initially. Not to say SNCC wouldn't have done that whether they did voter registration or not, but that is how it got into it. Also, out of that the . . .

ES: Do you know Tim Jenkins?

JS: Yes. Really, out of that trip and the requests that came out of those Southwest Mississippi counties and our trying to meet those requests, the concept of SNCC as a group of organizers to go to an area on request to do a specific job and then work themselves out of that job. This is a crucial, I think, idea that came out of that, those early days, and wasn't verbalized until very late. In fact, probably just a year and a half ago SNCC people said what we really are is a group of organizers. But this nevertheless was the trend in SNCC, beginning with when Bob went in there. Also, the necessity of a central office much more than an office secretary and a newsletter. The violence. The need for funds, all these things, and then after that the development of a real administrative staff which changed a lot of things about SNCC, raised a lot of problems, the whole question of structure, but it was necessary. If Jim Forman hadn't been on the phone when those guys were down in those counties in Southwest Mississippi there was no way they would have ever come out of those counties at all. So the role of a central office, communications, press, all these things. I think, third, a willingness in those days to at least try and work and have an integrated staff. Very early in the game a lot of the Negro kids in SNCC were dubious about this, were ill at ease, were resentful and some felt "this won't work," had nothing against whites, but for what we were trying to do we can't have whites in this organization practically. But in those early days very little—I mean we had a job to do and it didn't really matter if you were white or not if you were willing to.

ES: How about how SNCC's policy of nonviolence developed?

JS: Well, it was always a tactic. It was never for SNCC. That is to say for most people in SNCC. That's what I guess I mean by SNCC. It was never a philosophy of life or a way of life. I think people felt that it was. Some people outside, maybe some people inside, felt that it was because that's the way the statement of purpose was stated. Jim Lawson wrote that statement of purpose and I don't think SNCC people really thought in terms of love and reconciliation.

ES: That reminds me of another question. SNCC's first conference was sponsored by SCLC and it was sort of the student wing of SCLC, or I think SNCC was thought of that way by SCLC. Why did SNCC go away from SCLC? What were the biggest areas of conflict?

JS: Well, I think there were people in SCLC who hoped that would be how SNCC would view itself. No question that SCLC wanted to be regarded as the parent of the kids who were going sitting-in, doing all this. SCLC was able to use that to raise funds for the Southern students. Also, there were people like Ella Baker and others who didn't see that this was necessary, who felt that the students knew what they wanted to do and could do it. That they didn't have to be a part of an organization. You know, call them what you want to call them, but that wasn't important, how they were tied to SCLC.

ES: That has a fund-raising advantage.

JS: Right. SNCC people didn't talk the same language that SCLC talked, which is to say they didn't have the same things in mind.

ES: Could you expound on that?

JS: I don't think SNCC people, even in the early days, were interested in brotherhood, in reconciliation, in integration. SNCC has not changed radically, taking the position of Black Power. I think SNCC wanted desegregation, they wanted Negro rights, they wanted to go to Woolworth's and eat, but they simply didn't say the same things that Dr. King has said and I don't think they wanted the same things that he seems to want. They also were in a bigger hurry than SCLC. They were also alienated by SCLC's big office and office staff and all the red tape and the same old kind of organization, bureaucracy thing, that stayed in Atlanta and really didn't have much contact with the grass roots, or so it seemed then and still does, really. That this is just another Negro organization, is what they would say. Very cynical about it and just really didn't want to have anything to do with it.

ES: Did SNCC think of itself as a democratic organization?

JS: Yes. Also, SCLC wanted to make some decisions that SNCC really felt that they didn't have the right to make. Like who was going to speak at our meetings and this sort of thing. SCLC was helping us to raise money. We didn't have anything. I mean we used their stamps and their envelopes and their everything else. The first newsletter was run off on SCLC paper. We didn't have a dime. So we were dependent on them, but then in turn they wanted to say, "Well, this person can't speak at your conference because he's a communist," or "He's going to cause you all kinds of problems" and try and control them. Well, SNCC was never the student wing of SCLC, never wanted to be. Within a few months it was clear that the organizations were doing two entirely different things and they'd never get together, probably. Unfortunately, in some ways, but nonetheless.

ES: Where did SNCC turn for funds then?

JS: Turned to the North, started fund-raising, college campuses and all the individual people who were writing to us. There was no systematic program of fund-raising in those days, but just whatever contacts we had we explored them on our own.

ES: Is that still true that they are going to the North on college campuses?

JS: Right.

ES: You were talking about the big developments in those first few years. Do you have any more about that?

JS: Well, I think the concept of the organizer and the move into the political sphere were the really significant things. And the decision on the part of the white kids who were involved with the movement to be involved with the movement as a Negro movement and not really at that time try and get out and organize whites, was a crucial decision. Some people felt then that the white kids ought to be organizing whites and trying to get the two things together. I mean it was pointless, I think, to really talk about it because the white kids weren't ready and I think most of them stayed in SNCC in order to learn from SNCC and learn from Negro kids in the movement how the thing can be done, and now some of the white kids are trying to organize whites.

ES: Did people talk about that much?

JS: Not really.

ES: Skipping back to about where we were before in '63, do you remember how the decision to have the '64 summer project was made?

JS: Yes. This is an oversimplification but it went something like this. All right, here's Mississippi. We've been down here three years and we have gotten nowhere. The only way Mississippi is going to change is if there's a lot of pressure from outside and it just cracks this damn wall, and the only force that can exert that much pressure is the federal government. The federal government is not going to move until certain people get hurt. They're not going to move because Negroes are getting killed. They never have. And they're not going to move because white beatniks that have joined up with the Negroes are getting killed because they're weirdos. So it's got to be a respectable, important somebody and it's got to be a lot of those somebodys, probably. So there are two ideas: it's got to be somebody and it's got to be a lot of people, but not a lot of Negroes because that doesn't matter. So what are we going to do but settle on this move in Mississippi. We're going to get a lot of kids to come down here. We're going to have a statewide voter registration program, Freedom Schools, whatever, going this summer and we'll recruit those students and we'll screen them and we'll try to get kids who can take it and we'll be careful, and somebody's going to get killed, probably, just because if that many people come to do that kind of thing somebody's sure to get killed. But we've been being killed for all these years and maybe some more people have to die so that a lot of people don't have to die, kind of thing, in the future. It was a very, very, very hard decision to make to issue the call for kids to come down and risk their lives. We also had questions about—very real questions which proved to be true—about kids coming down who were well educated and white who would simply reinforce the same old thing. They're going to be able to type. They're going to be able to teach. They're going to be able to do all these things. How are we going to develop local leadership among the Negroes if we keep bringing in these educated white kids? It was finally decided that we had to try it. We had to get some kind of attention focused on the state and if focused on that state, then hopefully focused on the other Southern states. So that decision was made in November to go ahead and make plans for such a project.

ES: What did the people who didn't want the project say?

JS: Well, at the conclusion of that week-end meeting I don't believe there was anyone there who was still strongly opposed to that, because we did talk about it and we ironed it out, and everybody had questions about it. But I think the general feeling at the end of the meeting was that this was what we had to do. We still had a lot of questions about it.

ES: What effect did the summer of '64 have on SNCC?

JS: Well, it did focus some attention on the state of Mississippi. People did get killed. It did reinforce the old ideas. It did put the cap on the development of local leadership to some extent. This varied from project to project, depending on what kind of white kids had come in there and what kind of local people were there to begin with. Most of the white kids tried to be sensitive to this kind of thing; some of them were not sensitive to it. But it did impede that. I think the biggest lesson SNCC learned from it was that you can't bring in white kids to help develop Negro leadership. It's an impossibility. I think that's true, too. And it was after the summer project that I learned that I could not help develop Negro leadership because I was white. There was no other reason. Because I would go in and talk to Mrs. Brown about registering to vote and why she should and so on and she would say, "Yes, ma'am. I will," and if she did that would be why she did. I mean as far as really talking about it, really understanding it, no.

ES: After the summer a bunch of white people stayed on. About how many were there?

JS: Of the volunteers? The people who came down?

ES: Yes, the volunteers.

JS: I don't have any idea how many people really stayed. I'll say thirty or so who stayed any significant time. I think some stayed possibly a semester. Dropped out for the semester, intended to stay for the semester and stayed a week or a month or so, but people who really stayed a year and dug into one community, there weren't that many. Twenty or thirty maybe, if that many. They didn't all stay in Mississippi, but stayed in the south, stayed in the movement.

ES: Was that group connected with the dispute over structure that we talked about before; did their presence affect it?

JS: Do you mean did it have anything to do with the fact that the debate arose, or how did they figure in the debate? What's your question?

ES: What role did they play in that debate?

JS: Well, they advocated a looser structure, I think, on the whole, but these kids did not play as important a role in the debate as the white kids who had been with SNCC much longer, before the project. There were a half dozen, say, white kids who had been with SNCC for quite a long time who were very vocal about structure, who submitted proposals for alternate structures, this kind of thing. Gave a lot of thought to it, in other words. But these were people who had been out. Mendy Samstein and Casey Hayden. People who had been there for quite a while.

ES: Yourself?

JS: I did not go with the first conference on structure. I was still in the state, but I was writing and I was pretty much out of it. I was for a rotating loose structure, but I was not on SNCC staff then. I didn't go to the meeting. Mary King, Casey Hayden, Mendy Samstein.

ES: She left?

JS: Yes. These people had been with SNCC for quite a long time. But the volunteers who stayed, I don't think had that much to say about the structure issue.

ES: Was their presence one of the reasons that other people were upset about the structure issue?

JS: Well, their presence made some of the Negro people angry. I mean there were some Southern Negro kids who were on the SNCC staff who were just as insecure as local Negroes and the fact that a white kid came in and could do this or that, the other, made them mad as hell. Again, you talk about black power and black this and black the other, which is not what Stokely's saying or why Stokely's saying what he's saying, but there was some personal antagonism towards them. The more whites that came in, the greater this antagonism. "This is our organization. This is our identity. Why the hell does this kid have to come and join it," kind of thing. The more that came in, naturally, the madder they got.

ES: How does that differ from what Stokely's saying?

JS: I don't think Stokely's saying what he's saying because he got mad at the white kids who came in, because Stokely is as competent as anybody can be, and as articulate and capable and as well educated. I don't think. He might have been, but he had no need to be really threatened by these kids' ability. Whereas, some Negroes at SNCC did have some reason to be threatened in terms of: "This person can speak better than I can." If you ever had a reason to be threatened, they did. I'm not sure you do, but—When they talked about Black Power they were really talking about their own needs and their own fears. I'm not saying that Stokely doesn't have his own needs tied up with what he's saying—everybody does—but I think he's talking about what he thinks is the only program that Negroes can adopt in this country that's going to get them anywhere. He's talking about a program. He's talking about a strategy. He's not pouting. He's not lashing out at whites. I think Stokely's not too concerned about whites. He's concerned about Negroes. He's not saying what he's saying in order to get back at whites, which a lot of Negroes have done. He's saying what he's saying because he wants to.

Ella Baker

New York City, December 27, 1966.

[Ella Baker is a middle-aged woman, a graduate of Shaw University in Raleigh, North Carolina. She has worked for the NAACP and SCLC and it was she who called the conference at which SNCC was founded. She was a strong influence over it in its early years.]

Q. What is the basic goal of SNCC?
A. To change society so that the have-nots can share in it.

* * * * *

Q. Could you discuss in detail SNCC's move from the sit-ins to other things?
A. In the early days, there was little communication, except on a highly personal basis, as between friends and relatives, in the sit-in movement. I had originally thought of pulling together 120-125 sit-in leaders for a leadership training conference—but the rate of spread of the sit-ins was so rapid and the response so electrifying, both North and South, that the meeting ended up with 300 people. Many colleges sent representatives; there was a great thrust of human desire and effort. The first sit-in took place February 1, 1960; the meeting in Raleigh was around April 17, 1960, for three days. Nineteen colleges above the Mason-Dixon Line sent representatives, most of them white. There were so many Northerners that at the meeting it was decided that Northerners could not participate in decision-making. This decision was made sort of by mutual agreement after discussion, because the Northerners recognized that the thrust of the action came from the South. They had been drawn magnetically to the movement because of their great admiration for the wonderful, brave Southerners. The Southerners wanted it that way, at that meeting, because of the divergent levels of political thinking both within the Northern group and between the

North and the politically unsophisticated Deep South. (There were many representatives from Georgia, Louisiana, Alabama, although only token representation from Mississippi.) There was an outstanding leadership group from Nashville. It was a basic insecurity that caused the South to keep the North out of decision-making. The North and South used different terminology, had trouble communicating. This has cropped up again in SNCC. It became more subdued in the summer of '64 when there was a real program to be carried out.

Q. What else was decided on at the meeting?

A. That the coordinating group (SNCC) was not to be part of any other organization. Some tried to make it the student arm of SCLC, which had put up the few dollars to hold the meeting. They decided that it was too early to fix the structure of the organization, but the feeling was that it ought to be independent from adults.

* * * * *

Moreover, some of those who took part (I realize in retrospect) saw a basic difference in the role of leadership in the two organizations. In SCLC, the organization revolved around King; in SNCC, the leadership was group-centered (although I may have had some influence). Southern members of the movement were somewhat in awe of each other. There was a feeling that it was the "dawn of a new era," that something new and great was happening and that only they could chart the course of history. A strong equalitarian philosophy prevailed. There was a belief you could just go into an area and organize if you had had no leadership experience. SNCC rejected the idea of a God-sent leader. A basic goal was to make it unnecessary for the people to depend on a leader, for them to be strong themselves. SNCC hoped to spread into a big movement, to develop leadership from among the people. At first it had a rotating chairmanship, for periods of about two months. Marion Barry was the first chairman. He was selected at the Raleigh meeting as temporary chairman with no opposition. This was in deference to the role of the Nashville movement, of which he was a leader. (Nashville had already had mass arrests after which the demonstrators had decided to stay in jail.) Marion had already demonstrated his capacity both to suffer and to confront the white man. He was seen as a real martyr. The Nashville group brought with it the influence of the Reverend James Lawson, who believed in nonviolence as a religious principle.

A continuations committee of two representatives from each state was chosen. It met in Atlanta once a month from April to August 1960. Then in Atlanta in October there was another general meeting at which SNCC was chosen as the name and Barry was retained as chairman. The next chairman, elected in '61, was Chuck McDew, who served for two years and was succeeded by John Lewis.

*****

Q. How did the office of executive secretary evolve?
A. Jane Stembridge was then studying at Union Theological Seminary and she expressed to Rev. Shuttlesworth (of SCLC) her special interest. In June she became the "office secretary" and was accepted as such by the Continuations Committee. Many of the Southern students lacked certain kinds of experience, e.g., of conducting a meeting. Jane (who was white) could type, write, etc. Her first job was to prepare, with me, a statement for the Republican and Democratic National Conventions. Barry, with Bernard Lee, went to the Democratic Convention in California to deliver it. The simplicity of their presentation had its impact. Several papers in Tennessee (where Marion came from) carried stories.

At the October meeting, Jane asked to be relieved because certain things did not please her. Anyway, Southerners were no longer worried about competition for their leadership roles from people with greater skills, and then Jane had had no actual experience with confronting the enemy in the field.

Ed King of Kentucky, who had been working in the office, took over then and stayed till the following spring. It may have been he who first had the title executive secretary. The office was in Atlanta right from the start.
Q. What were the powers of the executive secretary?
A. From the beginning, executive secretaries were the ones who spoke to the press. Jim Forman took over in fall '61, and the office under him acquired more powers because of his background. He is an excellent strategist under pressure. He was effective and therefore people deferred to him. There was no obvious period of resentment against him.

*****

Q. What is SNCC's basic goal, that makes it unique?

A. The NAACP, Urban League, etc., do not *change* society, they want to get in. It's a combination of concern with the black goal for itself and, beyond that, with the whole society, because this is the acid test of whether the outs can get in and share in equality and worth. By worth, I mean creativity, a contribution to society. SNCC defines itself in terms of the blacks but is concerned with all excluded people.

Q. Has there been a change in SNCC's goal over time?

A. During the sit-in movement, we were concerned with segregation of public accommodations. But even then we recognized that that was only a surface goal. These obvious "irritants" had to be removed first; this was natural. Some people probably thought this in itself would change race relations; others saw deeper.

* * * * *

Q. Would you tell in detail how SNCC's policy changed after the sit-ins?

A. From the start, there were those who knew sitting-in would not bring basic changes. Youngsters who had not thought it through had not bargained with the intractable resistance of the power structure. The notion of "appeals to the conscience" assumed that there is a conscience, and after a while the question began to be raised, *is* there a conscience? Students, because they were most out front in the movement, began to see this and its political connotations. People began asking who *really* controlled things. The realization arose in Georgia that the rural areas had control because of the county unit system and that change had to be in the direction of political action. The NAACP had long been conducting voter action through the courts. In the process of internal communications, the question of the vote arose. SNCC people began to go to Washington to talk to the attorney general, at first about Interstate Commerce [Commission rulings]. Kennedy [Attorney General] tried to sell them on the idea of voter registration. Jenkins, McDew, Jones were in on this.

Some people in SNCC thought voter registration was it; others liked the nonviolent resistance effort and feared that it would be sacrificed to voter registration. It was later decided that you couldn't possibly have voter registration without demonstrations, as Sherrod believed and said from the first.

* * * * *

At the Highlander Folk School meeting, some people felt Jenkins, McDew and Jones were setting themselves apart as those "in the know" because they were in contact with the Attorney General. Marion Barry, Diane Nash, James Bevel and the Nashville group in general were zealously supporting the nonviolent philosophy and resisting changes. Basically, they felt involvement in voter registration would end the demonstrations and cause involvement in the political machine.

At that meeting the decision was made to go into the hard-core areas under minority rule.

Diane Nash actually proposed there that SNCC split into two organizations. I opposed the split as serving the purpose of the enemy. It would have been tragic to have two organizations at a time when we could barely maintain one. Some of the adults thought that those who wanted voter registration were being Machiavellian.

A director of voter registration (Charles Jones) and a director of nonviolent direct action (Diane Nash) were chosen. She then approached Forman to become executive secretary, because she thought she could trust him to be impartial in the office. (They even approached me for this, but I thought it should remain in the hands of the youngsters.)

*****

In the development of the program, it became obvious there was no irreconcilable difference between the two tactics. Charles Jones and Diane Nash agreed a few months afterward that there was no more need for separate chairmen. All later clashes within SNCC were of a more local nature; this was the only time the organization was split.

*****

Even on the issue of nonviolence versus self-defense there was never such an open split. This issue came up in connection with the preparations for the summer of '64 and was never really discussed before. Then there were discussions in executive committee meetings over such questions as what a SNCC man should do if a man he lives with wants to defend his home with a gun. But no edict came down, and therefore this decision was left to individuals.

269

* * * * *

Q. What were other sources of disagreement?
A. None, really, It was a pretty unified organization up to the summer of '64.
Q. What about the issue of whether or not to have the summer of '64?
A. In January '64, there was a big demonstration in Hattiesburg, where it first came out that there was a lot of feeling in the Mississippi staff of not wanting Northerners to come to Mississippi. Bob Moses was in jail at the time, but Jim Forman carried the ball at the meeting in favor of the summer, and it was agreed to. This was in January '64.
Q. What were the reasons for disagreement about the summer?
A. One reason was a doubt that Northerners could fit into the policy of developing local leadership (or maybe this was a rationale developed after the summer). There was some element of protection of your own leadership position. During the Freedom Vote, there had been some experience of Northerners who came down for a couple of days and seemed to be "taking over."

* * * * *

Q. How were whites in SNCC dealt with before the summer of '64?
A. It was not a major problem. Anybody who wanted to help was welcomed. After '64 the problem arose not in terms of whites but in terms of the right of the individual to make his own decisions in SNCC (this was Freedom High).

At a staff meeting in November '64, the issue of structure versus non-structure arose. Some wanted structure; others thought the real genius of SNCC was in the scope given to the original organizer. Some people said nobody should ever be fired. I thought this was unrealistic, that people were thinking in terms of a small closed society. It was a tragedy . . . people finding their personal need was not SNCC's purpose.

Old radicals have a saying: "You can't make the new world and live in it too." The young people in SNCC wanted to live in it too. This was all part of a general thing about young people not conforming. At first we dressed in work clothes in order to identify with those with whom we were working, but later this became a part of our *right* to identity.

Q. Was the Freedom High connected with the white-black problem?

A. I'm not sure. I think maybe it was—because there were more whites in Freedom High, especially whites who felt their talents hadn't been well used, for reasons of their philosophy or their psychological problems. In those days, resentment against whites came not from black nationalism but from a feeling that it was the whites who brought in these ideas (Freedom High) and who perhaps had trouble accepting leadership.

* * * * *

Freedom High was an effort to develop a nucleus of the "pure" in which you could disregard the outside world.

* * * * *

Q. Would you discuss the impact on SNCC of the '64 Democratic Convention?

A. Some people had been extremely optimistic; others weren't at all surprised at the outcome. Moses was among the more hopeful ones. I myself had never expected that we'd be seated. The fact that the liberals and most of the black civil rights leadership were committed *first* to electing Johnson was crucial. The delegates acted on nothing important. Even though they sympathized with SNCC as people, they were capable of being maneuvered by politicians.

But it wasn't the convention that caused SNCC to lose a lot of its vigor. It was the exhaustion after the summer and then the Freedom High conflict. Too much (i.e. the assimilation of hundreds of whites *and* the convention challenge) had been attempted in too short a time.

* * * * *

Q. Is there anything you'd like to add?

A. SNCC has played the role of *gadfly*—partly consciously, partly because of circumstances. By irking people and by getting down to basic issues, it has done this. Its members are not yet ready to give up this role. They understand the need for someone to keep pointing out the difference between rhetoric and reality—and also the importance of *changing* society, not just adding a few more people to it.

Q. In what way has SNCC fallen short of its goals?

A. It has not been successful in developing basic leadership in Mississippi, Alabama, Southwest Georgia. Its greatest difficulty has been in reconciling its genius for individual expression with the political necessity for organizational discipline. I myself approve of group discipline in general. The trend is more toward discipline, because the members of SNCC are a smaller and smaller band. This is because SNCC is no longer "the thing" and the civil rights movement in general is no longer "the thing."

*****

An important part of SNCC's impact has been on its individual members, who later continue the work in other ways, through other groups.

James Bevel

SNCC's early goals were concerned with dignity for the Negro. Even when SNCC became interested in voting, at first it was not using voting to seize power but as a handle for teaching people to have dignity, to stand up for themselves.

* * * * *

[Highlander Folk School Conference]

Marion Barry favored both voter registration and direct action. We favored direct action because we felt this was a better way to get people involved and because the proposed VEP was a research project to find out if Negroes wanted to get involved and we knew they did. In fact, the voter registration wing did spend a lot of time doing research and developing suits for the Justice Department. But you can't bring about real change through the courts, because they are an institution set up to preserve the status quo. [Later, in an angrier mood]: VEP was supported by the CIA. The foundations were conduits. All those guys who favored voter registration back then are now working for the government.

* * * * *

The voter registration wing went to Southwest Georgia and the direct action wing went to Mississippi. But it turned out the programs worked out the reverse. In Mississippi, the towns were too small and the people too frightened to have effective direct action.

In Georgia direct action was possible and was often a more effective organizing handle than voter registration.

*****

The trouble with SNCC is that it has never had any clear successes.

*****

In early '63, I left SNCC to work for SCLC. SCLC was better because it gave you more freedom to do the kind of organizing you wanted to. In SNCC, there was a lot of group pressure to do a certain kind of organizing, plus there was an unwillingness to give resources to anyone who was not going along with the general line. Also, Martin Luther King provided a good method of getting national attention.

*****

Nonviolence means not just "turning the other cheek" but learning to live in a community and to love yourself and thus to love all other human beings. I believe that carrying a gun for "self defense" is a hostile act and therefore not a nonviolent act. Man should present himself naked and defenseless to those who threaten him with violence and then he can love and live.

*****

Around early '63, all of the early group—Barry, Lafayette, myself, etc.—left SNCC and went to work for other organizations. A new group, mainly Northern Negroes, began to come in. These people were less at peace with themselves and more arrogant than the Southerners. They always had to be belligerent, to prove themselves. This gave them trouble as organizers.

*****

Selma did most of the organizing. SNCC's work there was completely ineffective. SNCC people talked a good line, but couldn't organize because they weren't in touch with what the people wanted.

Julian Bond

Diane Nash and James Bevel had met Forman in Fayette County. They told him that they would not work for SNCC any more unless there was someone in the office they could trust. (Charlie Jones had been running the office.)

Q. What was the most important change in SNCC's history?

A. The most important change was that Forman turned out to be a fantastic administrator and fund-raiser. Under him we moved from a tiny corner office to our present one.

When I first started working for SNCC (around October '61), there was a lot of romanticism, a great mystique of working with the rural poor under great danger. This mystique never disappeared, but Forman helped to make it more serious. He instituted field reports, a fund-raising apparatus and a no-nonsense attitude.

* * * * *

Q. In general, have Northerners played a different role in SNCC than Southerners?

A. Carmichael, Cox and Moses were all Northerners. In general, they are more articulate, better educated, have a wider view and are more interested in international questions. They were the first to develop anti-war feelings. Northerners in general are better able to promote their own ideas.

This caused tensions in the organization between those who thought of themselves as organizing a faceless mass and those who thought you ought to let the faceless mass decide what to do.

Almost all the Northerners, and most of the whites, believed in loose structure. Black Southerners wanted a tight organization.

Q. Why?

A. Because the Northerners were more philosophical. The Southerners might have needed more authority. The Northerners tended to jump from project to project a lot, whereas the Southerners would settle in one place and work. Since the Northerners were more restless, they felt the need for more freedom.

Q. Perhaps another reason was that an informal structure gave more arbitrary power over resources to the people in Atlanta, who tended to be Northerners and to favor their Northern friends.

A. Yes, I definitely agree. The tight-structure people often felt that they did not get their share of the resources. Also, whites tended to be for loose structure and Southern Negroes were the ones most resentful of whites.

* * * * *

One reason for the loose-tight structure debate was the question: where does SNCC's responsibility lie—to the organization or to the people with whom we work?

* * * * *

The dispute over loose versus tight structure was somewhat racial. Bob and Donna Moses, Mary King, Mendy Samstein, Casey Hayden, Mike Sayer, were all strong advocates of loose structure. The people who tended to be against whites in the organization were the most likely to be tight-structure people. Southern Negroes, especially. They were irritated because they often could not follow the arguments at staff meetings when whites were speaking. These meetings sometimes went on for seven days and nights. I wanted very tight structure.

The debate never really came to a head. The loose people sort of gave up and drifted out. This meant the loss of some very creative people.

* * * * *

Q. Is SNCC more Northern now since May '66?

A. No. The Northerners are not in a majority, nor are there more Northerners now than there were before. However, in '66, the Northerners were much more in leadership positions than they had been in '61.

An important difference between Northerners and Southerners is that many Northerners had been active in campus politics and therefore had more experience in political maneuvering.

(I consider Diane Nash [Bevel] a Southerner, even though she's from Chicago, because she went to college in the South and was part of the Southern faction.)

* * * * *

The Northerners who did fund-raising in the North came back frustrated because they couldn't say what SNCC's policy on Vietnam was.

The McComb project put out an anti-Vietnam leaflet before the organization as a whole took a stand.

Then came the death of Sammy Younge, a SNCC worker in Tuskegee. He had lost a kidney while in the service and then was killed trying to use a segregated bathroom [January 3, 1966]. This touched off the feeling that SNCC had to say something about Vietnam [January 6, 1966].

* * * * *

Q. When did the resentment against whites in SNCC develop?
A. Before the summer project. It was not necessarily racial but rather based on the fact that white people brought trouble wherever they worked. (Some people felt that way about SNCC in general.) Then, during the summer project, whites took over so much that they reinforced the feeling among the local people that you *had* to have them.

* * * * *

There was a lot of opposition to having the summer of '64, particularly from the native Mississippians. The only reason we had the summer project was that Bob Moses insisted on it. He believed that this was the only way to break the back of segregation in Mississippi.

After the summer of '64, SNCC sort of died. It never did anything new after that except Lowndes. Maybe the summer was just too much effort, too much tension. A lot of people were burned out after it.

* * * * *

The FDP failure in Atlantic City was a crushing blow. Many people felt that the FDP had all the right—legal, moral, etc.—on its side. *I* personally

277

had thought the convention would seat them. This was probably naive, but I was very disappointed.

*****

The FDP Challenge turned a lot of people off. It seemed you couldn't do anything if you couldn't get through such a clearly *right* challenge.

*****

The Atlanta Project started in January '65, at the time I was expelled from the legislature and ended about a year later, having accomplished nothing. The idea was to build a political base in my constituency. [Bond was a Georgia state legislator.] There were a lot of tensions between the Atlanta Project and the office about the use of funds, etc. The Project never did anything. They spent most of their time talking about black consciousness, black power, etc.
Q. How did the Atlanta Project affect SNCC?
A. It was more militant than SNCC as a whole. When it started it had a white member, Mendy Samstein.

*****

I resigned from SNCC in September '66 because I wasn't doing anything. I was spending all my time on my own, campaigning, etc. My resignation had nothing to do with the drift of the organization.

*****

The main office was always here in Atlanta, even during the summer of '64. That was just a publicity move, saying the office had moved to Mississippi. All of the records and equipment were still here.

*****

The summer of '64 enabled us to move into parts of Mississippi we'd never been in before.

* * * * *

Q. Has SNCC's over-all purpose changed?
A. At first SNCC just wanted to coordinate lunch-counter sit-ins. Its second focus was voter registration. The third was organizing in general, e.g., for rent strikes. The fourth was helping prepare Negroes mentally for the day when there will be open racial warfare, or for taking advantage of some of the tools which they've won, e.g., the vote. It becomes less a matter of doing something as of preparing people psychologically for something, I don't know what. That explains why SNCC is doing less now. [Another explanation for this last is that is has a smaller staff.]

* * * * *

The '64 and '65 Civil Rights Acts took the pressure off the country. People weren't as concerned about civil rights because they figured they'd done what they should do for it.

* * * * *

There were tensions in SNCC between people who thought of themselves as organizing a faceless mass and others who thought you ought to let the faceless mass decide what to do. But what if the faceless mass just wants a TV set?

* * * * *

For some people, like Charles Sherrod and John Lewis, nonviolence was a way of life. For others, it was a tactic. The situation in Mississippi—where local Negroes carried guns for self-defense as a matter of custom—raised difficult questions. From 1960 on, the number of people in SNCC who believed in nonviolence as a tactic only began to increase, as new members joined SNCC and the sit-in people faded out.

* * * * *

The biggest change in SNCC came in '63-'64 when we decided to build political organizations as well as just trying to get people to register to vote.

279

The reason this was so important was because of the increase in size. We acquired a fantastic, two-story office with printing press, darkroom, etc. Around the time of the summer of '64, our *paid staff* was about 200.

* * * * *

Q. How did Stokely Carmichael come to power?
A. Jim Forman decided not to run again. John Lewis's version of the election is probably correct.

Most people probably didn't care between Lewis and Carmichael. The ones who wanted Lewis probably wanted him because he'd *been* chairman and because he was a Southern boy.

* * * * *

At one period, in '60-61, the Atlanta student movement had financed SNCC (paid Ed King's salary, etc.). SCLC only gave SNCC money when embarrassed into it, e.g., when a SNCC man caught Wyatt Tee Walker making a deposit in the bank.

Barney Frank

[November 11, 1966, Cambridge, Massachusetts. Frank is a graduate student in government at Harvard. He worked for SNCC in Jackson, Mississippi, for six weeks during the summer of 1964, concerning himself mostly with organization, recruitment and planning for the seating challenge of the Mississippi Freedom Democratic Party at the Democratic National Convention in Atlantic City that August. He did not attend the convention. 1989: Frank is now a U.S. Congressman (D-MA)].

Q. Did the Freedom Party expect to have its delegates seated?
A. The leadership in Jackson did not; they expected to be kicked out. However, in Canton [Mississippi] and probably other places, people were more optimistic. The pessimism of the leaders was not communicated to the rank and file. Therefore, some of these people were deeply disillusioned by what happened in Atlantic City.

The leadership suspected the existence of a deal between President Johnson and the regular Democratic Party of Mississippi, and their suspicion was justified. In exchange for seating the regulars, Johnson was given a guarantee that his name would be on the November ballot in Mississippi as the Democratic candidate. Otherwise, there would have been an election in Mississippi in September for the slate of electors, in which both the Mississippi State Democratic Committee and the Democratic National Committee would have put up candidates. The state committee candidates would almost surely have won and Mississippi voters in November would then have had a choice between Goldwater and Goldwater. [Frank learned of this deal from "someone high up in the Democratic Party"—Rep. Hale Boggs of Louisiana.]

However, things did not go quite so smoothly at the convention as the President had expected. Pressure from Northern and Western liberal Democrats forced the President to offer a compromise to the FDP, which was the seating of two of its delegates as delegates-at-large (in addition to the seating of the regular Mississippi Democratic delegation). He had to offer this or else risk a bitter floor fight, which he might even have lost. SNCC refused the proffered compromise.

Q. What effect did the Atlantic City experience have on SNCC?

A. After Atlantic City, the civil rights movement in Mississippi split. Before that it had still been possible for SNCC, CORE and the NAACP to work together under the umbrella of COFO (Council of Federated Organizations)—even though there was already open warfare between SNCC and Charles Evers, the state head of the NAACP. In August, Lawrence Guyot, a SNCC man, replaced Aaron Henry, an NAACP man, as chairman of the FDP—but Henry was still one of the delegates to Atlantic City. The FDP platform resembled that of the ADA [Americans for Democratic Action] (not too surprising, since Joseph Rauh wrote the brief); it called for freedom throughout the world and condemned the East German regime as well as that of South Africa. After the convention, Rauh split with SNCC over the issue of the challenge to the seating of Mississippi's Congressmen, which was planned for January '65. The SNCC people wanted to demand that the regular Congressional delegation from Mississippi not be seated and that the FDP-elected Congresswomen (Fannie Lou Hamer, Victoria Gray and Annie Devine) be seated instead. Rauh maintained that you could only in good conscience ask to have the regulars unseated. To demand the seating of the FDP delegates, whose election was also slightly irregular, was too much. SNCC won and Rauh went home to Washington.

Actually, by early '64, the radicals (those who rejected the American system) were already in power in SNCC. Staughton Lynd had opposed from the start going to Atlantic City. The motive of those who favored the convention challenge was to *prove* the Democrats didn't mean what they said. The COFO alliance was motivated by the fact that SNCC felt it needed to obtain mass white support through the summer project, that it could not hold out forever alone against fascist Mississippi. With the huge influx of organizers into Mississippi (800), SNCC needed to have something to organize *for*; therefore, the Atlantic City plan. The motive of the Congressional challenge in January was to embarrass the national administration still further, to further confirm its hypocrisy [in answer to a question]. Therefore there was much less bitterness after the January challenge than after the August one. Another reason to go through with the January challenge was that the Congressional delegates had already been elected and it was logical to follow through.

*****

The conflict between Forman and Moses went back to the summer of '64, when Forman, the national chairman, was working in the Greenwood, Mississippi, temporary national headquarters, while Moses, the director of the Mississippi Summer Project, worked in the FDP-COFO office in Jackson. At that point, the official national leader had less power than the project leader, which created enormous conflict.

The Mississippi faction (under Moses) thus lost out when voting came in, and this was when activity in Mississippi began to die down. Moses's friends Mendy Samstein, Marshall Gans and Casey Hayden, who were the best whites in SNCC, left the organization.

*****

Q. Discuss SNCC's political activities since 1964.
A. The Black Panthers were formed. SNCC is apparently now almost inoperative in Mississippi. Its main base is Alabama. SNCC and FDP are now completely separate. The FDP is losing ground to Charles Evers, who controls the two counties in Mississippi with a Negro voting majority. But SNCC probably doesn't care. Stokely Carmichael once said, "Majority rule stinks!" Or, as Bob Moses put it, "The best way to keep a man a slave is to give him a vote and tell him he's free." (Moses is "a philosophical poetical anarchist.") SNCC believes that the electoral process is a sham—and even if the majority did rule, it is composed of a lot of selfish bigots. SNCC under Moses is the only organization in my experience that really tried to exercise the "general will" of Rousseau. Moses opposed voting in principle. In late '64 and early '65 there was a big conflict in SNCC between the Moses faction and the Forman faction over whether to vote or not. Although the Moses people may have had a majority, they lost in the voting because they did not believe in voting. It was at that point that Moses changed his name to Bob Parris.

*****

Also, a conflict developed between SNCC and some of the older local Mississippians in the FDP, which eventually led to the FDP leaving SNCC's orbit.

Betty Garman

. . . involved—these twenty people then elected the chairman as their spokesman. So in the spring of '64 John Lewis was reelected. . .

Q. Twenty people—that means there were ten states?

A. Yes. There were approximately ten—and the District. But I'm not sure—I'm sure it varied—but in the spring of 1964 there were not anywhere near twenty elected state representatives who came together as the coordinating committee. The organization had grown to about fifty or sixty people working full time in the field, whereas the decisions were made by this appendage of the sit-in movement, the coordinating committee who were full-time students, so there was a real conflict. The staff in December of '63 had . . .

Q. I don't really understand. The decisions were made by . . . ?

A. The decisions were made by full-time college students who were left over from the old sit-in protest groups. They were not the full-time field workers who were doing the voter registration and the political organizing, and so forth. In December of '63, the coordinating committee—these full-time students—decided to allow the full-time staff to elect two representatives to sit on the coordinating committee, plus each state project director—so it meant that Bob Moses, who was the Mississippi director, and Bill Hansen, who was the Arkansas director, and so forth, were also on the coordinating committee. And I guess it was a total of six, five or six then, of the full-time staff, were added to this coordinating committee. And the first meeting of the expanded coordinating committee was held in April of '64. But it was still a very unrepresentative body, because the full-time college students had a larger representation than the full-time staff. And the work of the organization was really done by the staff, while the decisions were made by these people who were old-time sit-in leaders.

Q. It's amazing to me that the staff tolerated that for so long.

A. Well, see, what happened was that the coordinating committee didn't really make crucial decisions. The formal structure was that, but the staff made their own decisions while they were working in the field, and the hang-ups of the conflict never really came to the surface within the organization because people were not so much concerned with structure as long as they were autonomous in their various projects—which was also a policy: that projects would be autonomous, that people would have the right to do and experiment with what they wanted on the local level. So there was this individual autonomy that was always protected and probably still is. It was a very important part of SNCC.

Q. Then how did the influx of new people . . . ?

A. The influx of new people was largely white Northern and I think what happened . . . well, then there was a great deal of concern over *who* made that decision, or *who* made that decision, so in October of '64 there was a decision to plan a . . . well, it was a tentative suggestion really, it wasn't a decision . . . to plan a Black Belt Summer Project for the summer of '65 that would include eight or nine states. And this was presented in proposal form in a long research memorandum to the staff at its October '64 meeting, and a lot of the problems of . . .

Q. About how many were there who stayed on?

A. Well, there were about 100 summer workers who stayed on. Not all those 100 were added to SNCC staff, but a good fifty of them were. And in addition you have to understand that up until the spring of 1964 SNCC was structurally organized around the college unit, left over from the old protest days, of two people from each state coming to the coordinating committee. And those two people from each state were to have been elected by two representatives from each college in the state that had a protest group. And then the coordinating committee, which was these twenty people, I think, approximately, how many of the Southern states were . . .

* * * * *

Q. What were the backgrounds of SNCC workers in those days?

A. Well, in Mississippi, there were Jesse Harris, Willie Morris, Willie Peacock, Emma Bell—all Mississippians.

Q. There were also non-Mississippians. What was their role?

A. They brought integration—showed the country that black and white could work together for a common goal.

Q. Now you said you joined SNCC in '63, '64?

A. Well, I went South in March of '64.

Q. What effect did the '64 Summer Project have on SNCC as an organization?

A. A great deal, because up to the summer of 1964 SNCC was largely an organization of Southern and Northern Negro students and some white students sprinkled in. The fact of the summer created a psychological problem as well as a real practical problem of how would the organization cope with decision-making, those kinds of problems, during the summer, particularly since in a lot of cases you had white Northern liberal college types coming down, who thought that they knew everything that was going to happen, or confident to the extent that they felt they could cope with the problems, and you had them put . . . you had to make them understand that they had to take orders from, so to speak, or take directions from the Southern Negro natives, who were less well educated and not as articulate by any means, and that caused a great deal of friction, both in the organization and in local project areas. And then in September, SNCC was faced with the question of expanding the staff, in September '64, and including all of these people who had been good workers during the summer.

. . . when this proposal was presented a lot of the problems from Summer '64, a lot of the resentment from Summer '64, a lot of the troubles of Summer '64, had never been discussed openly, or as a group, and so the immediate reaction to the Black Belt Summer Project was, look, I was in such-and-such a position during summer '64, we can't have a Black Belt project if this is the way it's going to be next year. Part of it was a problem of Southwest Georgia and Alabama and Arkansas being slighted during the Mississippi Summer, because Mississippi got all the money and all the focus and all the attention and all the care and so forth, and the other three states kind of dwindled . . . well, Mississippi got all the staff too, pretty much, and the other three states were kind of left to run their projects as best they could on a little bit of money and only a few staff and not very much attention from the Atlanta office.

Q. The Black Belt project wouldn't have excluded anybody, would it?

A. No, no, it wouldn't have excluded anybody, but, see, then there was all this "how are we going to pull off a Black Belt project if I, my project, my Southwest Georgia project, say, only got $1,000 this summer to spend, and Mississippi spent such-and-such an amount," and, you know, we couldn't get ourselves together in terms of allocating funds and resources. How are we going to run a Black Belt project? Then there was the whole Mississippi

resentment and kind of hang-ups and problems with the white college kids
. . . then as a result of these issues being raised, the whole question was
raised, who made this decision that we should have a Black Belt summer
project? Not that it was a decision yet, but just the fact that there was a
group of people pushing the idea . . . People raised that question, who made
this decision? And then another part of that same meeting was to determine
procedure for putting people on staff, so there was also a question raised
about *who* made *this* decision. And then people began to look internally and
discover, not that they didn't know it but discovered they didn't have a
structure to deal with any of these questions and they had no way to have
decisions get made. And as a result of that a meeting was called for
November of '64, where structure would be the topic of discussion. And at
November '64—it's very hard to describe a whole meeting.

Q. Where was the meeting held?

A. It was in Mississippi, Waveland. Briefly what happened was that two,
there were two sides to the structure issue. One group of people . . . and
it's not a . . . one group here and one group there kind of situation. It's a
lot of people in the center, a lot of people favoring a middle road, a lot of
people who also, to whom it depended upon the issues and the
circumstances as to what policy they supported, but the two extremes of the
issue were one group of people who were for a very loose, practically no
structure at all situation, and another group of people who were for a fairly
strong executive committee that would be able to make decisions in-between
coordinating committee meetings and that would be able to decide policy
and have people responsible for carrying out that policy and so forth. The
loose structurists were people who believed that everybody could be
responsible for their own actions and that people would function if you
didn't pressure them and that the work couldn't be defined and various
things like that. The strict structurists were more for, let's get on the move
and not let people kind of float around and take ten years to decide what
kind of program they want and five years to carry it out. Let's move
forward, let's have more of that emphasis—I *think*. It's very hard . . . the
debate went on for such a long time and the issues were not as clear as I
have made them seem still. So it's very hard to put it . . .

Q. Who were some of the leaders of the two groups?

A. Again, see, they weren't leaders. Bob Moses played an important role. He
was a spokesman for the loose kind of structure. He played an important
role until March, I guess, or February. I don't believe he came to the May

'65 staff meeting. And Forman was one of the leading figures on the tight-structure side. But that's about all you can say, in terms of leaders and so forth. Again, it wasn't so much a question of leaders and followers but a lot of people—maybe as many as thirty or forty people—having very strong opinions and being very committed to having particular kind of things carried out. And Forman and Moses certainly didn't go around and twist arms to get votes, because the debates went on for weeks at a time. And there was no question in anyone's mind that we could come to a vote and cut off discussion. It was more sort of that we reach a consensus. Consensus has always been the way that SNCC has operated.

Q. I'm trying to identify the people who were saying these different things. Do you think that in identifying them, you could say that whites tended to favor one position, and Negroes . . .

A. Yes. Yes, I think you could say that, with reservations and qualifications, that the Northern whites tended more to favor the loose structure, and that the . . . it's hard to say that . . . there were so many people . . . there were people who changed their position in the middle of the debate. There were three staff meetings on this question, and each one was a week to ten days long. So it was maybe a total of twenty-five days of debate, stretched out over eight months. In that period, people shifted and changed. But, pretty much, the Northern whites were the loose structurists and . . . I can't say much beyond that. There were Southern Negroes and Northern Negroes on both sides. It's hard to say that they were for or against the one thing or another.

Q. You couldn't make any generalizations about Southerners and Northerners?

A. No. No.

Q. How about the problem of educated people versus relatively uneducated people?

A. I don't know. I don't think that people chose sides on that basis. There were discussions about people who had education and people who were less articulate, people who had gone to college and people who had not gone to college. The concern on most people's part, anyway—and this was not so much a knock-down, drag-out fight—but the concern was that all of the debates and the discussions and so forth were . . . a lot of them were excluding people who were less well-educated and less articulate and who couldn't dig what was happening. And then there was also an issue of how do we make SNCC open enough so that less articulate, less well-educated people can participate on an equal basis with people who are educated. And that was a problem that I don't think the orientation really ever faced. I think that people were pretty honest about that and tried to grapple with the problem, but I don't think that the problem was ever resolved—and I'm not sure there is a solution anyway.

Q. Was there any split between male and female on this issue?

A. Not that I was aware of.

Q. Did all these debates eventually result in some structural changes?

A. Yes. In February of '65, at the staff meeting in Atlanta, an executive committee was elected. There was a decision made that SNCC should have an executive committee comprised of two representatives from each state and ten people elected at large.

Q. None of this on the college unit system?

A. No, nothing college. Two representatives from each state, one of whom will be the project director, ten people elected at large, plus the executive secretary, the chairman and Miss Baker as the . . . they all had votes. [Interruption]

Q. We were talking about the structural reform. You were talking about the executive committee and who was on it. Were there other structural reforms, other changes?

A. Not really. Well, see, I should go back to October—at least in October or November, I don't remember at which meeting, there was a firm decision which was not disputed by anyone that the coordinating committee would be the basic decision-making unit, and the coordinating committee was every member of the SNCC staff, everyone who worked for SNCC—put it that way, because there were some people who didn't get paychecks who were considered SNCC staff. Then, once the coordinating committee was recognized as the basic decision-making unit, the felt need was for this executive committee, to carry on things between meetings and to do administrative kinds of talks rather than making basic policy. In other words, they would decide how to and who was going to carry out certain decisions of the coordinating committee. The other structural change was the establishment of a secretariat, which was a three-man . . .

Q. This was in February '65?

A. Yes. This was a three-man administrative committee, that included the chairman, the executive secretary and the program secretary, and they were all of equal . . . they would all have equal power, equal vote, equal as spokesmen for the organization, although their job functions were defined in different ways. The chairman was the spokesman, the public figure, the one who appeared in publicity and so forth and so on; the executive secretary was in charge of fund-raising and Northern programs; and the program secretary was in charge of the Southern organizing program.

Q. Had there been a program secretary before?

A. There was a program something . . . chairman? . . . something . . . before, and it never really amounted to very much, but there had been . . . that job had been filled.

Q. Did these changes correspond to any shift in the actual people who were leaders of SNCC?

A. Not really. There has always been, and I suspect continues to be, . . . well, to the extent that there are leaders and followers, there have always been a highly articulate, hard-working, strong leadership group. Now there have been severe differences of opinion within the leadership group, so it's not a solid body, but the names of the people who stick out as the people who are recognized nationally, and so forth, as SNCC field secretaries, are primarily that leadership group, and by that *only* I mean they're respected, listened to, looked up to, by people who have been with SNCC a few number of years, or who haven't had the experience, and so forth—but again there's no set direction for that leadership group. Everything I say really relates to before March of '66. I really just have no way of saying this is such now or this is what's happening now. There's just no way for me to tell.

Q. What role did Bob Moses play in all this?

A. It's very hard to say. I'm not sure I know how much effect and influence he really had. But Bob was a different kind of person, because he was . . . well, he was the kind of person who inspired awe and a great deal of respect, and commanded himself in such a way that you respected him. So, for example, in a meeting situation, he would never get involved in the kind of petty details of the problem at hand that was being discussed, but he would hold back all of his comments until an appropriate time when he felt he could summarize and direct the entire course of the discussion. And he was capable of doing that. He would come in with a brilliant statement, which just clearly cut through all of the mess and all of the tangle and all of the debate, said exactly what probably three-quarters of the people wanted to have said and allowed the discussion to move on. Beyond that, there's no doubt that he was influential because of the qualities that he had. I mean, he has real leadership qualities, probably still does. But beyond that all I can say is that he had a great deal of influence and a great number of people listened to his every word and developed their philosophies along the line of his and so forth.

Q. Do you think SNCC looks for different kinds of qualities in its leaders now than it did back then?

A. No.

Q. Or in the beginning?

A. It's hard to answer. The reason it's hard to answer is that there's always been a suspicion of leadership, there's always been a tendency to . . . by leadership, what I mean is this sense, when I say a suspicion of leadership, I mean a suspicion of any strong, central authority that says, "You must adhere to such-and-such a policy because this is the organization's policy." Leaders, people who are capable of articulating something in a good way or people who are capable of helping and giving ideas and suggestions, working with people on their organizing, are leaders and they've always been respected, but they're not thought of as leadership in the traditional sense that the structure has a president and that's where the leadership . . . So it's hard to say and I really don't know now what it means, look for qualities in a leader. Yet I'm not so sure that . . .

Q. Well, there are types of leadership other than authoritarian.

A. Sure there are, sure there are. I'm not sure, as I say, whether there's any change in what qualities people respect about someone.

Q. Now these structural changes in '64-'65; at that time, were there real changes in the kinds of relationships that existed between the staff and office?

A. No. The first structural changes alleviated some of the problems of resources and personnel and communication and so forth, but didn't alleviate the problems enough so that they didn't . . . so that they recurred. The same problems recurred again and again and again and, I suspect, still recur now. And there was another structural change in November of '65, which was very minor, really. And that was a change in the manner in which the executive committee was elected and I can't even remember what it was changed to. I know it was ten people at large. Maybe the other had fewer people at large or more people at large, I can't remember. Anyway, it was changed some way. It wasn't really crucial. One thing that did happen was that there was a finance committee and a personnel committee established, I believe in the spring of '65. Those two committees did function, particularly the finance committee. It functioned for a while in alleviating some of the financial problems. They set up good systems of allocation of money and made certain that requests were reasonable in terms of the amount of money that we had coming and tried to keep it balanced so that everybody would get his share.

Q. What was the significance of the Freedom High?

A. Well, the Freedom High, you could call them the loose-structure people. The significance in terms of SNCC was, I think, that it put SNCC . . . well, the fact of the Freedom High movement and its existence over a period of this year, put SNCC in a position where the organization did not move forward in terms of actual gains in the broader community. That's not really true, I don't mean it that way, I don't mean there weren't any gains, but I mean that the organization's ability to develop new programs, the organization's ability to get more people involved was curtailed in some ways by the debate over the structure.

Q. Did the Freedom High movement have other concerns, other than the actual structure of the organization?

A. Sure, but I think that the other concerns . . . it's very hard to sort this all out, because probably a Freedom High person would say, "Well, I care that people . . . when people work they can choose the kind of work they want to do and they don't have to work under pressure and so forth and so on." Well, the non-Freedom High people will say, "Sure, OK, I agree with that, but the question is when you're in a movement situation, you know, and you've got scarce resources and you've got only a certain amount of money to allot to people, do you let a cat who's trying to find himself in some way stay on the payroll for a year and do nothing?" See, so . . . well, I mean, that's not even a good way to put it. The concerns of Freedom High people also were . . . well, what I'm really trying to say is that I think that anything that a Freedom High person says, "This is my concern or this wasn't my concern," that the non-Freedom High people will say, "Sure, that was a concern of mine, too." And it's very difficult to say that the Freedom High were the people who wanted no exploitation and the people who wanted all these marvelous, wonderful, idealistic kinds of things . . .

Q. Was there any disagreement on what short-range goals to go for between . . .

A. There was *never* any discussion of real goals, never any discussion of real goals, never really any discussion of program, so there were never differences over program, because they were never brought out in the open, because structure hung us up so much. There was an attempt, or there was a feeling . . . I would say this . . . the Freedom High people were concerned that we discuss program first and structure second and the non-Freedom High people wanted to discuss structure first and get it out of the way and then discuss program. And we always ended up discussing structure first, because people wanted to get rid of it, get it out of the way. The Freedom High people felt that structure flowed from program—which I agreed with—but on the other hand the structure seemed to overwhelm so many people because the structural problems in their functioning were real to them. They didn't have money, they didn't get communications, they didn't have typewriters, they didn't have cars, cars broke down, couldn't get 'em fixed, all those kinds of things. Those daily frustrations overrode their concern about what kind of program they were running. They wanted to get structure out of the way, figuring that if a structure were there, then these little frustrations would be solved and they could run a program. The Freedom High people said, "Well, we better talk about a program first and *then* we talk about structure because it flows from the program."

Q. Did the loose structuralists tend to be people who just worked out in the field, whereas the tight structuralists were office people?

A. No. No, absolutely not.

Q. Was it the reverse?

A. It wasn't the reverse and it wasn't that way either. I think there was probably a good representation of office and non-office people on both sides—although you can't say things, but it doesn't really mean anything, but most of the Atlanta people were tight structuralists or tighter-structure people. Most of Southwest Georgia wanted a tight structure. Most of Arkansas wanted a tight structure. Alabama wasn't really on its feet enough to have representation. Mississippi was split because Mississippi was where all the people were added to the staff and where this new influx of people had come, so Mississippi was split, down the middle practically, and there were field people in Mississippi, of course, but they were even split—so it wasn't Mississippi against Georgia, Arkansas and Atlanta. And there were some Atlanta people who were Freedom High also. I mean, it was all mixed up and I don't think that it's . . . people did say that all the office people were for tight structure, all the field people were for loose structure. That's not true. It's just simply not true, because some of the biggest arguers for tight structure were the Southwest Georgia, Arkansas, and a few (at that point) Alabama staff people, who felt they were getting screwed because there was a loose structure and their needs weren't being met and so they couldn't function in the field.

Q. This is sort of part of the thing you mentioned before about resentment against Mississippi for getting all the resources.

A. Right, right. Part of it. On the other hand, there were Mississippi projects who complained and were penniless and couldn't function, they felt, because they didn't have funds and they didn't have such-and-such and so forth. They were for tight structure too. So it's just not easy to put it in one bag or another.

Q. Was SNCC at this time sort of in a transition period, looking for new projects to work on?

A. Sure. Well, it wasn't so much looking for new projects to work on but looking to expand. SNCC always had ideas about where they were going to go next, if they only had the staff. We want to move into South Carolina, move into North Carolina, move in here, move in there. It wasn't a question of looking around for new places, it was a question of getting the new places under way. And Alabama did get started in the fall of '64. A great number of staff from Mississippi went into Alabama. No, I'm sorry. Around the time of summer, we started putting staff in Alabama and after the summer was over, that's when people like Stokely and George Green and so forth stayed in Alabama—spring '65. There was a hope that people would move into Alabama in the summer '64, but I guess it never materialized until the spring and then people moved in.

* * * * *

Q. Would you like to add something to this, to complete the picture?

A. No. I don't know what I'd add—unless you want to know about specific areas.

Q. Well, one specific area comes to mind and that is the whole question of whites in the organization. What do you think were the times when important things happened which changed that, the important events that occurred?

A. Well, OK. Summer '64 was the biggest, I think. Before summer '64, there was conflict between whites and blacks, yes, but I believe at that point the whites that were working were more conscious of their role in a sense, and therefore less conflict arose around them. Summer '64 brought all kinds of smart-aleck kids into Mississippi. I mean there was just no question about it. Not only were they smart-aleck to black organizers but they were smart-aleck to anyone. They set themselves up as experts on community organizing, people who knew what was happening, tried to direct things, and so forth and so on. And because of whatever superior education they had, and so forth, they felt they were in a position to do this. And it really destroyed a lot of the trust that, I think, had been built up between blacks and whites in SNCC up to that point. OK, well, that was one turning point. And then the whole influx of white workers in the fall of '64, most of whom were college-educated, that was part of that whole thing. The next turning point I don't know. I'm sure it was building up before I left but I'm not sure that it happened before that. I'm not sure I can pin it to an event either.

* * * * *

[Disillusionment of SNCC with white workers after summer of '64.]

It was also a change that was coupled with, I think, changes in the real political world, like the continual disappointment with the federal government, continual disappointment that the white liberals didn't come through, the continual disappointment that the Democratic Party wasn't interested in shaking the power structure, wasn't really for social justice after all, made people more and more and more suspicious of whites in general and then, when that happens, you turn on the nearest white person to you and that's a guy that's in the organization with you and you see him as a representation of that big of a thing, even though somehow he's there working with you.

* * * * *

Q. And even though he [the white worker] is as much against the white power structure . . . ?
A. Right, exactly. On the other hand, there are legitimate concerns, fantastically legitimate concerns and have been so through SNCC for a number of years, and need to be reinforced, I think, that it's bad to set up for people in the South, whom you are organizing—or people in the North, for that matter—whites as the experts. In other words, to bring a white kid down to teach a Freedom School is bad because it reinforces the image of white people being the teachers and knowing everything and black people being the ones who are always taught. The same kind of thing happens with the organizer. The same kind of thing happens with a lecturer. The same

kind of thing happens with policy-making, and so forth and so on. That kind of thing has come more and more to be . . . well, that was always important but I think it's used as a . . . you know, one of the reasons whites are being de-emphasized. The other concern, I think, is important and is real and I happen to think that this is really crucial and that whites really haven't recognized it, is that, dammit, why don't the whites go—and I include myself in this—why don't they go and work in the white community instead of having to hang in the black community. What is it about their own back yard that they can't see the importance of cleaning *it* up and going out and organizing around whatever issue would appeal or be the most radical for a particular area that they're in, either poor whites or . . . in fact I happen to think that organizing middle-class whites against the war is a pretty radical issue at this time in terms of how it affects the government and so forth. So that's a real concern, and it was always, you know, "how come you have to come into the civil rights movement and come into the Negro community" and that's effective and that gets people together so that there can be coalitions, because this whole business of working together is nonsense if there's nobody to work together with.

* * * * *

Q. You mentioned "bigger problems" after '64. Was that one of them?
A. Well . . . not really. I mean the political was always still there. The tactics changed. For example, up to and including '64, the federal government was always the focus of . . . a person's focus. This is where we go, we go to Washington to protest. We get the government to carry out its responsibilities, SNCC people began to see that the government wasn't the panacea, wasn't going to be the instrument for curing the ills.

* * * * *

There was a concern that the Lowndes County Freedom Movement was a different kind of thing for SNCC. Never had SNCC people conceived of actually taking over power in counties. SNCC people kind of shied away from taking power, because there was a notion that power corrupted and that the whole structure of government of the counties was corrupt and...

So . . . then in Lowndes County, the people were really committed to taking power in that county . . . but it was, again always couched in terms

297

of, "the people deserve that power, because they were the majority," kind of thing. I mean, it wasn't a take power by force.

* * * * *

Q. Well, they did run candidates for office.
A. Right, but that was much more on a protest bent, not really to take power. Well, to the extent that we knew that nobody was going to win, we never had to face the question of what do they do when they get power.

* * * * *

Q. Have there been major changes in SNCC's methods?
A. Well, the changes in methods are kind of historical, I mean, the sit-ins worked for a while and nonviolence worked for a while, and then they became worn-out kinds of tactics and then people needed to be organized politically so things like the FDP and the freedom organizations in Alabama or the C. B. King campaign in Albany took place . . . where it was a different style of organizing, where issues were raised of a different sort and where political workshops or educational kinds of things took place more often than the nonviolent workshops, so to speak, and the picket lines and the sit-ins. And then, as far as more recently, as far as I know, there haven't been any really new organizing developments. It's kind of . . '64 set the tone for organizing tactics.

* * * * *

Over the years, however, the goals went from, I think, more idealistic in the very early stages to, first, a political thing in, say, '63-'64, where the whole focus and orientation was the right to vote, the right to travel on an interstate bus, the right to do certain constitutional kinds of things . . . and then, in the year after, say, 1964, to a position where constitutional rights were important, yes, but where the bigger problems of people related to each other were more important and also the question of economics became important: how do people live? So what if you can sit at the same lunch counter with a white man, but if you don't have the quarter to buy the hamburger, what good is the lunch counter? That kind of thing.

*****

Q. On the question of nonviolence: when you were in SNCC, was there a lot of talk among SNCC people about nonviolence? Was it a problem that people worried about?

A. No. Nonviolence was seen as a tactic and nothing more, very little more, and that was about it. Self-defense was important. People should be able to protect their homes if their homes are fired on, protect their family if their family was shot at. In demonstrations, though, there was no question: it was always nonviolent. But if you were living with a family in the rural part of Alabama, [tape ends] . . .

*****

Q. There was something else? Oh, when Northern offices started to organize their own programs.

A. Right, right. Now . . . Chicago had very early organized a direct action program around the school situation in Chicago. That was done in '63 and '62, I'm not even sure when, and it still continued . . . it kind of died out in the spring of '64. Chicago had a peculiar history, since that was where Jim Forman was from and there was a very strong support group. Then from there . . . I'm not sure if Washington was the next place or not. Well, Washington has always had a program, that is, the NAG, the Nonviolent Action Group, and they had done organizing in Washington. Washington was also considered like a Southern city, so it really doesn't fit in. The "Free D.C." program in Washington, which started with a bus boycott, was in January '66. January 24, 1966, was the bus boycott, and then from there the Free D.C. movement developed around that. The boycott was because they were raising the fares; it was highly successful. They didn't raise the fares from twenty-five to thirty cents then, but they're raising them now—or, I guess they raised the transfer fee. That's it. If you want a transfer, you have to pay a nickel, and that hurts everybody in the ghetto, because they're the people who have to go long distances on the bus. But anyway . . . I'm really not sure what kind of a program San Francisco started. L.A. had things like freedom schools for a while and I don't think they ever had a program that got off the ground. Philadelphia's program was started much more recently. I don't know what's happening in Chicago or what's happening in Detroit. I don't think there's any local action in Boston.

*****

Q. When did SNCC decide to expand into Northern cities?

A. I really don't know. It happened after I left, I know that. I mean, the actual decision—although there had been a decision made at one of the staff meetings, I don't remember when, that if there were a Friends of SNCC office in a city and that group wanted to involve themselves in some way with the local political scene, then it was all right. And that was a battle that had been fought over a period of years. A lot of people said that fund-raising groups should be independent, they were to raise money, not to take political stands. At first they were volunteer groups, and that caused a lot of problems, because the volunteer groups were either liberal or too radical or represented some faction or something like that, so every time they made a move in the North and used SNCC's name, SNCC got called for it. Like some Trotskyists organized a Friends of SNCC group in Detroit in very early '63 and they had a bank sit-in. It was a flop and the Detroit papers blew it up big, that this was a SNCC group and so forth. And SNCC really had no knowledge of who these people were, had never met them, and so forth, but they had just decided that they would form this little Friends of SNCC group and use SNCC's name for their little direct action campaign. So this was a battle for a time. Once the Northern offices began to have full-time SNCC staff in them, people felt more comfortable about saying, "OK, go out yourselves."

*****

Q. When was that?

A. Well, let's see, the first full-time staff people were in New York and Washington. Miss Baker would know this better. And they were . . . well, it must have been fall '63 that the first Northern office people were paid. I mean they were given regular SNCC salaries to work in the Northern offices.

Q. This helped resolve that whole conflict?

A. Right. And then as of, say, fall '65 there were thirty people full-time in the Northern offices. They came to staff meetings and people knew them and they were close enough to the organization and committed enough to it that they wouldn't go off half-cocked and do some stupid thing that would, you know, that wasn't consistent with the direction SNCC was going in. Of these thirty full-time people, ten were in New York. Make that number twenty-five, because there were never really thirty; there were twenty-five, ten of whom were in New York, which was the biggest fund-raising operation, and two of them were in Boston, two in Detroit, two in Chicago, three in Washington, three in San Francisco, one in Philadelphia, one in Canada, two in L.A.

Q. You don't know exactly when these people started organizing their own programs?

A. Well, yes, I can give you some idea.

Q. What percentage were they of the total staff?

A. The total staff, the total paid staff—and this was never an accurate measure of who were on SNCC staff, because some people worked for nothing—so . . . the total paid staff at the highest point was something like 210 paid field workers—and at the point at which we had 210 field workers, there were twenty-five Northern office people. [around spring '65]

* * * * *

Q. That was in spring '65? [that SNCC had 210 paid field workers, twenty-five Northern office people]

A. Yes. Oh, I'm not even sure that there were that many paid people in '65. I guess there were. Summer '65 and after the summer, a lot of people dropped out.

Q. Why?

A. Well, people were either tired—they'd been working for a year, a year and a half—people left, some people got married, some people, you know, their projects were dwindling, some people were asked to leave—not too many, maybe four or five.

Q. When was that?

A. I'm not sure when, but they were for large kinds of things, like one kid was really out of it psychologically and so went to California to recuperate. Another kid had trouble with . . .

* * * * *

Q. Skipping back a little to the convention challenge in the summer of '64; what do you think was the effect of that on SNCC?

A. Not a whole lot. I'm sure it had an effect on the MFDP, but the MFDP was a much different organization than SNCC. On the other hand, I'm not in a very good position to answer that question, because since I went back South and I was working in Atlanta, I was not very close to the Mississippi situation, at least that fall, so I don't really know how Mississippi reacted. I can only say that I think that most SNCC people expected it and they weren't completely disappointed and demolished and so forth.

Q. People in Atlanta expected it?

A. Well, yes, people in Atlanta, but I think most SNCC people expected it, except maybe people who had been down for the summer were more hopeful. But I think most of the full-time SNCC people who'd been there before the summer knew even at that point that the federal government was just a . . . kind of a fake and that . . .well . . . a fake to the extent that they didn't come through ever and that the Democratic Party wasn't really serious about shaking the power structure in Mississippi because so much depended on it.

*****

Q. Sort of a more broad question: what do you think has been SNCC's greatest success? Its contribution?

A. Oh, heavens. I can't answer that. I don't know. OK, I will make one statement about that. I think that the biggest contribution—and this applies to Mississippi and Alabama and everywhere—or one of the biggest contributions is that so many people have become involved in some way in some kind of political activity and that what it has done is it has made people understand and realize that they can have an effect on their own lives. I think that the recent CDGM battle, for example, and the way in which the CDGM Executive Committee, or whatever it was, stood up and demanded that money and got people demonstrating in Jackson and got people demonstrating in Washington and that they stuck to it as much and weren't content to have the money taken away, was partly a carry-over from the spirit of you-can-do-it, you can have an effect on your lives, that SNCC really developed, with the MFDP and with later kind of work.

The people were always . . . their hopes were raised on the one hand, but also we found it necessary to say to people, "not only should you hope, but also you've got to do it on your own hook. Nobody's going to get your freedom for you but yourself." And that moved people to work and to be involved. And in the initial program it was that people who've never voted or never participated in politics somehow can't comprehend that all of a sudden they might be able to vote. I mean like it's a complete radical change for them. Overcoming the fact of people's unfamiliarity with the electoral process or unfamiliarity with what politics is all about and their feelings of inadequacy in face of that was important.

Q. What has been your greatest disappointment about SNCC?

A. I really . . . I mean, there were a lot of problems. But one of the most beautiful things about SNCC, to turn that question around, was that people kept slugging and working and trying to grapple with the problems. There were huge administrative problems, personality problems, huge interracial kinds of problems, huge problems of people just physically existing and being able to face the pressure, and so forth, but that there . . . that SNCC was really a place where some honest attempts were made to deal with these problems. Not that they were solved, . . . but the daily frustrations were the thing that kept you down, kind of, but when you look at the big picture, when you look back on it, it's really, it's one of the most exciting kinds of experiences of people pulling together and trying to grapple with the problems that the bureaucrats, for example, faced, because I'm sure there's inefficiency in the government and problems of administrative detail and so forth and so on, but the honest grappling with those problems I don't think is there.

Fannie Lou Hamer

[Interview on September 2, 1967, in Ruleville, Mississippi.]

Q. When did you first become involved with SNCC?
A. In 1962. I had never been involved in civil rights before. In fact, I had hardly ever heard about these things. I was too tired from working in the fields to keep up with the news.

My pastor told me about the first mass meeting. James Forman, James Bevel and Reggie Robinson were there. They talked about how it was our constitutional right to register to vote, to be a first-class citizen. [Mrs. Blackwell reported same.]

Q. Did they give other reasons for registering?
A. [hesitates] Well, yes, they said you could vote people out of office if you weren't satisfied with them. Then they asked for volunteers to try to register. I was one of eighteen volunteers. The same day I tried to register, I was fired from my job. The landlord told me straight out it was because I had tried to register.

* * * * *

Q. What was SNCC trying to do that was different from what the NAACP was trying to do?
A. The NAACP talked big, but they weren't doing anything. They just weren't going out in the local areas and getting people to do things. I had never even heard of the NAACP before SNCC came on the scene. Since then, I've also worked with CORE and SCLC.

* * * * *

Q. Were you ever on SNCC staff?

A. Yes, I was put on staff in '63. I worked on voter registration. I hoped and I still hope to use the ballot to get our share of the control. We [Negroes] are 60% of Sunflower County [where Ruleville is]. I think the white man respects power and would change his ways if we had power.

Q. Do you remember how the FDP was founded?

A. In '64, after we had tried to go to the Democratic Party precinct meetings and been barred from them, we held our own precinct meetings. Then, on April 26, 1964, the MFDP was officially organized in Jackson. It was organized because we could not get into the regular party. I have learned a great deal through it.

Both the people in SNCC and the local people wanted to go to Atlantic City. I didn't actually expect to be seated, but I believed we'd get *something*, and that compromise they offered us was nothing. After the convention, some people became bitter, some became disillusioned, some became discouraged. I myself was shocked by what happened. I was educated by what I had to fight. I found out there was no trick too low that a man wouldn't stoop to it for power.

But I think blacks and whites still got to work together. I'd like to see democracy work—I haven't given up yet. I'm not one of those who go around hating all the time. If I was like that, I'd be a miserable person. I keep remembering that righteousness exalts a nation; hate just makes people miserable.

I remained a member of SNCC until last December. I wouldn't work even with FDP if it didn't function for people. The races have got to try to understand each other. I feel sorry for the suffering of the poor whites too.

* * * * *

Q. FDP has had a lot of the same experiences of beatings and jailings and so on that SNCC had. How come FDP has not taken the same path as SNCC?

A. Well, SNCC was an organization, FDP was a political party. And then FDP did not become anti-white, maybe because it was made up of Mississippians, who were never taught to hate, or rather were never taught to hate a whole category of people. It's a question of how you were reared.

My religious background kept me from hating and helped me to see hating just makes you miserable.

* * * * *

Q. How did SNCC get to this position, where it hates white people?
A. People were thrown into jail time after time, and brutally beaten—and the Justice Department would say, "We can't put guards everywhere." Even in the Schwerner-Chaney-Goodman case, where two whites were involved, nothing was done. The kids got more and more angry. Stripping [Rep. Adam Clayton] Powell of his power got people mad. SNCC was just trying to get people to register—and for that, its workers were called Reds, radicals, beatniks, everything. And they never got credit for what they did. The NAACP would get the credit. This country made the problems and then used SNCC as a scapegoat instead of doing something about the problems. They run *studies* of the riots—when anyone can see there's only one possible cause.

* * * * *

Q. What was Bob Moses' role in SNCC?
A. I never met anyone I had more respect for than Bob Moses. He was so kind. Anyone could love him like their son. He was a great organizer. But it happened to Bob like anyone else—he saw so many things he believed in that weren't there. I don't know where he is now.

* * * * *

Q. Do you remember how the decision was made to have the summer '64 project?
A. Bob spearheaded that project. The NAACP was not in on the founding. It was the only group that disagreed—I don't know why. But after the summer was a success (and I think it was a success even though people got killed), they ran a summer project themselves in the summer of '65. The big thing about the summer of '64 was that people learned white folks were human.

* * * * *

Q. What was the effect of the summer on white workers in SNCC?
A. They got on very well. They did pretty good work organizing.

*****

Q. What was the distinctive thing about SNCC?
A. It got to the *people*, not just the middle class. It worked to develop grass-roots leadership.

*****

Q. What was SNCC's greatest problem?
A. I couldn't say.
Q. What did SNCC set out to accomplish and not accomplish?
A. To get a coalition between whites and Negroes.

*****

Q. What do you think was SNCC's greatest success?
A. Making people with little or no education see themselves as human beings. You could always feel at ease, let yourself go. If SNCC hadn't ventured into Mississippi, nobody would be in here now, doing all these things.

Notes

INTRODUCTION

1. Gene Roberts, "From 'Freedom High' to 'Black Power'" in the *New York Times Magazine*, September 25, 1966.
2. Ralph McGill, "This New Snick is a Travesty," *Boston Globe*, September 10, 1966, and other columns.
3. (Boston: Beacon Press, 1964).

CHAPTER ONE

1. Interview with Donald Harris.
2. Interview with Curtis Hayes.
3. Interviews with Bill Hansen and Charles Sherrod.
4. *National Guardian*, August 8, 1964, Vol. 16, p. 4.
5. Interview with Charles Sherrod.
6. Interview with Ella Baker.
7. Interviews with Peggy Day and James Bevel.
8. Technically, the summer project was sponsored by the Congress of Federated Organizations (COFO). See Chapter Two.
9. Interview with Julian Bond
10. Joanne Grant, "The Negro Movement Debates its Course," *National Guardian* (January 9, 1964), p. 8.

CHAPTER TWO

1. See James Silver, *Mississippi: The Closed Society* (New York: Harcourt, Brace & World, 1964).
2. Jacob R. Fishman and Frederic Solomon, "The Psychological Meaning of Nonviolence," *Psychiatry*, Vol. 27 (May, 1964).
3. Interview with Peggy Day.
4. Interview with Bernard Lafayette.
5. The whites are Schwerner, Goodman, Reeb, Mrs. Liuzzo and Daniels.
6. Zinn, *SNCC*, *op. cit.*, pp. 89-90.
7. *Look* (May 21, 1963).

8. John Fisher, "A Small Band of Practical Heroes," *Harper's* (October, 1963), Vol. 227.
9. SNCC press release, August 8, 1963.
10. Zinn, *SNCC, op. cit.*, p. 183
11. Willie Rogers, quoted in Zinn, *op. cit.*, p. 97.
12. Jesse James Glover, *Ibid.*, p. 97.
13. Interview with Bob Zellner.
14. Interview with John Perdew.
15. Interview with Michael Sayer.
16. Interview with Miriam Cohen.
17. Interview with Frank Smith.
18. Interview with James Bevel.
19. Interview with Cordell Reagon.
20. Interview with Howard Zinn.
21. Interview with Miriam Cohen.
22. Interview.
23. Interview with Miriam Cohen.
24. Interview with Curtis Hayes.
25. Interview with Claude Weaver.
26. *National Guardian* (January 9, 1964), Vol. 16, p. 8.
27. In Mississippi before 1965, a person who wished to register to vote had to interpret a section of the state constitution, and it was completely at the discretion of the registrar to determine whether the interpretation was adequate. Whites were passed as invariably as blacks were flunked.
28. Nicholas Von Hoffman, *Mississippi Notebook* (New York: David White Co., 1964), p. 12.
29. *Ibid.*, p. 14.
30. Interview with Willie Blue.
31. Belfrage, *op. cit.*, p. 10.
32. Interview with Barbara Brandt.
33. Interview with Worth Long.
34. *Ibid.*
35. Interview with Bob Zellner.
36. Freedom Information Service, *Notes on the Condition of the Mississippi Negro*, 1967.
37. *Ibid.*
38. Fannie Lou Hamer, *To Praise our Bridges: an Autobiography* (Jackson, Mississippi: KIPCO, 1967), p. 12. Such economic reprisals were forbidden by the Civil Rights Act of 1960, but the Justice Department never attempted to enforce this provision of the Act.
39. Freedom Information Service, *op. cit.*
40. Zinn, *SNCC, op. cit.*, p. 86.
41. Interview with Sylvia Fisher.
42. Interview with Charles Jones.
43. Donald R. Matthews and James W. Prothro, *Negroes and the New Southern Politics* (New York: Harcourt, Brace & World, 1966).

44. Interview with Don Harris.
45. Matthews and Prothro, *op. cit.*, p. 451.
46. *Ibid.*, p. 454.
47. *Ibid.*, p. 176.
48. "Freedom School Notes," by Jane Stembridge.
49. Stokely Carmichael, "Who Is Qualified?," *New Republic*, January 8, 1966, pp. 21-22.
50. Carmichael and Hamilton, *op. cit.*, pp. 117-119.
51. Interview with Charles Sherrod.
52. Interview with Miriam Cohen.
53. Interview with Betty Garman.
54. Memo to SNCC from Charley Cobb.
55. Newfield, *op. cit.*, p. 100.
56. Interview with Jesse Morris.
57. Interview with Betty Garman.
58. Interview with Bob Zellner.
59. Zinn, *SNCC*, p. 74.
60. Interview with Charles Jones.
61. Anthony Lewis, *Portrait of a Decade* (New York: Random House, 1964).
62. Leon Friedman, ed., *Southern Justice* (New York: Random House, 1965), pp. 59-60 *et passim.*
63. Interview.
64. Stokely Carmichael and Charles Hamilton, *Black Power, The Politics of Liberation in America* (New York: Vintage Books, 1967), p. 104.
65. *New Republic* (August 21, 1965).
66. *Ibid.*, (April 16, 1966).
67. *Ibid.*, (October 15, 1966).
68. Mississippi Action for Progress also continues to receive federal funds.
69. Stokely Carmichael in *Massachusetts Review* (Autumn 1966), Vol. 7, p. 646.
70. Interview with John Lewis.
71. Pat Watters and Reese Cleghorn, *Climbing Jacob's Ladder: The Arrival of Negroes in Southern Politics* (New York: Harcourt, Brace & World, 1967), p. 14.
72. *Ibid.*, p. 15.
73. Interview with John Lewis.
74. Watters and Cleghorn, *op. cit.*, p. 15.
75. Interview with John Lewis.
76. Interview with William Higgs.
77. Watters and Cleghorn, *op. cit.*, p. iv.
78. Interview with Fannie Lou Hamer.
79. Interview.
80. Interview with Elizabeth Sutherland.
81. Watters and Cleghorn, *op. cit.*, p. 291.
82. The regular Democrats of Mississippi supported Goldwater.
83. Interview with William Higgs.
84. Interview with William Higgs.

85. *New York Times* (August 25), p. 23.
86. Interview with Barney Frank.
87. *New York Times* (August 27).
88. Interview with Michael Sayer.
89. *National Guardian* (July 10, 1965), Vol. 17, p. 9.
90. *Congressional Record.*
91. *National Guardian* (September 25, 1965), Vol. 17, p. 7.
92. Abbie Hoffman, "Another Look at the Movement," *Village Voice* (December 22, 1966), p. 30.
93. *The Voice* (August 30), p. 3.
94. Interview with Julian Bond.
95. All of the organizations that had urged changes in Lewis' speech at the March on Washington or acceptance of the compromise at the Convention (the NAACP, the AFL-CIO, etc.) were giving tacit or explicit support to President Johnson's Vietnam policy. This fact further alienated SNCC from these groups.
96. "Power Structure, Integration, Militancy, Freedom Now!", *Life* (November 29, 1963), Vol. 55, p. 86.
97. *Ibid.*, p. 87.
98. *Ibid.*, p. 86.
99. Andrew Kopkind, "New Radicals in Dixie." Quoted in *The New Republic* (April 10, 1965), pp. 14-15.
100. *Now!* (May 4, 1964).
101. *National Guardian* (May 23, 1964), Vol. 16, p. 3.
102. *Boston Globe* (September 7, 1966) and other columns.
103. *National Guardian* (June 27, 1964), vol. 16, p. 7.
104. *New York Herald Tribune* (March 12, 1965).
105. Jimmie Garrett, in Jack Newfield, "Revolt Without Dogma: The New Student Left," *The Nation* (May 10, 1965), p. 493.
106. *Newsweek* (May 30, 1966), Vol. 67, p. 36.
107. Interview with Ivanhoe Donaldson.
108. James Forman, quoted in the *Jackson Clarion-Ledger* (March 20, 1965).
109. Jack Newfield, *A Prophetic Minority* (New York: New American Library, 1966), p. 28.
110. Interview with Gerald McWorter.
111. Interview with Willie Blue.
112. Interview with Barney Frank.
113. Interview with Charles Fishman.
114. Len Holt, *The Summer That Didn't End* (New York: William Morrow & Co., 1965), p. 33.
115. *Ibid.*, p. 32.
116. *Wall Street Journal.*
117. Interview with William Higgs.
118. October 14, 1966, p. 27.
119. Howard Zinn, *Albany: A Study in National Responsibility* (Atlanta: Southern Regional Council, 1962), p. 10.
120. Interview with John O'Neal.

121. Watters and Cleghorn, *op. cit.*, p. 251.
122. *New York Times* (March 22, 1965).
123. *Ibid.*
124. Interviews with John Lewis and Elizabeth Sutherland.
125. *New York Times* (March 22, 1965).
126. *New York Times* (March 21, 1965), p. 74.
127. *New York Herald Tribune* (March 23).
128. *National Guardian* (May 8, 1965), Vol. 17, p. 8.
129. Ingeborg Powell, "Ideology and Strategy of Direct Action: A Study of CORE" (Unpublished Ph.D. dissertation, Berkeley, 1965; University Microfilm).

CHAPTER THREE

1. Most people got $10, a few $20 or $40. The highest salary, for a married man with children, was $60 a week.
2. Interview with Jesse Morris.
3. Interview with Donald Shaw.
4. Interview with Miriam Cohen.
5. Bryan Wilson, "An Analysis of Sect Development," *American Sociological Review*, Vol. 24. (February 1959).
6. William McCord, *Mississippi: The Long, Hot Summer* (New York: W. W. Norton & Co., 1965).
7. *New Yorker*, "Meeting" (April 11, 1964), p. 33.
8. McCord, *op. cit.*
9. Mitchell Cohen and Dennis Hale, editors, *The New Student Left: An Anthology* (Boston: Beacon Press, 1966), p. 55.
10. Interview with Timothy Jenkins.
11. Belfrage, *op. cit.*, p. 74.
12. Interview with Curtis Hayes.
13. Film, "Black Natchez" and interview with its producer, Edward Pincus.
14. Interview with Worth Long.
15. Belfrage, *op. cit.*, pp. 182-183.
16. Newfield, *Prophetic Minority*, p. 80.
17. Newfield, *op. cit.*, p. 105.
18. Newfield, *op. cit.*, p. 105.
19. Interview.
20. Newfield, *op. cit.*, p. 104.

CHAPTER FOUR

1. Zinn, *SNCC*, *op. cit.*, p. 10.
2. Interview with Reggie Robinson.

3. Jacob R. Fishman and Frederic Solomon, "Youth and Social Action, I: Perspectives on the Student Sit-In Movement," *American Journal of Orthopsychiatry*, October 1963, p. 880.
4. Interview with Mary Varela.
5. Interview with Mary Varela.
6. Interview with Elizabeth Sutherland.
7. Bruce Payne, "SNCC: An Overview Two Years Later," *The Activist*, November 1965, p. 5.
8. Interview with Michael Sayer.
9. Interview with Don Harris.
10. Interview with Allard Lowenstein.
11. Belfrage, *op. cit.*, p. 82.
12. Interview with Jane Stembridge.
13. Interviews with Claude Weaver, Reggie Robinson, Peggy Day.
14. From *Some Aspects of Black-White Problems as Seen by Field Staff*, SNCC mimeographed sheet, no date.
15. Interview with John O'Neal.
16. Alvin F. Poussaint, "The Stresses of the White Female Worker in the Civil Rights Movement in the South," *American Journal of Psychiatry*, Vol. 123 (October 1966), p. 403.
17. A "Bwana" is a white colonial "boss-man" who regards help to the childlike black folk as the white man's burden. Interview with Charles Fishman.
18. A "missionary" in this context is one who seeks to lead others, usually regarded as inferiors, to enlightenment. *Ibid.*
19. The "White African Queen" complex refers to the white woman's "tabooed and repressed fantasy of the intelligent, brave and beautiful white woman leading the poor, downtrodden, and oppressed black man to freedom and salvation." Poussaint, *op. cit.*, p. 404.
20. Robert Penn Warren, *Who Speaks for the Negro* (New York: Random House, 1965), p. 97.
21. Interview with Jane Stembridge.
22. *New York Times* (March 11, 1964).
23. Interview with Gerald McWorter.
24. Warren, *op. cit.*, p. 175.

CHAPTER FIVE

1. Interview with Bill Hansen.
2. The phrases "alternative politics" and "new politics" are used in the New Left. They were not used in SNCC, but the concepts behind them owe a good deal to SNCC thinking.
3. Watters and Cleghorn, *op. cit.*, p. 291.
4. SNCC mimeographed sheets.
5. Interview with Ella Baker.

6. Interview with Charles Sherrod.
7. Interview with John O'Neal.
8. *The Wretched of the Earth* (New York: Grove Press, 1963).
9. *Ibid.*, p. 57.
10. *Ibid.*, p. 73.
11. *Ibid.*, p. 117.
12. *Ibid.*, p. 39.
13. *Ibid.*, p. 48.
14. Chicago: A. C. McClure & Co., 1903.
15. Some immigrants, such as these in the Socialist and Communist parties and IWW, did become radical.
16. Interview with Bill Hansen.
17. A similar conflict had split the Industrial Workers of the World into two factions, those who wanted a centralized organization that could eventually seize control of existing labor unions (the Marxist wing) and those who wanted a decentralized organization that would eventually attract the members of the old, conservative unions, in the manner of a parallel institution. (Patrick Renshaw, *The Wobblies: The Story of Syndicalism in the United States*, Garden City, N.Y.: Doubleday, 1967, pp. 164-5.)
18. Interview with John Perdew.
19. Quoted by Staughton Lynd, *The Activist* (Fall, 1964), p. 12.
20. Interview with John O'Neal.
21. Interview with Curtis Hayes.
22. Interview with Fannie Lou Hamer.
23. *The Activist* (Fall, 1964), p. 12.

CHAPTER SIX

1. Martin Diamond, "Socialism and the Decline of the American Socialist Party" (University of Chicago Ph.D. dissertation, 1956).
2. Irving Howe and Lewis Coser, *The American Communist Party, a Critical History, 1919-1957* (Boston: Beacon Press, 1957).
3. Robin Moore, *The Green Berets* (New York: Avon Books, 1965).
4. Since 1964, the Army has partly shifted the Green Berets from counter-guerrilla operations to "stability operations" and civic action. It was apparently not willing to tolerate the discipline problems created by what a Green Beret colonel called the "unconventional warfare mystique."
5. Both moralist and ideological organizations are subdivisions of the "purposive" organization in the typology that includes purposive, solidary, and material organizations set forth by Peter B. Clark and James Q. Wilson in "Incentive Systems: A Theory of Organizations," *Administration Science Quarterly*, VI (September 1969). Moralist organizations have more solidary features than most other purposive organizations.

6. R. A. Knox, *Enthusiasm: A Chapter in the History of Religion* (Oxford: Clarendon Press, 1950), p. 2.
7. *Ibid.*, p. 565.
8. Renshaw, *op. cit.*
9. Except for a profound suspicion of the powers-that-be, SNCC seems to have shared little with the American Populists, who fairly quickly became an organization of national political scope, able to exert considerable influence on the Democratic Party's selection of a presidential candidate. C. Vann Woodward, *Tom Watson, Agrarian Rebel* (New York: Oxford University Press, 1963).
10. Walter B. Miller *et. al*, "Delinquency Prevention and Organizational Relations," in Stanton Wheeler, ed., *Controlling Delinquents* (New York: John Wiley, 1968), pp. 61-100.
11. I am not equipped to evaluate the influence of SNCC on black people during the Black Power period.

Bibliography

Ahmann, Mathew, ed., *The New Negro* (Notre Dame, Indiana: Fides Publishers, 1961).

Armstrong, Richard, "Will SNCC Overcome?" *Saturday Evening Post*, Vol. 238 (August 28, 1965).

Belfrage, Sally, *Freedom Summer* (New York: The Viking Press, 1965).

Bennett, Lerone, Jr., "SNCC: Rebels With a Cause," *Ebony*, Vol. 20 (July 1965).

Bond, Julian, "Memoirs of a Southern Gentleman," *Ramparts* (January and February 1967).

Braden, Anne, "The Southern Freedom Movement in Perspective," *Monthly Review*, Vol. 17 (July-August 1965).

Camus, Albert, *The Rebel* (New York: Vintage Books, 1956).

Carmichael, Stokely, "Power and Racism," SNCC reprint (Fall 1966).

_____, "Toward Black Liberation," *Massachusetts Review*, Vol. 7 (Autumn 1966).

_____ and Charles V. Hamilton, *Black Power: The Politics of Liberation in America* (New York: Vintage, 1967).

Clark, Peter B. and James Q. Wilson, "Incentive Systems: a Theory of Organizations," *Administration Science Quarterly*, Vol. 6 (September 1961).

Cohen, Mitchell and Dennis Hale, eds., *The New Student Left: An Anthology* (Boston: Beacon Press, 1966).

Congressional Record (September 17, 1965).

Dammond, Margaret T. "The Doctrine of Satyagraha and Nonviolent Struggle of the American Negro in the Southern United States, 1960-63." Unpublished paper.

Diamond, Martin, "Socialism and the Decline of the American Socialist Party." University of Chicago Ph.D. dissertation in political science, 1956. (Unpublished).

DuBois, W. E. B., *Souls of Black Folk* (Chicago: A.C. McCLure & Co., 1903).

Etzioni, Amitai, *A Comparative Analysis of Complex Organizations: On Power Involvement and their Correlates* (New York: Free Press of Crowell-Collier, 1961).

Fanon, Frantz, *The Wretched of the Earth* (New York: Grove Press, 1965).

Feldman, Paul. "The Pathos of Black Power." *Dissent*, Vol. 14 (January-February 1967).

Fisher, John, "A Small Band of Practical Heroes," *Harper's*, Vol. 227 (October 1963).

Fishman, Jacob R. and Frederic Solomon, "The Psychological Meaning of Nonviolence." *Psychiatry*, Vol. 27 (May 1964).

_____, "Youth and Social Action, I: Perspectives on the Student Sit-in Movement,"*American Journal of Orthopsychiatry*, Vol. 33 (October 1963).

Frazier, E. Franklin, *Black Bourgeoisie* (Glencoe, Illinois: Free Press, 1957).

Freedom Information Service, *Notes on the Condition of the Mississippi Negro*, 1967.

Friedman, Leon, ed., *Southern Justice* (New York: Random House, 1965).

Fruchter, Norm, "Mississippi: Notes on SNCC," *Studies on the Left*, Vol. 5 (Winter 1965).

Grant, Joanne, "The Negro Movement Debates its Course," *National Guardian* (January 9, 1964).

Hamer, Fannie Lou, *To Praise Our Bridges: An Autobiography* (Jackson, Mississippi: ZIPCO, 1967).

Hayden, Tom, "SNCC: The Qualities of Protest," *Studies on the Left*, Vol. 5 (Winter 1965).

_____, *Revolution in Mississippi*. SDS pamphlet, 1962.

Hoffman, Abbie, "SNCC: The Desecration of a Delayed Dream," *The Village Voice*, Vol. 12 (December 15, 1966).

_____, "Another Look at the Movement," *The Village Voice*, Vol. 12 (December 22, 1966).

Hofstadter, Richard, *The Paranoid Style in American Politics* (New York: Vintage Books, 1967).

Holt, Len, *The Summer that Didn't End* (New York: William Morrow & Co., 1965).

Howe, Irving, and Lewis Coser, *The American Communist Party, A Critical History, 1919-1957* (Boston: Beacon Press, 1957).

Jacobs, Paul and Saul Landau, *The New Radicals* (New York: Random House, 1966).

Jencks, Christopher, "Accommodating Whites: A New Look at Mississippi," *New Republic*, Vol. 154 (April 16, 1966).

_____, "Mississippi: From Conversion to Coercion," *New Republic* (August 22, 1964).

_____ and Milton Kotler, "A Government of the Black, by the Black, and for the Black," *Ramparts* (July 1966).

Kahn, Tom, and August Meier, "Recent Trends in the Civil Rights Movement," *New Politics*, Vol. 3 (Spring 1964).

Knox, R. A., *Enthusiasm: A Chapter in the History of Religion* (Oxford: Clarendon Press, 1959).

Kopkind, Andrew, "Bureaucracy's Long Arm: Too Heady a Start in Mississippi," *New Republic* (August 21, 1965).

_____, "New Radicals in Dixie," *New Republic* (April 10, 1965), p. 14-15.

Laue, James Howard, "Direct Action and Desegregation: Toward a Theory of the Rationalization of Protest," Unpublished Harvard Ph.D. dissertation in sociology (December 1965).

Lewis, Anthony and the *New York Times*, *Portrait of a Decade* (New York: Random House, 1964).

Lynd, Staughton, "Roots of Negro Militancy," *New Republic*, Vol. 150 (February 22, 1964).

_____, "SNCC: The Beginning of Ideology," *The Activist* (Fall 1964).

Mabee, Carlton, "Voting in the Black Belt," *Negro History Bulletin*, Vol. 27 (December 1963).

Marshall, James P., "Protest Politics in the Closed Society," Unpublished paper, 1965.

Matthews, Donald R. and James W. Prothro, *Negroes and the New Southern Politics* (New York: Harcourt, Brace & World, 1966).

McCord, William, *Mississippi: The Long, Hot Summer* (New York: W. W. Norton & Co., 1965).

McGill, Ralph, "This New Snick is a Travesty," *Boston Globe* (September 10, 1966).

Miller, Walter B. *et. al*, "Delinquency Prevention and Organizational Relations" in Stanton Wheeler, ed., *Controlling Delinquents* (New York: John Wiley, 1968).

Moore, Robin, *The Green Berets* (New York: Avon Books, 1965).

Nash, Diane, "Inside the Sit-ins and Freedom Rides: Testimony of a Southern Student," in *The New Negro*, edited by Matthew Ahmann.

New Republic, "Shriver Drops CDGM." (October 15, 1966).

New Yorker, "Meeting," under "Talk of the Town," Vol. 40 (April 11, 1964).

Newfield, Jack, *A Prophetic Minority* (New York: New American Library, 1966).

———, "The Question of SNCC," *Nation* (July 19, 1965).

———, "Revolt without Dogma: The Student Left," *Nation* (May 10, 1965).

Newsweek, "Black Power: Carmichael's New Politics," Vol. 67 (June 27, 1966).

———, "Buy-In," Vol. 63 (January 6, 1964).

———, "Growl of the Panther: New Voice of SNCC," Vol. 67 (May 30, 1966).

———, "Hotter Fires: Friction Between Organizations." Vol. 62 (July 1, 1963).

———, "Team Players," Vol. 66 (August 23, 1965).

Payne, Bruce, "The Student Nonviolent Coordinating Committee: An Overview Two Years Later," *The Activist* (November 1965).

Poppy, John, "The South's War Against Negro Votes," *Look*, Vol. 37 (May 21, 1963).

Poussaint, Alvin F., "The Stresses of the White Female Worker in the Civil Rights Movement in the South," *American Journal of Psychiatry*, Vol. 123 (October 1966).

Powell, Ingeborg, "Ideology and Strategy of Direct Action: A Study of CORE." Unpublished Ph.D. thesis, Berkeley, 1965. University Microfilm.

Powledge, Fred, "The New Fraternity," *Esquire*, Vol. 64 (September 1965).

Renshaw, Patrick, *The Wobblies: The Story of Syndicalism in the United States* (Garden City, N.Y.: Doubleday, 1967).

Roberts, Gene, "From 'Freedom High' to 'Black Power,'" *New York Times Magazine* (September 25, 1966).

Schardt, Arlie, "Tension, Not Split in the Negro Ranks," *Christian Century*, Vol. 82 (May 12, 1965).

Silver, James, *Mississippi: The Closed Society* (New York: Harcourt, Brace & World, 1964).

"Some Aspects of Black-White Problems as Seen by Field Staff," SNCC mimeographed sheet, no date.

Stembridge, Jane, "Freedom School Notes," SNCC mimeographed sheets.

"The Story of SNCC," SNCC pamphlet, 1966.

Sugarman, Tracy, *Stranger at the Gates* (New York: Hill & Wang).

Sutherland, Elizabeth, ed., *Letters from Mississippi* (New York: McGraw-Hill, 1965).

_____, "SNCC Takes Stock: Mandate from History," *Nation* (January 6, 1964).

Tucker, Shirley, *Mississippi from Within* (New York: Arco Publishing Co., 1965).

"Vietnam and Civil Rights: Two Papers," Nashville Southern Student Organizing Committee, 1965.

Von Hoffman, Nicholas, *Mississippi Notebook* (New York: David White Co., 1964).

Warren, Robert Penn, "Two for SNCC," *Commentary*, Vol. 30 (April 1965).

_____, *Who Speaks for the Negro?* (New York: Random House, 1965).

Watters, Pat, *Encounter with the Future* (Atlanta: Southern Regional Council, 1965).

_____, "Mississippi: Children and Politics," *Dissent*, Vol. 14 (May-June 1967).

_____ and Reese Cleghorn, *Climbing Jacob's Ladder: The Arrival of Negroes in Southern Politics* (New York: Harcourt, Brace, and World, 1967).

White, Theodore, "Power Structure, Integration, Militancy, Freedom Now!" *Life*, Vol. 55 (November 29, 1963).

Wilson, Bryan, "An Analysis of Sect Development," *American Sociological Review*, Vol. 24 (February 1959).

Woodward, C. Vann, *Tom Watson: Agrarian Rebel* (New York: Oxford University Press, 1963).

Wulbert, R., "Food for Greenwood," *New Republic*, Vol. 149 (July 13, 1963).

Zinn, Howard, *Albany: A Study in National Responsibility* (Atlanta: Southern Regional Council, 1962).

_____, "SNCC: The Battle-Scarred Youngsters," *Nation* (October 5, 1963).

_____, *SNCC: The New Abolitionists* (Boston: Beacon Press, 1964).

News articles in *New York Times*, *New York Herald Tribune*, *National Guardian*, and SNCC newspapers *Now* and *The Voice*.

Index

TITLES IN THE SERIES

Martin Luther King, Jr.
and the
Civil Rights Movement

DAVID J. GARROW, EDITOR